Ancient Poetry from China, Japan, & India

RENDERED INTO ENGLISH VERSE
BY HENRY W. WELLS

UNIVERSITY OF SOUTH CAROLINA PRESS

COLUMBIA

⊸§First edition. Copyright © 1968 by the University of South Carolina Press. Published in Columbia, S.C., 1968. Library of Congress Catalog Card Number: 68–9365. Manufactured in the United States of America. Designed by Damienne Grant. The University of South Carolina Press and the author are grateful to the editors of Literature East and West and The Literary Half-Yearly (Mysore, India) for permission to reprint versions of Ode to the Lute, Karna's Task, and a number of shorter poems that appeared first in those journals.

To William Hung

Contents

A
New
View of
Translation

Some fruitful questions are raised by two remarks on translation and rhyme by Arthur Waley. In his 170 Chinese Poems he wrote: "I have not used rhyme because it is impossible to produce in English rhyme-effects at all similar to those of the original, where the same rhyme sometimes runs through a whole poem. Also, because the restrictions of rhyme necessarily injure either the vigor of one's language or the literalness of one's version. I do not, at any rate, know of an example to the contrary." Certainly in all his translations of Asian poetry, almost always marked by great distinction, he remained faithful to this statement, made in 1919. Yet there is evidence that he felt uneasy in such an opinion. In his subsequent volume translating the Book of Songs (1937), he wrote: "I trust that some part of my delight in them, despite the deadening lack of rhyme and formal metric, has found its way to the reader of the foregoing translations." Few persons acquainted with Waley's works will doubt that he has faced a peculiar dilemma. His own art as a stylist unquestionably proves that he possessed many of the potential qualities for becoming a first-rate English poet. Yet all translation is a compromise between the genius of two languages. By the very nature of his task he was forced to compromise. Wishing to be read with pleasure in English, he could not strive for the most complete effort at literalness. Wishing to be faithful to the original, he could not be the unfettered English poet. Had he possessed less abundant gifts or been solely a linguist or a dilettante, his dilemma would not have been so sharp. No one reading between the lines of his translations can doubt that he highly valued all the major forms and conventions of English poetry, among which rhyme and other metric features are conspicuous.

He labored with some singularly unhappy instances of infelicitous translations staring at him from his shelves. It is certain that he felt their ineptitudes keenly. His objections to rhyme were beyond question strongly motivated. It is true that virtually no translations available to him at the time of his writing based on Chinese or Japanese verse used the stricter conventions of English poetry with any measure of success. The translators, such as Herbert A. Giles, fell into precisely the traps that Waley describes. They wrote bad English verse, at times almost execrable. Insofar as they used established verse forms they failed in the implied compromise. They misused English conventions at the very time that they also seriously compromised fidelity to their originals.

Conditions of translation from Far Eastern poets were at this time not greatly different from those of translation in general. Of course some loss of fidelity in the literal sense is inevitable where poetry is rendered into verse. Waley's versions, incidentally, are even here a compromise, for they are not prose; they have considerable metrical form and rhetorical form, in general accord with English poetic usage of the times despite their disregard for the stricter or more old-fashioned forms of English verse. In fact, modern poets have continually tended to converge upon the general usages selected by Waley himself. Their forms have been less formalized and abstract, freer and more sinuous than the romantic poetry as a whole admitted. Still, it is true that Waley rigorously and deliberately dismissed the older and stricter conventions from his own pages. Other equally successful translators have not done so, those such as George Chapman, John Dryden, or Edward Fitzgerald. The generalization always holds that, as Waley implied, the more numerous and binding the verse conventions in a translation may be, the greater are the liberties which are taken with the original. Yet in celebrated instances these liberties have been found justified by almost all readers. Possibly Waley was too austere as guide or example for all occasions. It may be argued that the conventions of one poetic literature, though different from those of a second literature, are of much aid to the translator, and that poetic formalities may better be used than not even where differing from the original. Verse translates verse; form translates form. A translation of verse into prose may itself be the graver contradiction. It is to be remembered that taste in verse-style at approximately the time when Waley began to write now seems to us to have been at an unusually low ebb. These pages plead for a reconsideration of these problems and for a more cordial view of greater formality in translation from Chinese, Japanese, and Sanskrit poetry.

If it be true, as here assumed, that all translation is compromise, then a translator may still hope that he is preserving the poetry, indeed lengthening its life and enlarging the number of its admirers, at the same time that he is inevitably engaged in a process of transposition. The old, original forms, let it be admitted, are unavailable in the new language. Very well, then, let forms native to the second tongue be used in their place. The spirit of formality may in itself be as important as oversolicitude for the literal meanings of the words. There is the old proposition that the translator writes as the original poet would have written had he flourished in the country of the translator and not in his own. This proposition, obviously, even if accepted, cannot be overworked. The poet could not have been what he was had he lived in another land or culture. This view is also somewhat specious and contains a contradiction in terms. But it also contains much common sense.

Mr. Waley himself was actually more conservative than he admitted. True, he did not use stanzas, sonnet forms, or couplets, but he did, when he deemed it appropriate, utilize what he so well appreciated of the alliterative eloquence of Old English in, for example, the savage poem "The Nightmare"; in an allegorical poem, "The Orphan," he introduced features of Chaucerian allegory; and in that exuberant poem "The Temple" he used aspects of the baroque style, such as that found in Richard Crashaw. In his many pieces of a distinctly colloquial style, he introduced nuances which he had acquired from his obvious acquaintance with English poetry of the easy grace and urbanity best shown, perhaps, in John Gay. He dipped freely into the rich resources of English verse. Had he so wished, he might safely have gone very much further.

In defense of his more literal and less poetic or imaginative method of translation, it may be argued that such versions have a special value—above all for the Asian languages—at an early stage in the practice of translation. Where only a relatively small group of scholars or persons especially interested in the language are to be presumed, a literal version supplies at least a hard, solid ground on which to fall back. The more poetic or imaginative the translation, the more personal or subjective it is likely to be. Each enterpriser will use a strategy of his own. The literal version, when it is available, may be used by anyone not acquainted with the language in question, yet who has some sincere interest in its literature, to check on possible idiosyncrasy. Many masterpieces of oriental poetry have now been translated into English —a statement that could not have been made at the beginning of this century. Clearly, in these instances times are more favorable now than hitherto for the bolder attempts.

It should be remembered that in the Orient advanced stages of formality constitute an especially important phase of the poetic experience and, indeed, of the aesthetic experience generally. This becomes most significant as far as the translator is concerned, since it is precisely these forms that are the least malleable in a Western language. Moreover, the content of an Asian poem in particular is likely to the less well-initiated Western reader to be misleading and to appear—as it generally is not— prosaic. To reassure him of the truth of the situation requires precisely these aids of formality in expression that restore to him the comfortable and pleasant assurance that he is reading what in its original is verse and not prose.

Of late the partial dissolution of the standard forms of English verse has frequently led to a superficial understanding of their true value. We find it hard to reconstruct standards of taste which include a large number of preconceived forms. A singularly idealistic, and often virtually mystical, aesthetic instructs us that each work of art possesses its own inner principles, which are unique, and, similarly, that the once widely accepted theory of genres is now obsolete. Whatever may be wise or viable for creative art today, it is certain that artists of all previous times and cultures have thought otherwise. The classical theories of art throughout the world presume an area of independence for each work and for each artist, but these areas are set off against forms or requirements for large groups of creative work. Verse forms and various rhetorical forms become obligatory. On beginning a poem its author is to choose established patterns and remain within them. His creative imagination is exercised in nuances which he is able to introduce within the framework which the conventions of his art present to him. He will have special types of meter, metaphor, and rhetoric to develop as best he can. Chinese, Japanese, and Sanskrit poets cling strongly to these conditions of their craft; indeed, it may be said that they accept them with uncommon enthusiasm.

Possibly translators overlooking any such conventions do so at a considerable risk. There is serious doubt that formalism can be successfully translated into a broad license. There is fair possibility that forms at least in tune with the original, though clearly those of another culture and tongue, may serve an imaginative translator well.

Another way of envisaging the problem is to consider the English language and the English poetic tradition as a highly developed instrument offering a great range of expression. It is further possible that forms of small use at present to living poets in their own compositions may still be of service to the translator. Moreover, formalism of various sorts does not seem decadent today to the degree to which it often appeared in the golden age of free verse a generation ago. Many leading poets, both British and American, have been eminent formalists, such as Yeats, Eliot, Pound, and Frost. The ideals of the line, the stanza, even of rhyme cannot as yet seriously be thought outmoded. Hence classical poetry the world over would seem best translated in standard forms, though never, of course, quite those of the original language. Poets, for example, writing in stanzas or strophes are certainly best translated by use of at least equivalent devices. Our poets through the ages have left at the disposal of poets today a vast number of still highly expressive forms, which it may well be that a translator disregards to his own loss. Such a one would really labor with hands tied behind his back. Do we really think that the best translation of the Rubaiyat would be in free verse? Fitzgerald found a form well known to serve the mood and meaning of his original. Almost everyone is glad that he did so.

Fitzgerald went far indeed in taking liberties. The truth is that his poem is materially unlike its "original" in both intellectual and emotional content and even in much of its imagery. To a large extent it is a Victorian poem suggested by a Persian classic, just as Tennyson's poems using the Arthurian legend were suggested by the work of Sir Thomas Malory. As a representative writer of his times, Malory himself took great liberties with his legends and probably did little or no direct translation from his "French book," which he claimed to be his model. He was, in our terms, using a source, not translating a text. On the whole, modern opinion, contrary to Malory's outlook, prefers a fair degree of fidelity in translations, and with this requirement there should, I think, be no quarrel. The differences of peoples and of individuals are sacred to us as they were not to the medieval thinkers. But what constitutes a fair degree of fidelity? What is the very conception of fidelity itself? Is it faithful to read an opera libretto and omit the music? Is it faithful to translate formal verse as free verse, omitting the chief appeal to the ear? The wisest rules are that in these matters there are no rules and that any number of premises are feasible provided that each is worked out fully according to its own presumptions. Arthur Waley stated that in general he used one English accent for one Chinese word. No lover of Chinese poetry, I assume, feels anything but intense admiration for his translations. But their rigidity still leaves much undone that, I believe, may be done to good effect. These pages outline a different way.

In the strategy of translation a question to be asked before a poem is translated is, simply, what English poet has come nearest to composing a work in a similar mood and form. This should not mean, of course, that any strict imitation of the style of an English poet is proper to use in rendering an Asian poet, but that through keeping such analogies in mind, and in some instances allowing the English master to modify the writing, the translation is likely to gain. In the process of the translation of poetry, the ideal condition is not a confrontation of a poem in one language with a pragmatic problem of its immediate transposition into another but a consideration of the original poem in relation to whatever of an analogous nature has already been achieved in the second tongue. There are more analogies than the man in the street supposes. The literature of the world presents a tissue of comparisons. Translation is a process of the imagination which at its best leans heavily on freshly discovered analogies. It is, ideally speaking, the transposition of a basic score from one instrument to another. A meditation on the potentialities of the two instruments, both their likenesses and differences, lies at the heart of the process.

On Chinese Poetry

The remark can be commonly heard about almost any major country that its culture is unique. Although the statement presumably has some validity, its force is clearly greater in some times and places than in others. For few countries, if for any, does the observation have more validity than for China, which for centuries has been the homeland of so many extraordinary institutions and rare developments in art, music, and literature. Its language, especially in its written form, is idiosyncratic; its modes of thought are highly original. At the same time that China has drawn much from its neighbors to the south and west, it has by tradition converted what has been taken into its own idiom. It has refashioned its militant conquerors into its own image so often that it seems that to be conquered by China it is necessary only to conquer it. The country is singularly loath to acknowledge indebtedness to other lands. Today its communism, is radically unlike that of Europe, just as a millenium ago its Buddhism was distinctly unlike that of India. In short, China with some justice regards itself as a heart-land, spiritually sufficient to itself. Even those Chinese who make their homes outside of China as a rule conduct their lives in the ways of their adopted country while still managing to cling to the spirit of their ancestral land.

The converse is also true inasmuch as Chinese civilization has given the world imaginative expressions in art and literature that to a remarkable degree seem basic to human nature. The preference in China for a secular, an ethical, or an aesthetic view of life rather than a religious or theological view has made the Chinese seem brothers to humanists in many parts of the world. No wonder that their values in literature, art, and decoration have been warmly received in regions geographically remote. Their ceramics and textiles have been highly popular; their moralists have been sympathetically read; their sculpture, painting, and poetry deeply admired. One notes a paradox here. In no art are their practices more idiosyncratic than in poetry, yet their poetry, even when read in translation, has proved singularly attractive.

Although its foreignness is obvious, its humanity has given it a magnetic force.

In any speculation such as the foregoing some caution is, of course, desirable. It should be recalled that when a literature as long-lived, extensive, and various as the Chinese is considered, generalizations are all too likely to be at best half-truths. Some of the earliest Chinese poetry appears to be the occult incantations of magicians; some of the latest and by no means the weakest is laden with social and political propaganda. It seems that Chinese literature supplies at one time or another analogies to almost any species to be found elsewhere, as, in Europe, in medieval, neo-classical, baroque, romantic, or modern periods. A poet such as Li Ho, who flourished about 800 A.D., affords striking analogies to T. S. Eliot; a poet such as Chu Yuan, who flourished in the fourth century B.C., bears some resemblances to Coleridge.

Nevertheless, a remarkable school of Chinese poetry, synchronous with a similar school of painting, developed by the eighth century A.D. and, to be sure, with decreasing vigor flourished for a millenium. It, in turn, owed much to an ancient tradition extending backward through at least eight centuries B.C. Yet it is from the early part of this period, roughly from 700 to 850 A.D., that the most memorable work derives. Although within these fertile years there is, admittedly, great diversity, some major lines can safely be drawn with reference to the aims of the chief poets. A few of Tu Fu's short poems, for example, perhaps present a better introduction for aesthetic values than any critical statements originating in the twentieth century. Moreover, the problems of translation should, of course, be clarified by an investigation of the expressed aims of the poets themselves. Their own words show better than any others why we cherish their work and wherein it not only differs from prevailing traditions in Western poetry but presents its translators with some unique difficulties. The West, naturally enough, is so much the more prone to misinterpret whatever is foreign to itself. Sanskrit poetry in translation is all too likely to seem bombastic, Japanese overmannered, and Chinese prosaic. All these appearances are fundamentally erroneous. At their best the Sanskrit is eloquent, the Japanese fastidious, the Chinese profoundly human. Since Asian poetry by almost any serious standards is in its classical achievements a great poetry, it inevitably possesses nuances. But the Westerner must pause and listen carefully to discover such refinements.

Most Chinese poetry affords an art for weekdays rather than for feastdays, an art firmly built into the lives of its people, directed not to a cult but to the community at large, intelligible but not vulgar, more an admirably cooked loaf of bread than an elaborately prepared cake. In the classical period all persons capable of the rather laborious achievement of literacy were expected to read and write verse. Only a few poets could by any extension of the term be called professionals. Poetry, in short, was one of the accomplishments of "the complete gentleman." Some merely wrote better than others. The ideal is voiced in the following poem by Tu Fu. (The English rendering here, as elsewhere, is my own.)

> I saw that Mr. Sung's old pond and villa
> Are now too desolate to entertain
> The Muse. Once one could only reach his house
> By devious paths across a wooded plain.
>
> Then, if one came, he was not reinvited
> Unless he left a well-turned poem behind.
> Now all is desolate, as I converse
> With aged neighbors holding this in mind.
>
> We sit in melancholy silence, facing
> The landscape, where we view a giant tree
> Suggesting the good general, but at sunset
> Cold winds sigh through its leaves lugubriously.

The following poem provides a vivid and convincing picture of Tu Fu reading his own poetry to neighbors and friends who have shared something of his own trying experiences in time of civil war:

> Cocks and hens are clucking in confusion,
> Fighting fiercely as our friends draw near.
> I drive my noisy chickens up the trees;
> Knocking at the gate shows guests are here.
>
> Several of our older villagers
> Come to inquire about my health and ask
> How I sustained my long and dangerous journey.
> They bring me gifts and many a brimming flask.

We pour our wines together, weak and strong.
They say, "Forgive the flavor of our brew!
Good grain is scarce. Our boys are at the front.
The war drags on. What can poor farmers do?"

"Let me sing my poems to you, old friends.
Times have been harder upon you than me."—
After my song I lift my face and sigh.—
Tears flood our eyes in mutual sympathy.

The poems quite surprisingly resemble entries in a diary or famil-
iar letters dealing with current events in the state, the family, or
in both. Here are verses by Tu Fu recording the manner in which
he and his household received news that their period of political
exile had come abruptly to an end:

The sudden news of the recovery
Of Yu-chou reaches me in far Chien-nan.
At once the tears of joy sprinkle my gown
Where earlier only tears of sorrow ran.

I turn to see the sadness vanishing
From faces of my children and my wife.
I roll my books at random, sing aloud
And drink to the new happiness of life.

I shall not grudge myself the richest wine.
Spring shall be our companion going back,
Sailing through gorges of Wu-shan and Pa,
Taking through Hsiang our homeward track.

The poets enjoy subjects too humble for the typical Western
poet. Here are Tu Fu's lines to an old horse:

I've ridden you long, far, far beyond the frontier,
Deep, deep into the winter, and yet still
You toiled ever the more. So now I grieve
That you at last are feeble, old and ill.

There was nothing extraordinary about you
Save love and loyalty you gave so long.
The noble spirit of a humble creature
Is touching and deserves a grateful song.

The Chinese relish not only didactic verse, which, to be sure, they welcome with avidity but also poetry that is fanciful, whimsical, and that, above all, presents neither life nor art as burdensome. These views are expressed in the following verses:

Worldly cares never pass by old age.
Fatigue along with poverty intrudes
On all my dreary travels but I cannot
Forget dear friends and their poetic moods.

The Eastern capital is graced with streams;
Against the Western mountains storms disburse.
What peril can a serious tract remove?
I had far better turn to whims of verse!

My hut beyond the town wears a new thatch.
You reach it by the well-known road along
The river's side, past jade-green country fields.
The site is fair and gladdened by bird-song.

Giant bamboos condense and then release
Mist that covers them like glistening dew.
Swallows form a curtain from the sun
And rustle when a cooling breeze sweeps through.

Rooks flutter, old and young; mad swallows fly
Chattering, and then nest in sure repose.
Some scholars might compare me to Yang Hsiung
But, unlike him, I write no serious prose.

On the one hand, then, the Chinese poets stand remarkably close to the manners and experiences of everyday life, which they illumine with a peculiarly penetrating light. Here is an instance:

A curve in a clear stream circles our village.
Everything smiles in these warm summer days.
Gulls upon the water flock together;
Swallows dart upon their several ways.

My good wife draws a chessboard upon paper;
Our small sons hammer fishhooks out of wire.
All that a sick man needs is medicine.
What further can a humble man require?

On the other hand, the poets are also dreamers:

Last night I slept inside the monastery
Though earlier I knew the neighborhood.
Music of stillness haunts the dark ravine;
Radiance of moonlight filters through the wood.

Mountain peaks are pressing on the stars.
Sleep in clouds leaves clothing moist and chill.
The prayer-bell rang when I was half asleep.
My senses stir; my soul is sleeping still.

A conjunction of Taoism and Confucianism doubtless accounts for much of this extraordinary scope. In Chinese poetry the common touch is achieved with uncommon skill.

Most of the celebrated Chinese poets combine intimacy with profundity, contemplating the common denominator of human experience while, by virtue of their nuances, shunning banality. They are acutely conscious of being artists at the same time that they escape the unhappy condition of being sterilized by either aestheticism or romantic self-consciousness. They combine Indian warmth with Japanese fastidiousness. Here, to conclude, is one of Tu Fu's several poems addressed to his friend and fellow poet Li Po:

Li's poems soar upward with unrivaled splendor,
Winged by consummate mastery of technique,
Fresh as Yu Hsin, subtle as Pao Chao;
In final mastery he stands unique.

Now he views evening clouds east of the Chiang
And I, spring foliage north on the Wei's shore.
When can we meet over a pot of wine
Again to study and talk of literature?

Through verses such as these one grasps best the aims and methods of the most celebrated Chinese poets and what peculiar adjustments in English style must be made to render translation refreshing and exhilarating, not, as it too often becomes, flat and debilitating.

On Japanese Poetry

Although the major arts and the literature of Japan were sired by China, the brilliant culture of the island even from its early, formative years exhibits impressive qualities of its own. In contrast with their Chinese predecessors, the Japanese appear highly self-conscious learners, extremely gifted in both acquisition and, up to a certain point, in invention, but in the latter respect not to the same measure as the Chinese, who were so conspicuously to the manner born. A youthful glow at all times lightens the happiest Japanese work, no matter how sophisticated it becomes.

At the same time that their productions may justly lay claim to a remarkable vitality, perhaps nowhere have the criteria of aesthetics as understood in virtually all highly civilized lands been pressed to such extremes. In other words, emphasis falls upon form, notwithstanding a substantial content. Japanese imagination flourishes in a singularly rarefied atmosphere. So it comes about that although the subject matter of Japanese art and poetry is very commonly nature, no confusion exists between the claims of nature and art. Presumably the philosophical and emotional depth of Chinese thought is not achieved; assuming its place is an unsurpassed polish and charm. Moreover, the singular vigor of the Japanese spirit leads to a notable development of the comic spirit as manifest in all major modes of expression, with a corresponding development in the realm of tragedy, austerely framed and contained within aesthetic laws. Few comedies are more delightful than the Japanese kyōgen, few tragedies more admirable as works of art than the finest of the classical Noh plays.

From a less evolutionary point of view one finds the Japanese modes of expression outstanding in three respects. First, as I have already indicated, artfulness and refinement are of the highest order; craftsmanship is unsurpassed. Second, favored by its insular position, Japan developed one of the most legitimately indigenous outlooks, provincial only in the most favorable understanding of that word. Although the Japanese may look through lenses made in China, it is Japan that they see. This condition is apparent first of all in their devotion to the extraordinary Japanese landscape. To be sure, we recognize its trees as trees, its flowers as flowers. The same ocean obviously washes the shores of Japan, China, and America. Yet the phenomenally sharp Japanese eye detects not only the universal but the particular. There is a seeming paradox here. Although the Japanese are among the foremost masters of audacious stylization, they are likewise masters of the keenest realism. This characteristic appears, of course, equally in their art and literature and even in their highly developed "program music." It extends not only to a study of nature but to a study of manners as well. The Japanese may prefer midnight scenes for their Noh plays, yet their eyes are wide open even in the darkness. Their meditations may not be the most profound, but their observations are for accuracy unsurpassed.

Inevitably, the Japanese should be viewed in the general context of Eastern Asia. The Indians are primarily concerned with the ultimate destiny of things and with all things seen collectively as well as individually. Their obsession—a word scarcely too bold to express their own conception—is with birth and death, in terms both of the individual and of the universe. Each of their great books or poems is at heart a book of genesis and an apocalypse. The Chinese may also explore the various conditions of nature and of man in a general context, but each bush or tree, each external object of any sort, exhibits a general principle which in turn is seen as a constituent part of a comprehensive view of human life. The focus at all times remains social and humanistic. Through severe discipline and well-established traditions in Chinese thought, nature becomes a symbolic reflection of man. Man is supreme; the universe is his world, whereas it is better said of Indian thought that the universe is God's world.

It is important to note that as Japanese thought developed it followed a path taken by neither of the great cultures which fostered so much of its civilization. Its Buddhism was not strictly Indian, its devotion to the ethical thought of the great Chinese teachers never followed strictly along the lines of the Chinese. The most popular cult of Buddhism in Japan, Zen Buddhism, favored especially an aesthetic view of experience; Japanese morals developed along lines especially adapted to Japanese life. The Japanese vision proved to be less philosophical than aesthetic.

The mind's eye studied surfaces rather than interiors. Its gift for the realization of the purest art forms notwithstanding, it was to an extraordinary degree realistic. Origins and symbols as understood either in Indian or in Chinese thought concerned it relatively less, while the particular incident as studied at any given moment became of supreme importance.

This point of view further connoted a love of place which was also reflected in an extreme provincialism or patriotism. A physical landscape by almost any criterion unsurpassed for its beauty was seen with the eye of a painter much less philosophical than the Chinese vision but certainly no less acute as regards the sensual image. Nature imagery in Japanese poetry by no means possesses the sensuous and tropical warmth of the Indian but proceeds from a mind in a sense even more observant and discriminating, in the way that in a colder air visibility is often sharpened. Here again the Japanese, as their painting and poetry show to an almost equal degree, are an astonishingly eye-minded people. They have created nothing approaching the subjective and spiritual depth of German or Italian music; they have, however, given the world some of its greatest drawings.

That the Japanese mind turns with singular devotion to specific scenes and places is easily visible in its ancient poetry. An extraordinary number of place names occurs in the first great Japanese anthology, the Manyōshū, and much the same characteristic appears in later collections. Especially the longer poems in the Manyōshū celebrate places, often the site of an imperial palace, a famous harbor, mountain, river, or town. Much the same quality appears in the dramatic poetry. The Noh plays commonly put great emphasis upon the scene. At times the scene even becomes the dominating factor. In one play a famous grove of cherry trees seen in full bloom converts a hardhearted man to human kindness; in another the beauty of a vista seen under the full moon of autumn restores a mad woman to sanity. Many of the chief Noh plays have their scenes at monasteries or shrines famous for the natural beauty of their surroundings. Sometimes the shrine itself provided the location in which the play was originally performed.

It would be erroneous to hold that the Japanese in their poetry or in the actuality of their history show a greater or deeper love for nature than the Indians, the Chinese, the British, or the

Americans but they are, indeed, devoted to nature both intensely and in a peculiar manner. Nature they see as a Zen garden; the reflection cast by nature upon their highly stylized poetry or upon their remarkable paintings on silk or paper is a nature much modified by the conventions of art but still highly recognizable. The image may appear to Westerners less nature than decoration but it is unmistakably related not only to the Japanese mind but to the Japanese landscape. The very robes which the Noh actors wore, in spite of their extraordinary artificiality, often celebrate the seasons of the Japanese year.

The third pronounced tendency of the Japanese poet or artist derives in large measure from the two tendencies just examined. Art is a reshaping of experience. Drama is by its very nature palpably artificial. Strictly speaking, as its present-day commentators are especially fond of reminding us, it is deliberately an illusion. If, as Luigi Pirandello so often observed, we believe even for a moment that the play is real, it ceases to be a play. Playwrights, at least in a country where the art is highly developed and sophisticated, do not copy life; they interpret it with aid of fresh, creative inspiration. How natural it is, then, that trends in the Japanese character from early times led to a singularly extensive productivity in this consummate form of the artificial. Moreover, drama can hardly attain the extreme limits of aesthetic abstraction since it is created by actors who find it hard indeed to become transformed into pure abstractions. A pure allegory transposed to presentational art is more likely to become a tableau or a dance than a play. Drama as almost universally understood requires dramatis personae.

To this extent, also, it becomes naturalistic. The inclination of the richly qualified Japanese to combine artifice with realism led them to create some of the world's most remarkable drama. The most memorable form of Japanese drama was, naturally, destined to be the form from one point of view the most poetic because it is presumably the most artificial drama anywhere known to us, the Noh. This is also the supreme lyrical drama, using the word as applying not so much to song as to words. The brevity and concentration of a Noh play, not to mention the extraordinary manner of its presentation with the aid of both vocal and instrumental music, lead to analogy with what is commonly taken to be the genius of lyric poetry. Here the coin may be seen from its two sides, the converse being as true as the obverse. The finest Japanese drama is in this sense lyrical, while many of the finest Japanese lyrical poems are in their spirit and inspiration also dramatic. They insist upon the qualities of theatrical contrast and surprise. In other words, they enjoy much of the peculiar vitality and excitement that characterize drama.

Thus far the description of the Japanese poetic mind has been without explicit reference to development or change. It is widely acknowledged that the history of Japanese civilization shows a remarkable degree of coherence, integrity, and continuity, with small evidence of stagnation. Nevertheless, even in the long centuries, exceeding a millenium, in which Japanese culture remained to a very striking degree conservative and insular, change was a necessary condition for the flourishing of life. Inevitably, the arts either create what is new or decline and perish. By the very nature of poetic inspiration and the dependence of any vital art on the individuality of its creators, some change is inevitable. If the change occurs by no other means, men of genius inaugurate schools of expression, which is almost certainly the case in a dynamic culture. Only to a superficial eye, then, do the successive schools of Japanese expression seem alike. Possibly the unusual continuity in Japanese classical thought was overemphasized by its first serious critics in the West. It has been found attractive to distinguish the Japanese from the Chinese manner and to stand with considerable admiration before a culture which so long remained vital with, undeniably, so few revolutionary changes. To speak of drastic changes in classical Japan may well be just, but one cannot speak of revolutionary changes. Since this book deals only with what is called "ancient poetry," some attention to this consideration where Japan is concerned becomes especially desirable. Presumably a qualitative difference exists between what may legitimately be called "ancient poetry" and what is not ancient. What, in general, is the distinction?

The two most clearly "ancient" forms of Japanese poetry are, naturally, the nondramatic and the dramatic, one best represented by the venerable if not "primitive" anthology, the Manyōshū, the other by the earliest drama now known to exist, the Noh. Here it should at once be observed that the nondramatic poetry now surviving in any considerable quantity precedes by almost five centuries the oldest Noh plays. Few persons concerned with such matters are likely to dispute the statement that the Noh represent the climax of both Japanese poetic and presentational art. Beside them the Manyōshū does, indeed, appear "primitive." By comparison it is undeniably naïve. Yet it shows great subtleties of its own in craftsmanship and art. Although it admits none of the learned and almost esoteric symbolism found in the Noh, there is clearly a remarkable integrity of art form. These poems by no means resemble the British "border ballads." In few cases does the childhood of a great culture present so much refinement and delicacy. One with difficulty resists here what is possibly a specious analogy. To Western eyes, at least, much as Japanese children so often possess a peculiar charm, having at once the attractions of innocence and of a surprising maturity in manners, so the poets of the Manyōshū are at once naïve and mature. No seedling has more clearly possessed the promise of lusty growth, or, to change the metaphor, no palace of art has rested on a more sound, solid, and auspicious foundation.

Few critics will care to hold that the Manyōshū remotely approaches in profundity the Confucian Book of Songs, yet few will deny it a place of high honor not only in the history of Japanese verse but in world literature. It breathes throughout an air of crystal clarity. The large number of place names which it contains in no way limits it to a merely local significance. In this respect it seems almost as universal as the Iliad. This, again, is not to claim for it the depth of Homeric poetry. It is only to maintain that it has at all times spoken clearly, though one is pleased to say not loudly, to all its readers. It may possibly invite annotations because of its many references to person and place; otherwise explanation is called for only to a minimum.

By a natural development, especially because of the aesthetic doctrine of intimation so attractive to the Japanese and best stated by the master of the Noh drama, Seami, Japanese poetry even at a comparatively early time left its original naïveté behind it. To a remarkable degree in the course of years it became a poetry of oblique, not direct, reference, of overtones, halftones, and diminuendos. To be sure, a popular style developed, coming to its startling climax in the triumph of the kabuki during the seventeenth century, which stands in sharp contrast to a truly sophisticated art.

Evolution in Japanese dramatic and nondramatic poetry presents, then, a scene upon at least two levels. The finest Japanese dramatic poetry, as already stated, is almost incontestably in the Noh drama and its variants. In comparison, the kabuki is vin ordinaire. Regardless of an invariable conjunction in the Noh of verse and prose, a Noh play is, seriously considered, one essentially lyric poem throughout. With the drama for puppets as perfected at the close of the seventeenth century, not only was there a conjunction of prose and verse passages, but only the verse remotely rivals the high standards established by Japanese poetry in the deeper sense of the word. Chikamatsu, the chief writer for the puppets, employs prose as the medium for almost undiluted naturalism. No major poet in the realm of drama appeared after the seventeenth century. Poetry's two competitors, namely, realism and melodrama, triumphed on the popular stage.

In nondramatic poetry, development proceeded on less complicated lines. The naïve temper of the Manyōshū yielded, as I have already observed, to a distinctly sophisticated art, destined to reach its highest development at approximately the same period as the dynamic years of the Noh, or, roughly speaking, the closing years of the Middle Ages in Europe. Thereafter, the nondramatic poetry became increasingly mannered and rarefied rather than imaginatively virile and vigorous. Inspiration undeniably remained. The most assiduously cultivated form, the haiku, one of the most succinct types of poetic epigram, certainly yields much that is pure gold. But an attenuation set in; the culture became inbred. Change had progressed along what now seems an almost inevitable course. The youthful bloom was left behind, and a glossy veneer took its place. Japan awaited new impulses from the West, influences which, as it has recently been proved, she was abundantly qualified to receive.

The preceding reference to the medieval period in Europe is not without some meaning that at first it is possible to overlook. Western civilization offers no especially strategic portal of which I am aware that leads to the art and poetry of China. The major Chinese works are neither esoteric nor perspicuous. On the contrary, Scholasticism, or the religious thought of the Middle Ages, offers many entrances to Indian thought and poetry. An understanding of the Divine Comedy, for instance, should materially aid an appreciation of the Bhagavad-Gita. Only in the twentieth century have the more advanced forms of Japanese verse occupied a position to attract Western readers. This they have indeed done. William Butler Yeats, for example, came abruptly upon the Noh plays as he might have embraced long-lost spiritual brothers. The haiku provided inspiration to a large number of Western poets, among them the American Amy Lowell, whose stature it is now the fashion, I believe, somewhat to underestimate. One can scarcely imagine so precious a form of verse attracting William Shakespeare or even Edmund Spenser.

It is to the age of Chaucer that one must turn for helpful analogies with the Manyōshū. This is not the place to pursue comparisons to great lengths. Nevertheless it may be noted, to begin with, that the verse-forms are often clearly parallel. The use of the "envoy" in lyric poems appears, for example, in both literatures. The clarity of tone in the earlier and more dynamic period of medieval lyric poetry, especially in Provençe and the Rhinelands, even a little earlier than the times of Chaucer, reminds one of the great purity of tone of the Manyōshū. In both literatures is much the same naïve optimism and much the same ironic melancholy, where youthful happiness is discovered, one imagines for the first time, to be fleeting and eminently perishable. There is, ironically, also, the same naïve acceptance of the physical world. Ideals and loyalties of feudalism appear much the same in both East and West. Striking parallels exist in the rituals of courtship. Hence in the twentieth century a Westerner translating this early Japanese poetry does well to keep the delightful art of the troubadours and minnesingers prominently in mind.

That the Manyōshū merits priority in any study of truly ancient Japanese verse is, I believe, inescapable. In this book Japanese dramatic poetry is represented not by a Noh play, as might conceivably be presumed, but by a work of what is, unhappily, a much less well-known form than the Noh, the kōwaka. The kōwaka stands, nevertheless, extremely close to the Noh in conception and equally close to the inspired narratives in both prose and verse that Japan produced during its feudal period. In short, the kōwaka occupies a position halfway between the epic or historical poems and the verbal texts for works that are at once lyrical and dramatic. It is less theatrical than the Noh but on this very account harmonizes even more closely with the nondramatic or pure poetry. Moreover, it is a much less complex form than the Noh, which has undeniably presented translators with what have as yet proved almost unsurmountable difficulties. From a variety of reasons, then, a kōwaka play, Atsumori, has been selected here. It clearly exhibits the qualities already described as typical of Japanese poetic inspiration. The brilliant descriptions of place, the intensely dramatic feeling, the luxury of pure color, the poignancy of the pathos combine to make it, I believe, an attractive specimen of the Japanese poetic genius very close to its highest achievement.

It is, perhaps, all but inevitable that the peculiar climate of Japanese poetic thought and feeling be analyzed by some comparison or contrast with the parent art of China. The differences are almost always subtle, and on this very account they are more readily felt than analyzed or explained. Why, for example, are the following brief poems so clearly Chinese and not Japanese, even when seen through the dusky veil of translation?

> The same moon in Fu-chou brightens her wall.
> From the window she will watch it all alone.
> Our children are too little to recall
> When we were once together in Ch'ang-an.
>
> Night-dew will fall upon her perfumed hair;
> Her frail arms shiver in that chilly place.
> When can we both lean on the window there
> And watch the tears dry on each other's face?
>
> TU FU

> After the cold winds blew the snow came soon.
> Roads were hard; flutes blew their dreary tune.
> Three hundred thousand troops camped on the desert.—
> Suddenly all turned to see the moon.
>
> LI I

The very numerous quotations in the Noh plays from Chinese poetry, even without benefit—or injury—of translation from the Chinese would alone show how truly the Japanese themselves enjoyed and treasured their Chinese masters. In few cases has one country so fruitfully cherished the arts of another. But to duplicate the more philosophical and emotionally profound arts of China was not granted to the brilliant though essentially less

On winds of lightning, tortured as vast waves
Of ocean, infinite and depth-defying,
Shower gentle moisture on the scented earth
Piercing its verdurous beauty in all parts
With drops of rain so crystalline and clear
They gleam like diamond-pointed, kindly darts.

The world has closed its lotus eyes, that now
Know neither day nor night; lightning persists
To flare but earth has veiled its dazzled eyes;
The sky is drowned in slumber; nothing exists
But rain that pours from heaven's high palaces
Beneath its canopy of swirling mists.

Now when the earth is seen through lightning flashes,
Fragrant with rain-washed flowers, this woman has come,
By love exalted and with rain-drenched hair,
At last to visit her beloved one's home.
Quivering with lightning, deafened by roar of thunder,
She sighs for one whom she so thirsts to meet,
Even while cleansing mud-bespattered ankles,
The circling bracelets and the agile feet.

The poet's imagery not only with the boldest strokes encom-
passes heaven and earth; a single drop of water begets the follow-
ing remarkable stanza. The dramatic moment occasioning it oc-
curs, of course, after the lovers have met face to face.

The rain-drenched blossom of the cadamba flower
Nestling beside her ear releases one
Clear drop of moisture descending on her breast
Such as might fall upon the heir and son
Of some great king in regal ritual,
The consecration ceremony begun.

The sensuous character of this poetry is seldom so well repre-
sented as in the two stanzas with which the entire episode con-
cludes. Both are rarely, if ever, paralleled in Western poetry. In
the first of these the heavens are audaciously likened to the physi-
cal state of the expectant lovers: the rainbow embracing the sky
is like the lovers' embrace; an opening in the clouds is like the

mouth opened for a kiss; the lightning is the eager tongue; the heavens seem yawning with the languor that precedes fruition. The personal and universal are conjoined. To speak of tactile values here would, indeed, be an understatement. In the second stanza the various sounds of wind and rain falling upon dense tropical foliage are conveyed with phenomenal success. These stanzas are hard for any translator to render. Unhappily, the first is likely to appear merely grotesque; the second is likely to evaporate for want of adequate subtlety in language, especially in its vocal aspects. I have done what I can.

Does not the sky seem yawning languidly?
Its great tongue vibrates in its mouth through shrouds
Of darkness; it throws huge arms, a rainbow forth;
It opens up enormous jaws, the clouds.

The raindrops throb on palm leaves, sigh aloud
On branches, drum on rocks, hiss on a lake,
And all together resound as the rich tones
Artful players on strings and cymbals make.

It is hardly necessary to add that in the theater the orchestra which accompanied the performance on the stage performed as the last words of the second stanza indicate.

Finally, from the semi-dramatic poem, or verse dialogue, the Bhagavad-Gita, most celebrated of Sanskrit religious books, the image of God as destroyer, or God as cruelty, yields one of the most famous passages in Sanskrit literature. I feel that it even surpasses, in evocation of horror, the roughly analogous passage in the Divine Comedy, Dante's image of the Anti-God, or Satan:

I see you, powerful, endless, vast,
You, the myriad-shouldered one,
Whose face is but a blazing fire,
Its eyes, the shining moon and sun.

I feel I can no longer live
Because my heart is terrified.
No magic can restore my thoughts
By such a splendor stupefied.

Lord, saint of saints, prop of the world,
Seeing you with your gaping maw
Blazing with the fires of hell,
I cover burning eyes in awe.

Ah, my lord, please appear mild!
You have robbed me of all breath:
Bhisma, Drona, Karna, all
Seem hastening to your jaws of death.

All Duryodhana's family,
Warrior, priest and reverend sage,
Kings and princes, all as one
Are there consumed in war's hot rage!

Some of them now reappear
As if stuck there between your teeth,
Raw heads severed from their limbs,
All at last to plunge beneath.

Torrential rivers from the hills
Flow to the sea and know no drouth,
So the brave ones of this world
Plunge into your blazing mouth.

Minutest fireflies haunt the flame
Thinking to expunge its light,
So the great ones of this world
Haste to your jaws, crushed by their might.*

This awareness of evil attacking soul and body is, surely, enough to make any conscientious translator uncomfortable, though his reader may possibly derive a grim pleasure. It is typical of the peculiar power of Sanskrit verse.

The foregoing translations of dramatic stanzas have been chosen as keys to a reading and study of Sanskrit poetry when it is rendered into English. Quite apart from whatever intrinsic worth these "dramatic lyrics" may or may not possess, it is hoped that they may in some way serve to open the way to further enjoyment and analysis of the ancient masterpieces from which they spring.

* Translated by H. W. Wells and M. Srinivasan.

Tu Fu

๙Tu Fu (A.D. 712–770) is called by his leading biographer and commentator, William Hung, "China's greatest poet." He has probably been the most widely beloved of their poets by the Chinese. Some fourteen hundred of his poems have survived, a surprisingly large number of which have become to the Chinese people as familiar as their household treasures.

To an almost unique degree, these poems are autobiographical. They also give a vivid image of the social and political life in Tu Fu's tumultuous times. So descriptive are they in these respects that no extended account of the man or his career is required as introduction to works that are themselves our best introduction to him and to his country. Like a large number of his fellow poets, Tu Fu held several government posts, both in the capital and in the provinces, moving in and out of office as factions in the Imperial ministry changed. Because of civil war and repeated uprisings, he was frequently in exile and was at least once captured by the enemy. Some of his best-remembered poems deal with his wartime sufferings and with those of his fellow countrymen. Yet throughout the political chaos his literary fame grew steadily. By the time of his death he was the most widely known poet in the Empire. His position in Chinese literature has never been shaken.

In varying degrees poets or playwrights represent their native culture. Molière and La Fontaine are indisputably French. Whitman is more clearly American than Poe. There can be no doubt that Tu Fu represents to a remarkable degree the central current of Chinese thought, taste, and imagination. To be sure, no writer, however inspired, could be expected actually to summarize the breadth of a culture so eclectic and so long-lived as that of China. Chinese verse extends from the ultra-romantic and fantastic to the down-to-earth and colloquial. But its main stem is much closer to the unrhetorical and the familiar than to the metaphysical or the sublime. In other words, it reflects the central place of Confucian thinking in Chinese life. Accordingly, it implies an aesthetic very unlike that formulated by Aristotle or propagated by such representative thinkers in the field of English poetry and criticism as Samuel Taylor Coleridge and T. S. Eliot. The main stem of Chinese poetry is as faithful in capturing the image of daily living as Walt Whitman and as fastidious in its sense of form as Alexander Pope. It is as close to earth as Robert Burns and as elegant as Matthew Prior.

This image, never realized in the West, describes the poetry of Tu Fu better, perhaps, than that of any other Chinese master. Because he so well represents an outlook radically unlike that of most Western poets and yet a synthesis which no English poet quite achieves, he is given the leading place in this book. To no English poet is he closer than to Chaucer. But Chaucer is primarily a storyteller who employs a traveling lense. Tu Fu is the arch-master of a poetry that resembles still photography, snapshots that seem deceptively casual but that never seem to grow old nor fade. How much we have to learn from him! Seen from our own generally accepted point of view, his aesthetic is revolutionary.

In conclusion, something should be said regarding the arrangement of Tu Fu's poems on the following pages. For a chronological arrangement the reader is referred to William Hung's versions, accompanied by an extensive biographical commentary. Such a plan, though eminently valuable elsewhere, hardly suits the purposes of this book, where historical and biographical points of view are secondary and no new data in these fields is offered. The arrangement here is intended to aid in elucidating the nature of Tu Fu's poetry, his imaginative vision of life, and the principles of his art. Inasmuch as his exceptionally frank enjoyment of living is conspicuous, a group of his verses is first presented which express the poet's refreshing and positive view of experience. Since Tu Fu is also masterly in voicing compassion for human suffering, especially as experienced by a civilian population in time of war, a number of his poems are included lamenting the brutality of civil strife which he knew so well. His resilient spirit notwithstanding, he was no shallow optimist. That his imagination not only penetrated the intimate and homely incidents in life but also expanded to embrace much that was physically distant in time and space is revealed in still another group of verses. The largest group given here resembles in its topicality entries in a verse-diary, or suggests the outlook found in the tradition of the verse-letter, which has extended in Western literature from Horace to Alexander Pope and considerably beyond. The eighteenth-century use of the verse couplet has been very helpful to me in my rendering of the poetry. Finally, because despite the colloquial character of the verse a strong lyrical element is found—which is as a rule more familiar and attractive to Westerners than the occasional verse of the preceding section—a group of poems is offered designated "Odes and Elegies." It is hoped that this arrangement indicates something of the scope of Tu Fu's extraordinary genius. His work combines the metaphysical quality achieved in the verses of his friend Li Po with the ethical quality in the work of his most eminent successor, Po Chü-i. It would be hard to overemphasize the centrality of Tu Fu's position in the history of Chinese poetry.

These rhymed renderings of selected poems have been made with the generous assistance of William Hung and the permission of the Harvard University Press, publisher of Tu Fu: China's Greatest Poet, by William Hung, 1951.

The Good Life

Though fallen petals mean less of the springtime
And rude winds blow a thousand shreds away,
I'll let my eyes feast on such flowers as stay
And shall not grudge my lips the dangerous wine.

Kingfishers nest in ruined masonary;
A unicorn of stone smiles near a tomb;
In this fresh Park nature repudiates gloom,
So why should rank or honor trouble me?

Drink for one day is all my pawned clothes give;
From Court to Park my daily trip is made.
I well may die leaving wine-debts unpaid;
Seventy years men scarcely hope to live.

Butterflies drown themselves inside rich flowers;
Dragonflies fleck blue water now and then.
O wind and light and time, be with us men!
Let us not strive; long joy is never ours!

TRUE ENJOYMENT

I drink tea on the terrace at sunset all alone.
Spring breezes fan me as I moisten my brush on stone.
Sitting in perfect comfort, I write a poem on a palm.
A kingfisher chirps on a bamboo clothes-rack safe from harm;
A dragonfly clings to a fishing line, buzzing his warm refrain.
Now that I know what enjoyment is, I'll come here again and again!

⤳ HIS MAJESTY'S GIFT OF CLOTHES ⤵

So my name is on the list for the festival gift!
The clothes made only as the palace tailors know.
Their muslin sways as the lightest breezes shift;
Their fragrant silk folds up like layers of snow.

I notice their label is signed with His Majesty's hand,
Ink hardly dry; summer's heat will fly their face;
Their size precise—how do tailors understand?—
I shall always remember my Majesty's "fitting" grace.

⤳ THE AUDIENCE HALL¹ ⤵

Bells of the fifth watch resound and hasten the coming of day;
Peach blossoms blush as if drunk with too much April wine;
Embroidered dragons swirl on banners in warm sunshine;
High over palace walls the swallows dart and play.

On leaving the audience hall the incense clings to your sleeve;
Writing your poetry your thoughts and words flow smoothly together.
The Secretary's Office is the Phoenix' Pool, men believe,
For the son follows the father, as the Phoenix drops a feather.

⤳ MAGISTRATE TS'UI COMES ⤵

Around my hut pools gather
As the spring rain falls;
Gulls are the only creatures
Paying daily calls.

My path is strewn with petals
For my broom lies at rest;
My rustic gate's open
And you're the year's first guest.

Market's far; I haven't
Any fancy food;
I'm poor; but my only pot
Of home-brew's good.

Wouldn't you like to drink
With an old neighbor of mine?
I'll shout over the fence;
He'll help us finish our wine.

⊷ FACING THE SNOW ⊶

A sleet-storm falls like an invading power;
Out of the nip of the north its winds blow;
Gale-driven leaves are flying with the snow;
Flakes seldom show the pattern of a flower.

My money's spent; my purse itself is light;
But I can buy on credit readily;
Why doesn't someone share my jug with me?
I'll wait till crows come homing with the night.

⊷ EVENING AFTER THE SHOWER ⊶

Over the village at evening sudden rain-storms pass;
They sprinkle the fine garden and glitter over the green.
Now the setting sun is warming the new-sprung grass.
The river sparkles in view through the newly opened screen.

My books lie in disorder; I can tend to them later on.
This cup's empty; I may as well fill it again.
I hear certain comments about me down in the town
But as yet no one has blamed me for my life that is quiet and plain.

INTOXICATION OF FLOWERS

Flowers in confusion by the river shine;
Awed, I likewise stagger as I can;
I can subsist on poetry and wine;
But try not to undo a white-haired man!

HAPPY OVER RAIN

Drought; a glaring sun; months without rain.
This morning clouds arise thickening the sky again.
A sprinkle begins; swallows, ceasing from nervous flight,
Re-enter nests; forests gleam fresh and bright.
Rain continues at dusk. I shall hear it into the night.

TO ABBOT MIN

Abbot Min, I've not set eyes on you since thirty years ago,
Yet now in writing to you the warm tears blot the page.
Are you still the all-accomplished master whom I used to know?
To whom do you address new poems you write in your old age?

I see your chess pawns moving in the patterned shade and sun;
I recall the saffron cloak you wore when boating on the deep;
I hear that you've been praising my honors lately won.—
The best is just my dull white head, drunk and sound asleep.

❧ OUR SOUTHERN NEIGHBOR ❧

I had stopped at a neighbor's just down the road
And returning was told of the call you had made.
It's a long trip you took to my modest abode
And I'm quite overwhelmed by the honor you paid.

My country home seems miles away, I am sure.
That good company's scant in the village is plain.
But I'll maybe make bold to discuss literature.—
Would you knock on my shabby wood gateway again?

This Troubled World

⇜§ MOONLIGHT NIGHT [2] §⇝

The same moon in Fu-chou brightens her wall.
From the window she will watch it all alone.
Our children are too little to recall
When we were once together in Ch'ang-an.

Night-dew will fall upon her perfumed hair;
Her frail arms shiver in that chilly place.—
When can we both lean on the window there
And watch the tears dry on each other's face?

⇜§ RETURNING HOME [3] §⇝

From west of the purple horizon the sun makes its final dive
Beneath the western mountain; a bird by the gate appears
To welcome me home, but my family can't believe that I've come
    back alive.
When the shock is finally over, they're busy wiping their tears.

Storms have blown families apart; by luck I escaped their doom.
Neighbors climb walls to see me; they sob in the day's last gleam.
When the night has darkened, the candles shine through the gloom.
We look at each other and wonder whether we live in a dream?

ᵛᵍ HEARD ABOUT MY BROTHER ᵍᵛ

How many have returned since the war made
   A place unknown
   Seem better than their own?

That I am feeling bitter and dismayed
   Is that you are
   In exile and afar.

Your books are walled up from the roaming thief;
   Your second spouse
   Has lately left your house.

Only the old dog shares my sighs and grief
   With drooping head
   Sitting beside my bed.

ᵛᵍ WASHING AND POUNDING CLOTHES ᵍᵛ

I know that you will not come back from war.
   Still, on this stone
I pound your cloak while you must die afar
   And I alone.

Here in this bitter autumn chill I dream
   You may be warm
Although the heart's chill that I suffer seems
   An equal harm.

How can I cease from toiling, since I pray
   This coat may come
To the Great Wall you guard, while I must stay
   In our cold home?

Each sinew in my woman's body pounds
   Your garment fair:
Listen! You may even hear these sounds
   Out there!

DREAMING OF LI PO [4]

Grief can be swallowed when a life has fled
But absent friends mean dread anxiety.
I am much worried that Li Po should be
In exile where malaria is bred.

You have appeared to me in dreams which show
How fierce and deep the longings love has made.
When from this distance I perceive your shade
If you are live or dead is hard to know.

You came to me through woods green sunshine lit;
Through a black mountain-pass your spirit sped.
The prosecutor's net fell on your head:
How could you ever have escaped from it?

Starless heavens are a glossy blue;
In the wan moonlight I can see your face.
Vast monsters coil where the mad waters race.
Beware! Don't let the dragons swallow you!

A RECRUITING OFFICER AT SHIH-HAO

Once while traveling I came in sight
Of Shih village and passed the night.

There a recruiting officer came
To corral men for the old campaign.

My old host climbed his wall and fled;
His old wife jumped out of her bed.

When she opened the gate the officer roared
While the old woman wept and implored.

This is what I heard her say:
"Three sons have gone to the war away.

One has in his letter said
That both of his brothers now are dead.

Two boys are dead and forever gone,
So how can the third linger on?

There's only this suckling grandson left,
Of the other males our home's bereft.

His mother stays because of her son,
She hasn't a whole skirt to put on.

I'm old and of little use to fight
But I'll go with you, sir, this very night.

If I'm no use in battle, then
I can still cook meals for men."

Talk droned till the midnight bell had passed
And I seemed to hear only sobbing at last.

I resumed my trip at sunrise bell,
When only the old man waved farewell.

∿§ PARTING OF A NEWLY WEDDED COUPLE ৰ৶

A dodder clinging to a flax-plant finds
No long or sure support; marriage that binds
A girl and soldier cannot hold for long.
Such a cruel union is as wrong
As throwing out a girl on the roadside.
It's true that I am legally your bride;
My hair's tied firm, but, ah! I'm brokenhearted:
Married at evening and at morning parted!

Too hurriedly by far our union came.
It's true that we are man and wife in name.
The distance isn't what I have to fear;
The frontier station isn't far from here.
But since our marriage hasn't been fulfilled,
How can the beating of our hearts be stilled?
How can I now sincerely have the right
To be a daughter-in-law? By day and night

My parents guarded me and they did not
Give me away for such a wretched lot
Or think, when I was married, I would then
Be poor and lonely as a dog or hen.

You're marching to the frontier to be slain
While I am stumbling to a world of pain.
To go with you would make our trouble worse
For that would only bring our comrades' curse.
You'd better now forget about your bride,
Putting our tenderness and love aside.
Give yourself to the duties of the war;
That's what you should now be living for.
Love and gentleness are for a wife
And kind thoughts wrong in military life.
Silk clothes so long to weave are worthless now;
I wash the rouge and powder from my brow.
Birds fly in pairs while men feel misery;
Longing alone is left for you and me.

⊷§ THE SONG OF WAR CHARIOTS [5] §⊶

Chargers champ; chariots groan;
Men march with menacing weapons;
Wives weep; whimpering children
And parents push pressing forward
To embrace and bid the boys goodbye.
There's rumble and roar; rising dust
Blurs the bridge as battalions file.—
As crowds clutch clothes of soldiers
Shrill skrieks shatter clouds.
Passer-by puts his question:
"Who are you and where are you going?"
"Regular recruits," the reply comes.
"Some sent to secure the frontier.
First we were fifteen; we're forty now.
First a captain compelled us to wear men's caps,
Now, white-haired, we go again.

We've bled enough blood to bloat the ocean
While our Sovereign ceaselessly swells his Empire.
Haven't you heard in hundreds of counties
Thousands and thousands of villages thick in weeds?
Where strong women work the farms
No farmer can find his field to harvest.
Since soldiers from Ching-chao are celebrated for courage
They must be driven like dogs and downtrod chickens.
It's well enough for you to inquire of our troubles
But how can we have courage to recount our ills?
Our Kuan-hsi contingent continues to serve
Yet our governor continues to collect taxes,
But where in heaven will the taxes come from?
Now we know we never should have sons—
Better to have begot a bevy of daughters;
Girls given in marriage keep families together
But boys are born to blister in the sands
Of the Kokonor desert country where it's common practice
To let bones bleach unburied in the sun.
Young ghosts whimper while the old weep.
You hear them always on rainy nights."

~§ SILKWORMS AND COWS §~

There must be a thousand cities
   Peopled, alas, with fools,
Rich in iron weapons,
   But taught in folly's schools.
How good to beat those weapons
   Into farming tools!

Let oxen plow the acres
   Left barren far too long!
Let women tend the silkworms!
   Let farmers mend the wrong
To their fields with loving labor!
   Let each sing his song!

Our generals of the Renaissance are rescuing the East;
Reports of victory are now awaited day and night;
Towns on the Yellow River will soon find themselves released
And at his final fort at Yeh the foe be put to flight.
These gains are clearly owing to the Shuo-fang armies' might.
The Tatar's force is splintered as a keen axe cuts bamboo.
In the capital our captains ride war-horses as their right;
The Uighurs in the Imperial halls hold joyous rendezvous;
The Northeast gives the Emperor the homage that is due.

We well may now recall the days the royal Court moved back
And forth from Ling-wu traversing so many dreary miles;
For three years our men were saddened by songs that sang the lack
Of free communication but today, when fortune smiles,
Our countless armies sweep the foe as crisp and withered piles
Of leaves before the autumn gales. Ch'eng's Prince is truly wise
With caution even in victory; Kuo Tzu-i has countless wiles;
General Li Kuang-pi's mind is true as truth in mirrors lies;
General Wang Ssu-li's loyalty deep as the autumn skies.

Heaven dispatched such men to save a world with chaos vexed;
Our people now may live like birds reposing in a nest.
Officials no more need to shun their duties by pretext.
Courtiers' costumes shine again like earth with springtime blessed.
Fumes from a thousand incense-burners everywhere invest
The air with fragrance blended with a multitudinous store
Of palace flowers. The Emperor's chariot, lying long at rest,
Is all the night prepared, at dawn to issue through the door;
Our Sovereign will give filial thanks to the Old Emperor!

It seems at Court that the whole world's aswarm with dukes and
            lords.
But, parasites, remember that you have no rightful claim
To favor just for snatching at what fortune's hand affords;
To follow with the exiled Court is no just lease on fame.
Mere simple luck and bravery can never be the same.
At Court another Hsiao Ho becomes the lord of all;
In field another Chang Liang achieves a noble name,
Long versed in all the ways of men, he answers duty's call,
A man with jet-black beard and brows and truly nine feet tall!

He saved the crumbling Dynasty in its most fateful hour!
How many rebels now are left pretending to renew
Their war? Rejoice that the Imperial House now reigns in power
And glory, as of old the Houses of the Han and Chou!
We trust that from all lands on earth tributes will accrue
To grace the imperial treasure with magic that instills
Protective charms, propitious signs, gems wonderful to view,
White jade-rings out of fairy-tales, the work of fabulous skills.
Reports are heard of silver urns discovered in the hills!

Our famous scholar-hermit must from henceforward lay
Aside songs of retirement, poets sing instead in praise
Of peace and this sagacious rule. Our loyal farmers pray
For rain. Cuckoos are calling for good spring-planting days.
Let our valiant boys who long have fought in grim forays
Of battle in Tsi Valley return and soon regain
Their homes and dreaming wives. Today each faithful subject prays
Some man will pour the sky's star-river on the gory stain
Of arms and put them all away, never to rise again!

⊰§ OVERNIGHT IN THE APARTMENT
BY THE RIVER ◌⟩

Dusk shrouds the mountain, for the hour is late;
Clouds on the cliffside in the twilight gleam;
Here from my room beside the Water Gate
I watch the lonely moon fall on the stream.

I hear a wolf pack baying from afar;
I see a crane fly past the moon unfurled.
I cannot sleep because I think of war
And I am powerless to amend the world.

In a Lighter Vein

⊸§ CRICKET ๑∾

A tiny thing
With harrowing
Voice won't sing
To words; instead

For company
It's come to be
Indoors with me
Beneath my bed:

Its song a dart
Poignant to smart
A lonely heart
Moved to tears;

The abandoned wife
Feels its knife
Piercing her life
With keener fears.

No sound of strings
Or flute tune brings
Such bitter stings
As here belong

To this weird note
From Nature's throat,
Mystic, remote,
The cricket's song.

✑ FIREFLY ✑

Bothersome thing! remember, you come from rotted weeds;
 How dare you fly in the sun's light?
By your tenuous flicker no scholar really reads;
 You spot my clean robe with your tiny blight.

Windblown, you are barely seen through my darkened blind.
 In rain-drenched woods you stagger to and fro.
But in frosty winter I pity your feeble kind:
 Then, scattered and afraid, where can you go?

✑ THE SPOTTED DUCK [7] ✑

The spotted duck without a speck of mud
Stalks with a stately waddle past my door.
"Your plumage shows that you are very odd,
But what is all this independence for?

Great judge and critic of the black and white!
Though you yourself are not by jealousy marred,
Even when rating other birds the worst
Don't place yourself in a conspicuous light!
While you are never from your breakfast barred,
Make up your mind never to quack the first."

✑ THE AUTUMN GALE TEARS OFF MY THATCHED ROOF ✑

September's howling wind, frantic and rough,
Has rolled three layers of thatch right off my roof.
Most of the stalks were blown against the bank,
Some into soggy, rain-swept hollows sank,
Others were lifted to the tops of trees.

Village boys perceiving that with ease—
Because of my great age and feeble sight—
They could steal property in broad daylight,
Carried away whole armfuls to the wood.
I cried to them as loudly as I could
Until my throat was hoarse, my lips were dry.
At length I left them with a deep-drawn sigh
And, leaning on my staff, was forced to come
Indoors again to my much ravished home.

The gale subsided while an ink-black shroud
Of darkness covered all the sky with cloud.
Cold night crept on. Over my frozen feet
The old cotton quilt seemed like an iron sheet,
Moreover sadly torn, for on their beds
My much spoiled boys had kicked it into shreds.
The roof leaked on the couch; nothing was dry.
Rain fell like flax out of a freezing sky.
Wholly deprived of sleep, I tossed this way
And that, impatient for the far-off day.
I thought of naked wretches in the storm,
Wet to the skin, miserable, never warm,
And wished one sturdy, rainproof roof unfurled
Over all poor scholars in the world,
So an impervious shield might be conveyed,
Unshakable as a mountain for their aid!
O, could I suddenly see before my eyes
Such a huge house as my fond prayer supplies,
Although my roof fell and my life was spent,
Naked beneath that storm, I'd die content.

Distances

◄§ WRITTEN ON THE WALL BESIDE THE HORSES PAINTED BY WEI YEN [8] §►

Wei Yen who has come to call
Knows I love his casual art.
Look! horses suddenly start
To grow on my Eastern wall.

One has his head to the ground,
One neighs with look aloof.
Both are eager to pound
A thousand miles on the hoof.

How I would sound applause
Could he only give them breath
To serve our war-lord's cause
On the fields of life and death!

◄§ THE LUTE TERRACE IN MEMORY OF SSU-MA HSIANG-JU [9] §►

I sit on the "Lute Terrace," famous in memory
    Of Ssu-ma, sickly lover, who took Cho-Wenchun far off
    To these bleak mountains where they kept a tavern and bore the
        scoff
Of common folk who laughed at them, mocking their misery.

Perhaps these wild-flowers bound her hair; perhaps her silken dress
    Was color of these weeds? But in this cloud-dark, dim estate
    No more a lonely Phoenix sings crying for his mate,
No more a lute-song blesses deathly quietness.

High on a terrace near the break of day
    Moving moonbeams brush my knee;
A gust extinguishes the Milky Way;
    Gradual dawn tips roof and tree.

Earth's varied creatures wake from sleep's caress
    Bestirred in groups of twos and threes;
I, too, shall set my sons their tasks and press
    To selfish ends with all of these.

In winter, travelers hasten to their goals
    And all's agog the world of man,
Because men's passions have disturbed their souls
    Since first the world itself began.

Why, having filled his belly with supplies
    Sufficient for his life—why yet
Should government and education rise
    To trap him in their wretched net?

First criminal was he who kindled fire;
    Next, who distinguished wrong from right;
Men wrestle in the coils of fierce desire
    Like moths transfixed in candlelight.

Let your spirit soar beyond the span
    Of all illusions that we feel or see;
Beyond their tides of ebb and flow find man's
    Secret of immortality.

◆§ THE NEAR AND FAR §◆

Two brown orioles sing in willows; white egrets climb the skies;
My window holds far mountains where snow for ages lies;
Beyond my gate are anchored boats that sail a thousand miles.

REQUESTING YOUNG PINE TREES

Do willows tower so high?
Or bushes keep so green?
I think of shadows seen
As centuries go by.

I'll thank you for some shoots
And saplings rich in strength
Not for their branches length
But for their sturdy roots.

PAINTING A LANDSCAPE [11]

Ten days to draw a river, five for a rock or bush.
Wang Tsai cannot be hurried as he wields his leisurely brush.
He'll leave you in time a landscape to hang on your walls and span
From the far west K'un-lun Mountains to the far east sea of Japan.
The water between red banks of his river overflows
In the starry river of heaven whose bourne no mortal knows.
In vapors and clouds the dragons are eager to dive and sport.
Here are boatmen and fishers turning their prows to port;
Here mountain trees are bowing under the wings of the gale.
To compete with such distances others would labor to small avail.
There are hundreds of miles to the inch. I'd like to take my stout
Pair of northern scissors and snip half of his river out.

Biographical

A poor, obscure man, dwelling in Tu-ling,
Grew more impractical in everything
Until in madness, as the years went by,
His final, crowning folly was to try
To serve his country, as the best men did
In old days; yet grim destiny forbid
That anything but grief should come of it.
His wishes and the world just did not fit.
Though now white-haired, his ludicrous fixation
Is to persist in face of his frustration
And not until reposing in his tomb
Can he escape this self-inflicted doom.
He worries about people constantly,
Burning his heart out with anxiety,
And though old friends insist that he is wrong,
He pours his sad heart out in passionate song.
Poor foolish man! he can't forget his dream
Of drifting gently down a glassy stream,
Living a life merely of pastime, since
Fortune grants him a munificent Prince.
He loathes the thought of strenuous and rough
Public life and knows there is enough
Political timber for the ship of state
But yet he knows it is the sunflower's fate
To turn its blossom frankly to the sun,
A gesture he can neither choose nor shun.
He further knows each tiny ant and mole
Rejoices in its own peculiar hole.
So why should he in folly emulate
The whale who claims the deep for his estate?
Yet, for all this, his daily practice shows
He lives by far less wisely than he knows

And being preternaturally shy,
Lets the best fortunes of the world slip by.
He should better strive to emulate
Hermits in their inviolable estate;
Or let him find in wine his best relief
And by sad singing immolate his grief.

Toward the year's end the grass and herbs are dead
And the fierce winds tear at the mountain's head.
Midnight in the capital is black
As I set out upon the wagon-track.
Frost snaps the knot binding my girdle-chain
Which frozen fingers fail to tie again.
While I clamber the precipitous steep
Of the Li Hills, the Emperor's asleep,
Reposing in his palace at Hua-Ch'ing,
Unconscious of his people's suffering.
The banners of his generals fan the air;
Rough soldiers trampling on these pathways wear
Hard rocks to smoothness where their boots have pressed,
While courtiers in the palace take their rest.
Close to this mountainside the mists are blown;
As close the Imperial Guard clings round the throne,
The mountain pool, like jasper or like jade,
Bright as their uniforms in dress parade.
Now in his Court our Sovereign Lord confers
With his Imperial aids and ministers,
While music rises from the deep ravine
In which the royal palaces are seen.
Only high lords and dignitaries go
To baths and feasts no humble people know,
But silks the women of the harem wear
Were woven by poor women in despair,
Their husbands whipped by the Imperial Guard
To make these wretches labor long and hard!
His Majesty's munificent gifts were meant
To make the common people more content
But the Imperial ministers ignore
The vital principles he labors for
And these are therefore utterly displaced
By extortion, cruelty and public waste.

What consequence may follow brings a dread
Fear to the upright and the talented.
We hear that gold plates and rich tapestries
Fall to the hands of favorites' families.
The central hall's a harem where one sees
Girls less than women, more than goddesses,
Shedding fragrant perfumes as they move,
Filling the heavy air with dreams of love.
They entertain their guests with finest art
Of songs and strings and pipes to pierce the heart.
After assorted dainty bits, they dine
On richest meats and drink the rarest wine;
With pungent tangerines had at great cost
And golden oranges encased in frost.
They feast upon a broth of camel's pad.
Such decadent profusion here is had
That here within the gates thrown out, forgot,
These wines are left to sour and meats to rot
While past these laquered doors we find the bones
Of bodies starved and frozen stiff as stones.
The rich and withered are a foot apart.
Pondering on this ruin wrings my heart!

Traveling north to where two streams converge,
I find that where their stormiest waters merge
The ferry's changed. Torrents pour ceaselessly.
More I look, the higher they seem to be.
They might have come from mountains of K'ung-t'ung
Or in the fury of their anger flung
The highest walls of heaven upon the ground.
Fortunately, the footbridge still is sound,
Though it creaks as though its piers were split.
Travelers crawl on all fours over it.
Cursing the river itself for being wide,
I creep in terror to the farther side.

I left my good wife among strangers; then
Ill times dispersed our family of ten.
I cannot leave them longer without care,
So I am traveling from the Court to share

Their cruel hunger, misery and thirst.
I cross the wooden threshold and the first
Greetings I have are moans, not shouts of joy.
I hear that famine killed my infant boy.
Why should I be stoical and keep
Tears to myself when even neighbors weep?
I am ashamed of my own fatherhood
When a small son has died from lack of food.
How could I know rich harvest-times should be
No help against this curse of poverty?

I am a man in advantageous station,
Free from draft, impressment or taxation.
So if my lot is such a bitter curse,
How much the common people's must be worse!
I think how goods for taxes disappear,
How soldiers vanish on some far frontier.
Anxiety rises like that river in spate;
The mad waves swell, impossible to abate.

⊷§ FLIGHT FROM P'ENG-YA ৡ⊱

I well recall we left P'eng-ya in flight
Northward through perils in the depth of night.
The moon shone on the hills over Po-shui
While my whole family footed hurriedly,
Foot-travelers, much ashamed at being seen.
Here and there birds would sing in a ravine.
Through all the long and dreary second day
Nobody passed us on the opposite way.
When my youngest daughter tried to bite
My arm from bitter hunger, I took fright
Lest wolves or tigers at her piercing cries
Might rush out at us, or, worse, rebel spies.
I pressed her mouth against me to make sure

Of silence but she shivered and wailed the more.
My little boy played smart and angered me
By wanting sour plums from a roadside tree.

Half of the ten days' journey we withstood
Thunder-storms, toiling through thick muck and wood.
The road was slippery; since our clothes were thin
We were all drenched completely to the skin.
Struggling against hardship, with dismay,
We scarcely staggered on two miles a day.
Wild berries were our food; in that fierce welter
Of rain, low branches were our only shelter.
Mornings, we waded through the deep defiles;
Evenings, we searched the horizon miles on miles
For smoke to show some house where we might warm
Our frigid limbs and shield us from the storm.

At last we made our overnight abode
At the T'ung Marsh, south of the mountain road,
Sharp and precipitous, which in due time
It was our grim necessity to climb.
Among our friends here was the good Sun Tsai
Whose hospitable nature rose so high
It soared above the clouds. We reached his house
When it was pitch-dark. We were loath to rouse
The people there, but they were prompt to admit
Poor travelers. Gates were opened; lamps were lit.
To make their hospitality complete
The servants brought warm water for our feet
And kindly condescended to unroll
Bright banners to restore my wandering soul.

His wife and children, too, came out that night
To meet us and all wept to see our plight.
My children fell asleep, they were so tired,
But, wakened, were given food which they required.
"You and I shall swear," Sun said to me,
"To be true brothers to eternity."
The hall was set for us where we had come
And we were asked to make ourselves at home.

Despite the dangers, my friend even sought
To tell his secret plans and private thought.

We have been parted now for a whole year;
The Tatar hordes still plague our land with fear.
How earnestly I wish that from afar
I could take wings to bring me where you are!

THE TRIP NORTH [13]

Before His Majesty has reigned two years,
As the first day of the eighth month appears
Propitious to my projects, I, Tu Fu,
Hold a long journey to the north in view.
The high importance of my family
Leaves me in a great perplexity.
These are times of crisis; none is right
To see his actions in a private light.
I am conscience-stricken as I see
The Emperor's favor in allowing me,
As evidence of his Imperial grace,
The right to visit my poor country-place.
Though I have registered my travel-plan,
Lingering here in pensive thought, I scan
The palace gate and by its lofty wall
Think how far short my civic virtues fall.
I also fear there might be an event
For which a loyal courtier should present
His message to the throne. His Majesty
Tokens the rising of our Dynasty.
He rules and plans with ruthless thoroughness.
The Tatar rebels, causing such distress
To me, are conquered. So my eyes are brought
To tears at parting from the exiled Court.
The whole world writhes in universal riot.
When will anxiety give way to quiet?

I drag myself across war-ravished ground.
Smoke from cooking fires is rarely found.

I stumble over ravished field and fen.
Most of those I meet are wounded men.
They groan and bleed. At Feng-hsiang I turn right
And see pale banners in a fading light.
Then I begin to climb the mountain ramp,
Here and there passing by a cavalry camp.
The level Pin-chou plain spreads out below,
Cleft by the flooded Ching's tumultuous flow.
Ahead there looms the Tiger Cataract;
Its roaring must have caused the cliffs to crack.
Wild chrysanthemums droop in autumn's cold;
The rocks bear tracks where ancient carts have rolled.
On climbing through thin clouds my spirits rise.
In those pure precincts contemplation lies,
Deep peace and quiet reigning over all.
The wild, low-lying berries here are small.
They grow where spreading oaks and chestnuts are,
Some red as crystals of pure cinnabar,
Others black as lacquer. Rain and dew
Fashion them sour or sweet. My thoughts pursue
Visions of hermitages far from men,
Persuading me to vow never again
To share the turmoil human beings make.
I see my life has been a long mistake.

The highlands of Fu-chou form a redoubt,
Mountains and valleys winding in and out.
I hurry on along the river's ledge,
My servant following at the forest's edge.
Strange owls hoot among the rugged boles
Of mulberry trees; mice peep from scattered holes;
We pass a battlefield littered with stones;
A cold moon shines upon the whited bones.
I wonder why a million valiant men
Should vanish, never to be known again,
And half the people of North China, why
It thus becomes their destiny to die?

I, too, fell among Tatars, and despair
Caused me to return with snow-white hair.

More than a year, struggling through hill and plain,
It took to reach my low-thatched hut again:
My wife in rags with crazy-quilt designs,
Her voice like sharp wind wailing through the pines.
It is keen misery to see my wife;
My boy, who was the jewel of my life,
Now wears a different face, pale as the snow.
He wept and turned his back, as if to go.
I marked his bruises and disheveled hair;
His legs were dirty and his feet were bare.

Before his couch, as miserable as these,
Their patched robes barely reaching to their knees,
My two diminutive poor daughters stand.
Their robes were once embroideries with grand
Waves of the ocean on them for a dress
Worn at the Court, but, cut to less and less,
Now patches, they are lying upside down.
The dragon and the phoenix, once the crown
Of a rich garment, are likewise inverted
And to inglorious, short skirts perverted.
Who can blame me that my old heart bleeds
With sadness which this state of misery feeds?
Of course, packed in my luggage is a fold
Of cloth to keep my family from the cold.
There's bedding to be taken out of it,
With presents, too, and a cosmetic kit.
Once more my wife's face wears a healthy glow;
The girls begin to dress themselves for show,
Imitating their mother in everything.
They try to do their hair up with some string;
They drown themselves in make-up; on the cheek
They smear thick rouge to make themselves look sleek.
They paint their eyebrows heavy and askew.
But yet whatever it is my children do
Makes me forget my hunger and my thirst.
They ask me questions till my head will burst.
They pull my beard until its white hairs drop,
But who would have the heart to make them stop?
Remembering my long imprisonment,
Such pesterings are pleasures heaven-sent.

Rest and reunion are a vital good,
But yet we must discuss our livelihood.
An exile's dust covers His Majesty.
I ask the heavens how long this war must be!
I feel an end to this daemonic pest,
A bleak wind blowing from the cold northwest.
The Uighur cavalry begins to ride
Against the Tatars. Ministers decide
Such an alliance spells their overthrow.
Their custom is to rush and smash the foe.
They will dispatch five thousand to the war,
Driving ten thousand horses on before.
By a judicious counsel it's averred:
"Of Uighurs a small number is preferred."
This wise provision will decide the day.
Uighurs will fall like falcons on their prey.
Rightly His Royal Majesty relies
On them to smite swift as an arrow flies.
By such devices wars may well be won;
Yet much is still to be decided on.

Lo-yang is within reach. Our men will leave
The capital to gain the last reprieve.
Westward the Imperial infantry flows back.
Let them gain their positions, then attack.
Our first assault will sweep the valley clear
And bring the conquest of the northeast near.
Winter is augury of heaven's will
To breath a spirit to destroy and kill.
The month is coming for the rebel's fall.
We'll drive the Tatars back beyond the wall.
Heaven has not decreed our Dynasty
Must perish in this harsh contingency.
Our wicked minister was overthrown
And all his traitorous associates blown
To ruin. I know that dynasties must end,
But ours has learned one never should depend
On mercy in excess nor spare the breath
Of women culpable and fit for death.
We shall not liken our regime to one

That stumbled and that presently rewon
Its power and dignity at last but to
The mighty dynasties of Han and Chou.

We are proud of you, General Ch'en Hsüan-li,
Who used an axe in name of loyalty.
Our destiny without you were suspect,
With you the Dynasty will stand erect.

O quiet now stands the great Ta-t'ung hall
Where Emperors held their Court before the fall.
Deserted now the stately Po-shou Gate
Where once the gorgeous courtiers thronged in state.
But now the people of the capital—
After the downfall of the criminal—
Plead loudly for Their Majesties' return,
A rising sun in golden rays to burn.
The spirits of the Imperial ancestors
Ascend to greet our latest Counselors.
No more shall ceremonies and cleansings cease;
Our Empire stands, confirmed in strength and peace.

~§ FIFTY RHYMES SENT TO CHIA CHIH
AND YEN WU [14] §~

The monkeys' wailing troubles far Yo-chou,
Only strong birds reach mountainous Pa-chou.
Neither of you, dear friends, can be content
Suffering such distant banishment.
New life comes as our Emperor rules again,
Whose sovereign grace falls here and there, like rain.
Yet Chia is exiled, like his ancestor
And Yen likewise not with the Emperor.

I think how at the exiled Court we three
Stood near the throne to counsel anxiously
The choice of generals able to repel
The Tatar traitors, sorting out as well
Good embassies to Uighurs and Tibet.
It was a feeble Court to face the threat.

Our useless fleet was anchored near Ch'ang-an;
Our brave men scattered, while the foe had won
All major cities in the vast Northeast.
War-bugles sounded where the foe increased
His rule along the rivers; his war-horns rang
Where the chief demon reveled in Lo-yang.

Though ill informed, I knew the foe would fall,
While you foresaw recovery of all
Our Empire's wide extent and saw the doom
Destined the traitor in the years to come:
A bird who strives with pebbles to fill the sea,
Or man to down the sun with archery.

Then many armies rose to amplify
The Imperial power and cause; morale soared high;
Once the drums sounded, all gloom disappeared,
Over Feng-hsiang our skies were cleared.
Days brightened for our temporary Court
To which the faithful followers had resort.
Rebels at Wei-chou were chopped down like weeds,
Their Yu-chou fort split like bamboo. High deeds
Of the Emperor's armies near Ch'ang-an
And its eight rivers proved his campaign won.
So with his tide of fortune at the full
His chariot regained the capital.

I saw the approach of an auspicious hour;
Even I occupied a place of power.
All the Imperial guardsmen were arrayed
In shining armor; ornaments of jade
Adorned the lashes that impelled the steeds.
The guardsmen were as powerful as the breeds
Of fiercest tigers or of leopards known;
All courtiers kept their stations round the throne.
Even long-stabled horses were aware
Of new-won honors showered upon them there.
Snowflakes sprinkled the red-lacquered towers;
Evergreens merged into soft mist and showers;
Beneficent rains fell from a kindly sky;
Officials dreamed of sad events gone by;
The breasts of all the population burned
With ardor when His Majesty returned.

Lashed by a bitter wind, His Highness went
To the Imperial temple to lament.
Then on New Year's Day the sun shone bright
When the Court-audience made a splendid sight.
A monthly rice-gift added to our bliss
And, with the spring, a moneyed benefice.
Flowers brighter than brocade adorned the hall;
Grass soft as floss bordered the palace wall.
You and I together bowed as one,
Thanking our Lord for gracious favors done.
At audience at dawn or eventide
You and I commonly stood side by side.
Many an evening I ate and drank
In your great house, despite my humble rank,
Or, sometimes lingering, I would remain
To sleep beneath your broidered counterpane.
Our horses breast to breast ran early and late;
My pockets groaned beneath your letters' weight.

Whenever I heard of a high post vacated
I hoped to see you promptly elevated.
But when you stood a short step from the top
Fate suddenly conspired that you should drop,
Fallen as a bird with clipped wings from the sky.
I missed you much and was prepared to die.
His Majesty, taking pity on my age,
Only thrust me off the active stage,
Sending me as an exile to Hua-chou
Where well enough the pert young students knew
I was a poor man and too old to learn
(I was the victim for all men to spurn)
And if an aged scholar had so failed
Himself, why was it reasonably entailed
On them to honor him just for his years?
Now I survive in constant worries and fears,
Always remembering our happy years.

The green of the bamboo forming the piers
For the precarious road on the Pa Hills
Is faded and Yo-chou's pond-garden fills
With deep red lotus of rare loveliness.

Chia has spoken of his loneliness;
Yen has surely written many lines;
I know those poems offer wise designs,
But better not to have them widely read,
For much malicious injury is bred
By men who, like the weavers of brocade,
Pick up loose threads to weave in their own trade.
Let water-birds take care lest they be slain;
Cold-hearted vultures never strike in vain.
Whether you're in some warm miasmic mire
Or where cool, rugged mountain-peaks aspire,
You'd better spend your time in playing chess,
Dissolving dreary days in drunkenness.
Though my position as a Prefect's small
For Yen and a subprefecture is all
But nothing to Chia-chih, no nobles shirk
In nobleness in any honest work.
Even in humblest efforts don't despair;
Your own peculiar talents are too rare
To stand unused, though it is hard to see
What now the intention of the heavens can be.

I follow an old saw which says, "Be gone!"
I know my time of usefulness is done.
I've fled for refuge to remote Ch'in-chou.
Seeing the Yu-chou rebels have pushed through
To westward, and though my large family
Makes idleness a wild absurdity,
I am quite willing to let time go by,
Having no more experiments to try.
I have few friends or relatives to share
My grief, and war is spreading everywhere.
In this strange place I'm rich in dreams and sleep,
But even so, it's difficult to keep
The memory of friends, and illness drains
Fertility in my poetic strains.
It's made the writing of this long poem hard
And any major effort quite debarred.
You, friends, are still enjoying health and strength.
Take heart, and both of you will rise at length.

As strength declines, I became lazier,
More foolish and more willing to defer
Important matters of my livelihood.
I only think of meals when lacking food
And only of a Southern prefecture
When the weather here is cold and raw.
Early in November in Han-yüan
The weather still is moderate as June;
Autumn briskness animates the breeze
Yet there's no fall or fading in the leaves.
The landscape here enjoys a minor fame.
"Chestnut Station" is a pleasant name.
Plenty of yams grow in the farms around;
Excellent wild honey's easily found.
Young bamboos grace a vegetable dish
And lucid ponds abound in varied fish.
Although my family takes small pleasure in it,
It still appeals to my adventurous spirit.

Ch'in-chou's an important thoroughfare.
I dread the human complications there.
Superficial contacts irk my soul,
And mere sight-seeing lacks a solid goal.
No interesting rocks nor deep ravines
Nor other marvels make attractive scenes.
Farmers find the sandy soil unkind
And I, small comfort for the thoughtful mind.
I cannot linger on for further years.—

At dusk the lonely fortress disappears,
By night we leave the city in a cart.
High above its walls the ravens start,
Harsh croaking; horses drink from roadside streams.
Air is crystal in the full moon's beams.
Faint clouds and vagrant mists float here and there;
All the heavenly prospect offers fair;
Space in the universe stands clear and free;
The pathway opens on Eternity.

Dawn's smoke is cold over this city-scene;
Fall leaves turn crimson in the deep ravine;
Cold winds out of a thousand miles of space
Blow briskly on your shore-side dwelling place.

The yellow cranes of Crooked Beach alight
With raucous cries distressing day and night.
O strict and upright Censor that you are,
How long must you be exiled at Ch'ang-sha?
Even a monkey grieves to lose its nest;
A bird escaped from arrows feels unrest.
You must have thought with joy of your return
To home but as I brood my spirits burn
To recollect how you were driven out
And how your punishment was brought about.

In days when the plagued Empire had resort
To Feng-hsiang, you and I were friends at Court.
The dust of exile struck the Emperor;
The town was gloomy with the clouds of war.
Military vigilance clamped down,
For many spies crept sneaking into town.
A stern court for convictions was supplied
But you required each case thoroughly tried.
You could not bear to see injustice done
But probed the wrong and right in everyone,
Separated as the black and white;
Higher officials kept you in their sight,
Never for once pretending to resent
Yet sent you in the end to banishment.
Obstructiveness was the alleged defect
And odious exile was its harsh effect.
The whole Court knew the charges were untrue
But, save in cases of the very few,
Kept their mouths closed. And so the case for us
Was like the exile of Confucius,
For you knew it was not a personal loss.

I was then an ardent counselor
And therefore should have spoken all the more.

That I saw this injustice done and yet
Was silent is my imminent regret.
The shame of it I carry to my grave.
Since I have started my long trip, I have
Often been sad; leaving your present home
I feel that in this instance I have come
To saddest shame and, failing to do right,
Remorse will turn my hairs even more white.

⊷§ LEAVING FOR CH'ENG-TU §⊷

One of the greatest sages of the earth
Left behind him an unblackened hearth;
The greatest of all sages never sat
In one place long enough to warm his mat; [15]
How could a hungry, inept man like me
Hope to remain in one place peacefully?
When coming first to mountains in the West,
I looked for solitude and a long rest;
What have I to do with worldly cares
When one year set me on four thoroughfares?
Leaving this handsome region with aversion,
I start my next vague, undefined excursion,
I halt my horse for the last time to take
A view of clouds above the Dragon Lake.
I feel I cannot look often enough
At the high-towering, rugged Tiger Bluff.
Where the mountain road turns toward the sky,
Several men have come to say good-bye.
When I take their hands my warm tears fall
Not of necessity because they call
On feeling of strong friendship old and deep
But because old men easily grieve and weep.
Lazy and clumsy, I long wished to dwell
In such a place, ripe for a hermit's cell.
To leave or linger I find equally
Harsh, and envy every bird I see.

I entered early in my fourteenth year
Literary contests without fear.
The living masters promptly rated me
Equal to masters of antiquity.
Even in my seventh year I bent
My thinking to heroic precedent.
My first song, written in the Phoenix' praise,
Foretold the coming of Imperial days
Blent with great wisdom and sagacity.
At nine I practiced large calligraphy.
My writings were a veritable mine.
I was temperamental and loved wine,
Whose influence was needed to suppress
Too vehement a hate of wickedness.
I shunned the company of careless youth,
Seeking the grey-beards who themselves sought truth.
Inspired by wine, we held a high converse,
Oblivious to the world's applause or curse.

From Su-chou I went farther to the East.
I had proposed a voyage at the least
As far as foreign shores, even Japan.
The courtly culture covering the span
Of centuries at Su-chou had long been dead.
Inscriptions on the tombs could not be read.
The royal graveyard lay in fern and brake.
Yet rocky cliffs still lean over Sword Lake
And still the famous lotus plants unfold
Their blossoms by the sandbar, as of old,
While the memorial temple casts its cool
Reflections on the waters of the pool
Lying in splendor by the city gate.
There I recalled past glories of the state.
Each time I entered there my tears would flow
In ardent gratitude to Wu T'ai-po,
Who so magnanimously declined a throne,
And thought that he in this was not alone.
My tears would flow to think so gladly of
Our own Prince who displayed such brotherly love;

I think of brave King Chien, who looked askance
On sleep and for his pillow chose a lance,
Or of the Emperor of Ch'in who came
South of the Che and earned a valiant name,
Or of Prince Liao, whom assassins did
To death by knife in a fish belly hid,
Or of the hidden seal of Chu Mai-ch'en,
Respected by the worst and meanest men.

The Yüh-chou girls are the most beautiful;
Even in summer, Mirror Lake is cool.
I found strange beauty in the Yen Defile;
I kept these things in mind for a long while,
Almost reluctant when my trip was done.

I returned home by boat, journeying on
Past high hills, along a rocky coast.
In the prime of life I was the most
Promising candidate in my prefecture.
No scholar seemed a rival any more
Nor did I dread the greatest difficulty
In questions that were fairly put to me.
Yet for all the boldness I displayed,
The grave Examiners declared I failed!

Next I went alone to say good-bye
To the Prefect of Ching-chao and then I,
Having performed as rightly as I could,
Roamed and ranged about the neighborhood.
Clothed in rich furs, I rode the finest steeds,
Racing through the forests and the meads.
I sang at the gay taverns in the spring;
I reveled to the height in everything
That gladdens youth; in winter warmed my blood
At gallop whistling falcons in the wood.
I chased the prey through clouds on snowy heights,
Sent arrows winging on their farthest flights.
Each outstretched arm brought down a stork or crane
As we dashed fiercely through the rough terrain.
My friend, Su Yü, laughed as we galloped on,
Praising me as a boon companion.

Eight years of youthful liberty, and so
At length I journeyed back to Ching-chao.
The first of scholars were close friends of mine.
A prince himself invited me to dine.
Among such hospitable men as these
I felt myself entirely at ease.
I sent my compositions to the Court
Where they met instant favor and, in short,
The Emperor himself soon summoned me.
I met the lords and men of high degree.
It was as if to dodge a fatal net
That I left Court with small or no regret.
I drank so much, it mattered not a jot
Whether I was asked to Court or not,
Until humiliating poverty
Made me a miserable thing to see:
A greybeard at a banquet toasting others;
Yet my neighbors treated me as brothers.
Humble of rank, I suffered no neglect
For all the village granted me respect,
Though as a spent man my heart was dazed,
The ashes of a fire that once had blazed.

The region specialized in graveyard trees,
Tall poplars. I observed fit obsequies
For village worthies sadly laid to rest.
The peasants of the region did their best
To cheer me, set me in an honored place,
Dutifully summoned me to grace
Their birthdays, bridals, funerals, as these
Occurred among their many families.
This was a period of licensed crimes,
Murder and plunder marring troubled times.
In bitter feuds whole families were slain;
Taxes for cavalry consumed the grain;
Food had to be collected for the forces,
Crops commandeered to feed the officials' horses.
Still the warnings beckoned from the wall
How hate and waste induced an Empire's fall.
Storm and dust obscured the sky from view
Of the Emperor's car on its long road to Shu.

Two courts maintained their camps in distant places
Looking with love across vast, dreary spaces.
In P'ing-liang martial spirit was intense.
In Ch'ang-an peoples' hopes lay in suspense.
Having reports the Emperor was near,
And just as with the ancient Yü, so here
A deed of magnanimity was done,
The Prince resigning to his loyal son.
The Imperial staff now occupied Fu-feng
To drive the wolves and tigers from their den.
When the first death-grip of our army missed,
The foe was still more rampant to resist.
Twice the heavenly army acted ill
While Tatar cavalry was poised to kill.
The wounds we suffered almost passed all cure.

Then I became a courtier once more,
Charged with duty to advise the throne.
My dread and keen anxiety had grown
To fearful strength; I was much angered at
The rebels who had laid the temples flat
And grieved by sufferings of the population.
Just then I made an urgent protestation,
Persisting to remonstrate and impress
My royal Lord so fallen in distress.
In such a cause my life was a small stake.
I would risk all things for my Sovereign's sake.
His royal anger did not harm his cause;
The Sovereign only moved by kindly laws,
Gaining for his kingdom partial peace.
I joined the ceremony to release
From guilt the heart of a repentant nation
By pious prayer with fervent lamentation
Before the ashes of the Imperial shrines
And temples of our high Dynastic lines.
Heavy at heart, with weeping eyes, we all
Went once again to the great Audience Hall.

Now I, frail servant of his Majesty,
Discharged from all Court duties, wandered free,
An old, sick stranger in a distant land.

So sad I am, rightly to understand
My true condition, bring before your eye
A bird with wounded wing that cannot fly.
The autumn wind blows through the wild ravine,
Pale, perfumed orchids can't redeem the scene,
But Chieh Chih-t'ui asked no rewarding smile
For going with his Master to exile
And Ch'ü Yüan's fishers, after torrid strife,
Preferred to praise in song the hermit's life.
Even a well-earned glory can be lost;
Winter brings greenest plants the keenest frost.
I believe Fan Li as guardian of our nation
To be the wisest of his generation.
Many rebels have not yet been slain.
I trust his talents will be used again.

◆§ SENT TO BE WRITTEN ON THE WALL OF MY THATCHED HUT ໒◆

My soul is carefree. I have found it good
To live at ease in Nature's neighborhood.
I'm fond of wine and bamboo in the breeze;
I like to dwell near to a spring and trees.
War and disorder banished me from Shu;
Here sick are cured and invalids made new.
Ending my long-drawn troubles, I reside
In quietness by a peaceful river's side.

At first we cleared only a rod around,
Then made some use of the adjacent ground.
Two years ago we started building here;
Additions did not cease until this year.
We built our structure simply, as we should,
But the foundation's firm, the setting good.
House and porch flow as the grounds beseem;
The whole is spacious, by a lucid stream,
And though my sympathetic friends invite
Me out on fishing parties day and night,

As bitter war drags on, all of us keep
Estranged from singing and deprived of sleep.
Like the dragon to whom fate denies
A resting-place or cranes in stormy skies,
The wise and able men always resent
Freedom curtailed by harsh environment.
I'm a short-sighted and an unwise man:
Could I foresee these frightful risks I ran?

I'm taking my good wife away again,
Sadly exposed to wind and mist and rain.
This is, of course, a strict necessity,
With choice of interest or integrity.
I'm still concerned for my four little pines
That might become enmeshed in weeds or vines.
Their stems are slender though their hearts are good.
They should be pitied by the neighborhood.

⊷§ FAREWELL TO THE ACTING GOVERNOR GENERAL CHANG I ℥⊷

Since coming to Chien-nan years have flown by;
Not only have my children grown but I
Become much older through my misery;
I truly am a sorry man to see.
I fear that this straightforward way of mine
May lead to trouble through a cup of wine.
Recently I have shunned the tavern gate.
I trust that my reform is not too late.

When young, I leaped as fish jump in a brook;
Now I'm a lost dog with a haggard look.
Since no attachment counsels me to stay,
Why should I not be always on my way?
From friends I meet—half old friends and half new—
I take their gifts regardless of their view.
With sudden luck a boat has touched the strand,
Abruptly dropping fortune in my hand.

The Prefect graciously has spread his pillows
For a high feast here underneath the willows.
Before the tower strong horses take their rest;
Inside the curtain cluster many a guest.
Strong warriors dance as crimson banners wave:
Here is a merry party for the brave!
The sun drops underneath the purple hills.
At dusk small birds cheep on the windowsills.
I have no dread of the rough voyage by night
Nor think the Triple Gorge will give me fright.
I'm worried only where the brigand thrives;
Twice have high officers fled for their lives.
Out of the Central Plains comes not a jot
Of news whether the Court's now safe or not.

I'll probably go South where men are wild,
And, as Chuang-tzu commends, be reconciled
To what may follow, or I still may plod
To the far temple of the Eastern God,
Or set my sails to visit the South Pole.
I have no fixed or reasonable goal.
I'll always send you letters if I may.
Where messengers are none, I'll look your way.

ᴥ§ THE THATCHED HUT §ᴥ

I left my thatched hut when barbarians
Filled Ch'eng-tu city with their roaring clans;
Now I have returned because their bands
Have left the city to our quiet hands.
Let me tell you of the first surprising
Outbreak of this turbulent uprising.
After the general left the capital
Underlings conspired the Empire's fall.
They killed a sacred white horse at midnight,
Sealing their oath of blood by candlelight.
Some went west to fight near Chiung-chou;
Some cut the wooden north road to Chien-chou.
A score of wretches, vagabonds and clowns

Assumed positions in important towns.
Only when rivalries among them rose
Did Chinese and barbarians come to blows
And when these forces parted company
The Western soldiers rose in mutiny.
The rebel leaders flew at one another.
In that wild chaos brother slaughtered brother.
Who could have told that mad, internal strife
Would cost these bloody criminals their life?

All good men among us raged and wept;
Law and discipline were no more kept.
Rule of the thoughtless many proved a blow
To work that population's overthrow.
Suffering and terrorism and dissent
Claimed all; no man preserved the innocent.
Where chiefs emerged, crude torture ruled the day;
While nights were turned to music and to play
They ordered massacres, chatted and laughed;
While turgid gutters ran with blood they quaffed
Their wine with glee. Now, when the storm assails
The city, you can hear the pitiful wails
Of victims groaning where the axes swang
Or jubilations and harsh cries that rang
From victors who appropriated then
The wives and horses of the murdered men.
Our Empire's law and order disappeared;
Total anarchy was what we feared.

Escape was what I hoped for at the most.
For three whole years I sought the Southern coast.
Bows and arrows shadowed the Yangtze.
The Five Lakes offered scant security.
Since I find it hard to leave this home
I have come back to weed and stir the loam.
Entering the gate, I joy to see again
My four young pines. I find that there remain
Many aspects of the scene I love.
I walk in sandals through my bamboo grove.
My old dog barks and running up and down
Fawns and finally hides beneath my gown.

My neighbors all applaud and, since I love it,
Bring me good wine and many bottles of it.
The Governor General is happy, too,
And asks if there's a favor he can do.
All would assist. The city with one voice,
With visitors and guests, seems to rejoice.

Peace has by no means settled over all.
Soldiers' fortunes rise while scholars fall.
With wind and dust and sad uncertainty,
Can there be any place for such as me?
I know well now I am a parasite
But, in despite of all, I am not quite
Perished and so need modest food and drink.
Under these circumstances I must think
That though the best of life is surely spent
With this small succor I should rest content.

✑ THE GIFT OF A SATIN-BROCADE COVERLET ✑

My honored guest from the Northwest has made
A present to me of this bright brocade.
Opening the package somewhat gingerly,
I look on seething waves of a vast sea.
A whale among them lashes his huge tail;
Other creatures swim in shining mail
But at the distance it's too far to see
What their true identity may be.
My guest says: "This is for your cushion's seat.
Take it as a present, I entreat.
Doing so, your joy will be increased
When you sit on it at some glorious feast.
Sleep on it, and you will have dreamless rest.
Display it, and bad luck will be suppressed."

My guest's great kindness I appreciate.
But since I am no minister of state,
This could not be auspicious. I decline
To place it in this modest house of mine.

There is a fitting law of long duration
That gifts should be appropriate to one's station.
Since I'm a humble man, precedent shows
I should be satisfied with plainest clothes.
So exquisite an object's only fit
For the Imperial Palace. Surely it
Would never be appropriate in my home
And from it only much bad luck could come.
I am surprised how in these cursed years
Of fighting and disorder it appears
That many leading men in high command
Have snatched advantage of their power in hand
To stock themselves with finest clothes and horse.
Li Ting died in Ch'i-yang since in his course
Of governing he showed excessive pride.
Lai T'ien was forced to commit suicide
Because his arrogance hindered the war.
Both were known to have amassed a store
Of tainted wealth. It's no surprise at all
They met their sad, inevitable fall.

How can an old and common farmer dare [16]
Accept so sumptuous a gift or wear
Such fabrics? Let me fold this whale-brocade
Which you have with such courtesy displayed
And so return it to you, if you please.
Then only shall I feel myself at ease.
Let me dust off this mat. Please take your seat!
Only thus can my pleasure be complete.
Even so my shy and timid spirits droop,
Handing you this thin cup of vegetable soup.

*⊷§ TWENTY RHYMES TO DISPEL GLOOM:
PRESENTED TO HIS EXCELLENCY YEN §⊶*

The old man with white locks whose whiteness gleams
As the autumn crane beside his shining streams
Once held a fishing rod but now he floats

Gently upon a stream in quiet boats.
Why should Headquarters hold a charm for me?
Why mentioned in the legal Registry?
Even my fine green robe I owe to you!
My rheumatism turns my old wife blue.
My daughter often asks of my headache.
On level ground I constantly mistake
My footing. I'm not only blind and halt
But irk my colleagues and am much at fault.

Duty requires what strength I can afford,
Still more, for friendship's sake, to serve my lord,
Whose understanding mind in poetry
It's been my pleasure many years to see,
Whose military pride I now have shared,
Whose lofty generosity has spared
Blaming my many faults of clumsiness,
Whose friendly hand has softened my distress!
But when I think of my wisteria vine
Wet with dew or of large blooms that shine
Shedding perfume from my cassia tree,
I seem a song-bird in captivity
Or some rare tortoise lifted gleaming wet
Out of the sea, caged in a fisher's net.

The Western Mountains bend about the north
Of our village, the South River flowing forth
Around the eastern quarter of my land.
In vain dry cups by empty wine-jars stand.
Cold bamboo bark now bears its usual green;
Wet pepper-berries wear a crimson sheen.
My unused boat may crack where the wave heaves.
My path and gate are blocked by weeds and leaves.
Placing myself in servitude, I must
Perform such deeds as answer friendship's trust.
I thought I knew the lesson trouble taught me
But soon I found how carelessness has caught me!

When the red gate at morning opens wide
I come and leave as bells ring eventide.
As yet I have not reached my country nest
Nor dared to give my feeble body rest.

The magpie's a poor bird and therefore shy
To bridge the Starry River in the sky.
The inferior horse is easily shamed and swerves
From the rich saddle-cloth he ill deserves.
Let me hope my master will be kind
To estimate my weak and humble mind,
Granting long and frequent leaves to me
To lean against my ancient wu-t'ung tree.

⚜ THE SOJOURNER'S DWELLING [17] ⚜

The chief room of the traveler's dwelling-place
Backs up against a mountain's rocky face
Looking to where the river-waters roar
Beneath a rugged, rough, precipitous shore.
Dark waves congest to rapids, surge and leap
Underneath the canyon's dizzy steep.
Tree-trunks drenched in moisture brace their backs
Erect out of the cliffside's jagged cracks.
I hear the ominous cuckoos cry by night,
Moving even the bravest breast with fright.
Down through a thousand miles the great Gorge brings
Angry torrents from a thousand springs.
Men and beasts share this gloomy wilderness
In constant war, existing none the less.

The flax trade out of Shu long since has ceased
To reach the West; Wu salt shipped from the East
Has to be unloaded at Chiang-ling.
Merchants, observing that in everything
Trade is impossible, have left the land.
Now the Emperor, as we understand,
Has sent a new Commander on his way.
It is barely possible he may
Facilitate a rise in navigation.
Here I am lingering in my halfway station.
I hardly need discuss my livelihood.

Bedridden legs can do me little good.
Down the short garden-walks I slowly pass
Or mark some narrow patches of green grass.
Memories of that saddest ballad come:
"The Exiled Prince Who Never Reached His Home."
Phoenix after phoenix flys away,
Only the chattering, small swallows stay.
Even they make me think of war and pillage
And my own dear, remote, deserted village
That I have not seen now for long years.
This augury of birds augments my fears.
How many of us poor birds will return?
Still to the north of us the forests burn
With war. Under such ills I brood and chafe.
Those northern groves at dusk I fear unsafe.

Would I could send eight ocean torrents whirled
To cleanse the wickedness of all this world!
Good ministers are not difficult to find.
Such can easily pacify and bind
These wild barbarian beasts. And yet I see
My learning and ripe age in impotency.
Being my Sovereign's servant, I must feel
Anxiety for all the commonweal,
And just as long as I can wield my pen
I shall write warmly of my fellowmen.

⋆§ DIRECTING FARMERS §⋆

Rain in the village must be plentiful.
I dream of fragrance with the rice-plants full.
Since Heaven's impartial in its overflow
Of grace, strong reeds and tares will likewise grow.
Men find such growths unwelcome from the harm
They always do to those who work a farm.
Hence none of the good villagers can shirk
In seasonable tasks of weeding work,

Piling tares by the river in defense
Of cleaner crops. Grain is life's sustenance.
Even a visitor's aware of it.

These fertile fields in spring have had their fit
Attention and their soil is no more wild.
Our water-buffaloes are strong and mild.
We drive them breast to breast across the land
As ancient rules of husbandry command.
Whatever grows will rise in mad confusion
And toil must guide the crop to its conclusion.
I have not neglected to provide
The common peasants with a knowing guide
But still I feel a natural unrest
That such a foreman may not do his best.
So I have conscientiously conveyed
Messages by a servant and a maid
To farmers working in the farthest field.
We'll give the poor much of our harvest yield.
My gift is not to court the neighborhood
But in harsh times I thrive in doing good.

Soon a north wind will blow on withered sedge
And crickets chirp along the southern edge
Of our main hall. Labor will find relief
From pain and leisure ease the farmer's grief.

⋆§ JUST A NOTE §⋆

True literature lasts for a thousand ages,
An inch of conscience in the minds of sages.
We know it in the twinkling of an eye.
Though different types of poets diversify
The art, poetic fame is seldom due
To pure caprice. The ancient bard of Ch'u
Rose first and next crept on a tedious span
Of years before the classic poets of Han.

They were lords of poetry's best effects
And were, indeed, its primal architects.
By them the laws of poetry were stated,
By others it is merely decorated.
All later poets have kept the past in view
And yet each age clearly adds something new.

Confucius' school defined poetic truth.[18]
To that I have applied myself from youth.
I have, moreover, long delighted in
The brilliance of the masters of the Chin,
And much regret I'm a poor scholar of
The Ts'ao family of Wei I love.
The father and the son ran brilliant courses—
Yes, all the poets of Chin rode gallant horses.
I have merely built a scaffolding
And somehow lack the sovereign power to bring
The whole to its conclusion. Here and there
I've ventured judgment but I feel despair
At reaching greatness. So my lines dispense
Dark messages of doubtful elegance.

Much of my poetry is self-consolation,
Lamenting my sad times and minor station.
Despite protracted periods I have spent
In illness or in tedious banishment
I am ashamed that I have failed to serve
My country as its urgencies deserve
And that, an exile, I am traveling now
As a poor bird flying from bough to bough,
Meeting lizards and wasps in desert places,
Dragons and crocodiles where the rapid races.
Peace and prosperity belong to the past;
Wars and invasions swallow us at last.
The Court is forced in Ch'ang-an to admit
Brigands and rebels who sit down with it.
I live in K'uei-chou among barbarous bands
Whose modes and manners no one understands.
Among these boisterous people none gainsay
That many honest men are hid away,
Buried like sharp, bright weapons underground

Or powerful dragons hid in some dark pond.
While this divided country now has two
Headquarters, in Chiang-ling and in Ch'eng-tu,
While thousands of armed men are standing by,
Southward sound rule is challenged at Nan-hai,
And north, Ching-chao suffers from the threat
Of bold marauding brigands from Tibet.
Contrary to the saying that pretends
Magpies and crows bring letters from our friends,
None comes, but wild beasts howl incessantly.
I live on farming and on poetry.
I take what my environment can give,
Learning by compromises how to live.

Since the White Tower upon the Southern Hills
Lies far from scenes my narrow vision fills,
And the autumn waters of the Imperial Lake
Are only to dim memory awake,
Shunning magnificent versification,
I sing of melancholy and separation.

◁§ DRUNK, I FELL FROM HORSEBACK §▷

I was the Governor's old, welcome guest
Whose warmth of hospitality expressed
Itself in lavish feasting and strong wine.
Then, in one of those mad moods of mine,
I rose hilariously to sing and danced
The lively figure of "the Golden Lance."
Next, suddenly remembering my pride
In youth, I mounted a swift horse to ride.
Outside the K'uei-chou Gate steep highways go
To where the stream and clouds stretch out below.
Precipitously the canyon walls dive down
Nine hundred yards beneath the white-walled town.
Like summer lightning the white fort flashed past

My purple bridle. Faster and more fast
I rushed across the level plain beside
The rustic village at the river's side.
Across the plain and underneath the bluff
The hills are rugged and the pathways rough.
Easing the rein, letting the whiplash trail,
I galloped with the madness of a gale
Over red, dusty land.

    My foolish ends
Were always to surprise my many friends
And garner for a white-haired man the praise
Won by his valor in his early days,
Showing I still can ride and shoot as then.
Though I might gain some favor among men,
I was indeed a fool to think of course
My views of speed congenial to my horse.
The white foam on his lips and the red sweat
Along his streaming body might have let
Me grasp the matter clearly as I ought
And know he could not share my private thought.
A careless stumble left a serious hurt.
To follow impulse so is to pervert
The truth of nature and to court disgrace.
Now I confront my error face to face.
I've much to ponder as I lie in bed
Reflecting on sad follies time has bred.

Kind souls and neighbors come with searching eyes;
I must now shamefacedly arise,
Leaning upon my servants and my cane.
I tell my tale. Good friends cannot refrain
From bursts of laughter. Now they carry me
To fields beside a stream that pleasantly
Purls on and there a mountainous feast is laid
With music that weird strings and flutes have made.
All pointing to the West, profoundly say
Time passes and the sun will not delay.
They shout for everyone to drain his glass,
Sipping the sparkling moments as they pass.

But why, good friends, envoys of gentleness,
Give me this comfort in my late distress?
The author of GOOD HEALTH held prudence high
Until a headsman led him out to die.

✑ A POEM ON SEEING THE SWORD PANTOMIME DANCE ❧

A lovely woman long ago, Kung-sun,
Performed a Sword Dance, praised by everyone.
Spectators came in throngs and mute suspense
Watched her with a breathless countenance.
You felt that air and land gained a rebirth.
She bent, and nine bright suns shot down to earth;
She leaped, and gods rode dragons through the sky;
She advanced, you dreaded lightning from on high
And waited thunder; she stooped quietly
And mellow light spread over a vast sea.

Those rosy lips, those fluttering sleeves she wore,
Soon retired and now are seen no more.
Through all her later years her skill was sought
Only in a pupil she had taught.
Now in the Emperor's Palace at Lin-ying
Madame Li leads all who dance and sing,
Gleaning from Kung-sun the secret art.
I muse upon the change with heavy heart.

Eight thousand Palace girls once graced the Prince,
Kung-sun the chief, no one her equal since.
She in the Brilliant Emperor's golden time [19]
Performed supremely the Sword Pantomime.
But scenes of half a century disband
As swiftly as the turning of a hand.
Storm waves of war have plunged the Court in grief
And the Pear Garden's troup enjoyed as brief
A triumph as a disappearing mist,

For time's an enemy none may resist.
So the fading beauty of the Bright
Courtesan gleams alone in cold sunlight.
Shrubs by the Emperor's mausoleum sown
Rise as trees prolific, overgrown.
The feasts, the music and the dancing end.
All heights of pleasure and of joy portend
Sadness and a wan moon in the East.
I am an old man, all his joys deceased,
Moving too rapidly, not knowing where,
Pacing bleak hills, unwilling, in despair.

◆§ PRESENTING MY ORCHARD TO NAN CH'ING-HSIUNG §◆

I have always loved moss and bamboo.
Like down alighting, glistening with dew,
Or duckweed drifting on a river's face,
I have no permanent abiding-place.
My children have grown up while following me.
In our long wanderings several times have we
Left pleasant hamlets. Here the flower-beds
Hold competitions in the shades of red.
Buds are of so exquisite a tint
Brocades will not surpass their gleam and glint.
I have a boat to leave this Gorge at last.
Nostalgically I recall years past
When I set out this orchard with a hoe.
Orioles say that February must go.
The painted fishhawk on my vessel's prow
Must fly downstream today. I shall dream how
I once plucked plum-blooms by this very wall
The melting snow now covers with its shawl.
Let me give you this orchard for your own
In token that my best delights have flown.
I'll write of rural days nevertheless
And how these country joys can charm and bless.

Though I live on the Yangtze and the Han,
I shall be still at heart a country man
And of all human beings much prefer
The simple fisherman or forester.

ᴥᎦ YO-LU-SHAN AND TAO-LIN MONASTERIES [20] Ꭶᴥ

South of Jade Springs, hidden by cliff and wood,
Two Buddhist monasteries long have stood.
Yo-lu-shan's entrance looms above its strand,
Tao-lin's foundations rest on Lake Red Sand.
Cool air in summer freezes Buddha's bone.
Music rises with its heavenly tone
From figures clustering by fragrant urns
Where sacred fire perpetually burns.
Each foot of ground is decked with fadeless grasses
Plucked from steep and snowbound mountain passes.
Each monk is like a pearl from some far sea.
Shrines like palace walls shine gloriously.
The kitchen has the pungent scent of pines.
Gongs that overhang these sculptured shrines
Easily make you believe that when they strike
Two-headed birds and lotus sound alike.
Those boards inscribed with golden characters
Dazzle where the yellow sunbeam stirs.

I fear that it might take too long for me
To reach the fairies of the Eastern Sea,
Nor am I quite persuaded of the blest
Kingdom in the Heavens of the West.
So in this evening of my stormy days
I'm pleased with these serene monastic ways.
Sacred hospitality falls on
My brow like blessings of the warm spring sun.
Where else could a white-haired old man go?
Why should he longer wander to and fro?

Better to build his hut and find life good
Here in this peaceful, heavenly neighborhood.
Though many ancient costumes now decline,
Soil in this famous region still is fine.
Life in the placid T'an-chou Prefecture
Is still conservative, wholesome and pure.
No loud or boisterous riotings infest
The courtyard of the venerable Prefect.

Many good men have drawn themselves away
From this degenerate world and I shall stay
Here in this happy region, nor despise
Shelter among these monks, aged and wise.
I should have come here at an earlier date
But even now I find it not too late.
Why should I strive for honor, wealth or fame,
The vain illusions of a glorious name?
Having long been fond of poetry,
I am accustomed to live quietly.
I'll read Buddhistic scrolls and at my side
Procure some monk and scholar for my guide,
Love of the landscape be my foremost end
And every bird and flower be my friend.
In time of exile the great Sung Chih-wen
Wrote on these walls a poem for future men.
I'm pleased the poet of that earlier day
Has left me something further to portray.

⋙ STAYING IN THE BOAT ⋘

Stupidity and long ill health appear
Twin causes of my miserable career.
I am so deaf my friends talk with their hands.
My thin hairs frustrate what my comb commands.

We have been waiting for these streams to flood
Which all the summer have been merely mud.

So while we pray for it to rain once more
I move my boat to dykes along the shore.

Though I first journeyed northward, I thought best
To go not to my home but towards the West.
It's bitter in the evening of one's life
For one to leave his family, home and wife.
My children more than once have written that
Their broth is meager, savorless and flat.
How did I come to such a sorry state?
Now, as this world goes, it is far too late
To look for justice. Here in bed I lie,
Propped up on pillows, gazing at the sky
Watching cold moonlight and keen starlight gleam
Upon the midnight waters of this stream.
I seem to hear the somber sounds that come
From the dull beating of the Governor's drum.
Wild beasts seem crying when the night-wind lulls,
While I'm companion to the ducks and gulls.

I find my side-trip served no useful ends
But only kept me from my usual friends.
This boat to me has proved no benefit;
Too many sleepless nights I've spent on it.
Gentlemen of this city, you have made
Large fortunes. Many come to you for aid.
To quench a mortal hunger, I implore
Only a handful from your ample store.
But my predicament will not admit
That I should wait a longer time for it.
The walk with staff in hand is much too far
For me to struggle on to where you are;
So weak are my resources that I can
No way afford the cost of a sedan.
While I grieve at this humiliation,
Will no one help my painful situation?
Can men fish in the sea of politics?
Or are there subtle, diplomatic tricks
To raise a ladder to the stately clouds?
Surely, no dubious suspicion shrouds

The purity or truth of my intention,
Discouraging your saving intervention?

Remember, ancients of a happier day
Gave even their whole granaries away,
While I recall a scholar who aspired
To dignity and honor and required
No final action should be mean or vile:
"A bridge should be recrossed in splendid style." [21]

Let it be understood that though my frame
Is weak, my loyalty remains the same.
I seek a place where, as I long have prayed,
No compromise with duty shall be made.

Odes and Elegies

ঙ PAINTING OF A FALCON ঙ

This painting of a hawk is truly rare!
From its pale silk issues a frosty breath.
Does he foresee a fleeing rabbit's death?
Why has he a vexed barbarian's stare?

Surely, we should unloose his ring and chain!
Now, as we call him, he must hear our words!
"When are you to strike those twittering birds,
Scattering blood and feathers on the plain?"

ঙ A VISIT TO THE ROYAL TEMPLE IN WINTER ঙ

The temple looms beneath the polar star;
Hill-fences hold all rude outsiders out;
Guards of the mystic shrine are strong and stout;
Priests keep what no vicissitudes can mar.

Green roof-tiles keep out early winter cold;
A central shaft upholds the cosmic soul;
Above, the sun and moon circle its pole;
Mountains and streams are on the door enscrolled.

Strong roots develop from the deathless plum.
Orchids' fragrance conquers time and space.
Though destiny denies him final grace,
Our Emperor is virtue's final sum.[22]

Famed colorists are common in these halls;
Wu Tao-hsüan excels them all by far;
Transporting nature's scenes from where they are
He makes them breathe again on palace walls.

Five stately seers in dragon robes march by;
A thousand petty clerks file past like geese.
Tassels and headgears shine like golden fleece.
Each banner sways and prances in its sky.

Cedars shade the spacious temple court.
Pears are reddish, tinged by heavy frost.
Jade-like tones from eave-hung wind-bells tossed
Make silver-frozen windlasses their sport.

The throne was barren where the Chou had reigned,
Yet all the laws of virtue were committed
To Han; if hollowness is so transmitted,
How may this clumsiness be still maintained? [23]

LI PO AND I CALL ON HERMIT FAN

Intimate poetry of my friend, Li Po,
At times suggests the classical Yin K'eng.
He's my heart's brother, and I often go
To meet him in the hills about Tung-meng.

Inebriate, we sleep in the same bed,
Blessed with the autumn coolness; or we walk
By day with hand in hand; or, if instead,
We seek a quiet rendezvous and talk,

We call upon the scholar-hermit, Fan,
Whose casual conversation breeds delight;
Even the gate-guard of this learned man
Is a youth handsome, gentle and polite.

The sun declines; then in that quiet scene
Save for one noise the city's without sound:
We know "The Ballad of the Evergreen,"
But hear the washer-women's mallets pound.

With peace and friendship in a hermit's bower,
Should men retire for paltry soup or ease?
Let us drop all speech of rank and power
While thoughts and feelings roam the distant seas.[24]

Ho Chih-chang rides his horse like a sailor sculling a sluggish
    boat,
Half-asleep and yet willing to fall in a well, sink or float.

Ju-yang drank three gallons, then going to Court and sight-
    ing a brewer's cart,
Declared: "To be Lord of the Wine Spring I'd give the rich
    blood of my heart."

Our Minister spends ten thousand a day which he gulps
    down like a whale,
Then explains: "I love things philosophic and whole, where
    severance may not avail."

Ts'ui Tsung-chih is a handsome young man with bland, blue
    eyes;
A jade-tree sparkling in wind, he lifts his cup to the azure
    skies.

At prayer at a Buddha's shrine, Su Chin is a vowed vegeta-
    rian,
But how he enjoys his lapses when turned a mad bacchana-
    lian!

Li writes a hundred poems to a gallon, then sleeps at a
    vintner's shop.
When the Emperor bids him mount a barge, he cries: "No,
    sir; I'm God of the Cup!"

Give Calligrapher Chang but three cupfulls, he dances crazy
    capers
Before the worthies themselves, making clouds ascend from
    his papers.

Chiao Sui will need five gallons to keep in a conscious state,
Amazing huge crowds by his eloquence in discussion and
    fierce debate.

✑ ON MEI-PEI LAKE ✑

Ts'en Shen and his brother relish nature's wonders
And take me for a sail upon the lake.
Suddenly the sky grows black and thunders;
Enormous waves like glass in fragments break.

We cast the boat loose on this crystal chaos
That threatens an extinguished universe.
Surely, huge whales or crocodiles will slay us
Or evil winds and waves be even worse!

But presently it clears. Our boatmen gladly
Unfurl the brightly-woven sails and sing.
Birds fly and call; the pipes and strings choir madly;
Deep sea-blossoms waver shimmering.

Then, as we gain the center of this ocean-
Like expanse of water, the waves cease.
There, inverted, without tremor or motion,
The dark shade of the mountain lies at peace.

Perhaps there is a just-observable shivering
As the inverted, somber shadow lies
Clear on the polished surface, but all quivering
Ends as the last breath of the tempest dies.

Will our boat collide with the far temple
Whose mountain-pinnacle these waters glass,
Or will our vessel inadvertently trample
The moon that swims out of the Lan-t'ien Pass?

Now is the hour when the Black Dragon rising
Above the waves will grant his fabulous Pearl.
Let the Guardian of the Lake, apprising
His followers, set all his drums aswirl.

And let the Princess of the Hsiang and choiring
Maidens of Han ascend in holy trance
While green and silver lanterns held aspiring
To heaven as an aurora light their dance!

Still, a fear lurks that thunderstorms may smite us
With blows when prayers offer no relief.
Age steels our youth with little to requite us:
How rapidly all pleasures turn to grief!

☙ FAREWELL TO K'UNG CH'AO-FU ❧

K'ung Ch'ao-fu shakes his head and will not stay;
He will follow the western clouds to the farthest sea,
While his poems themselves are admired, he has stolen away
And his fishing-line will hang from a coral tree.

The spring is cold and the sky is dense with gloom,
But the higher you climb, the farther you are from a pest.
The Fairy Maid has chosen the sky for her home
Proving the vacuous air of a summit is best.

How are the common people to know what is good
Or that you hold immortality deep in your bones?
We love you and want you here in our neighborhood
But forget that wealth passes like dew on grass or stones.

Ts'ai, the quietist, speaks through silence and keeps
A feast on his terrace to welcome the fine spring night.
I've finished playing my lute and moonshine steeps
The entire scene in its silvery, placid light.—
If you meet Li Po, inquire how he wakes and sleeps;
Tell him to write and that Tu Fu longs for his sight! [26]

☙ SUMMER OUTING AT CHANG-PA CREEK ❧

It is pleasant to board the barge as the sun sinks low
And a light breeze slowly beats the ripples up;
Now we enter shade where the bamboo thickets grow;
Cool winds will waft perfume from the lily's cup.

While young gentlemen mix their icy drinks for us
And pretty girls are slicing sweet lotus shoots,
I see dark clouds are gathering over us
And that rain must bring quickly to bloom my poetry's roots.

The shower dampens our seats; the wind beats hard
Against our sides; the girls' red skirts are drenched.
The painted cheeks of the Northern beauties are marred;
The mooring-line to the willow is badly wrenched.

I see the return will be a chilly affair.
Curtains are lashed and battered with flying spray.
Feelings are also drenched beyond repair.—
Summer has turned to a frosty autumn day.

ᵇ LO-YU PARK ᵇ

The old Lo-yu Park is open and spacious
With countless acres of soft, luxuriant sward.
Our aristocratic host, who is always gracious,
Has chosen a height for his picnic's sumptuous board.

We see a distant river smoothly flowing
Flat as our palm and shiny as sparkling wine.
We mount our horses and gallop like storm-winds blowing
Or sit with wooden ladles and madly dine.

The verdant spring is reflected in glittering ripples
On the Princess' Pond; drums from the Palace roar.
As we pass the gate by the river the sunshine stipples
Our cloaks while the Emperor's carriage rolls on before.

Many chariots are bright with a gleaming cover
Of silver plate. We watch the dancers' feet
And waving sleeves performing as sunlight hovers
Till shrill songs and cloud-reflections meet!

I note that each year I get drunk at this frantic season
But now I'm too sober before I am really drunk.
With this poor head and thin hair it were mortal treason
If I were not in a hundred forfeits sunk!

Heaven only feeds scholars, the Court finds them barren and
    hollow.
They must suffer long neglect and endless wrongs.
After the party is over, what must follow?
I stand alone in silence, lost in my songs.

◆§ TO HIS EXCELLENCY WEI TSI §◆

Men with silk underwear can never starve;
Academic dress ruins a man.
Listen, grave sir! I'll tell you how men carve
Successful lives after my humble plan.

When I was young I was a candidate
In all the Imperial ordinance required.
I read a thousand books at furious rate.
Took up my brush and thought myself inspired.

My prose was deemed to rival Yang Hsiung,
My poetry to equal Ts'ao Chih.
Even great Li Yung exalted me when young
And brilliant Wang Han wished to lodge with me.

I thought that I outdistanced all my brothers
And must climb quickly to a lofty station
Aiding my Sovereign to surpass all others
In the revival of true civilization.

But all these hopes were sadly dashed; I lack
Money to rent more than a hermit's stall.
I've spent three years upon a donkey's back
Fed by flower-perfume from the capital.

Mornings, I knock at doors of young or old;
Evenings, I breathe the dust where horsemen ride.
Leftover wine and roast I swallow cold
Together with my tears and humbled pride.

I failed my test but ventured my reply
Hoping to save my life and cure my grief
But proved a bird dropped out of a clear sky,
A carp thrown up upon a barren reef.

Wei Tsi, I know my present life depends
On unearned praise your charities consign;
I know that frequently among your friends
You have quoted good fresh lines of mine.

One moment I rejoice in your advance,
The next, commiserate my own retreat.
I know my heart beats a fantastic dance;
What can I do to rest its weary feet?

Now I am going eastward toward the sea
And so must leave Ching-chao in the West.
I shall dream of its river longingly
And of the Southern Hills I love the best.

A kind heart recollects a meal with tears
And can't forget the palace where you are.
When the white, swift seagull disappears
Who will there be to tame him from afar? [27]

◄§ FRONTIER DUTIES §►

We leave our village home with heavy heart
Bound for the distant regions of Turfan.
The government compels me to depart;
Torture or death awaits the fleeing man.

Has not our Empire a sufficient span?
What can His Majesty be thinking of?
We sob and march, following his general's plan,
Forever severed from our parents' love.

A magistrate is charged for everyone
And I am destined to the last frontier.
Life or death, we must go marching on.
You, officer, need not be angry here.
See, an acquaintance on the road appear
Who will take my letter home for me.
That we must part forever now is clear,
Hopeless of suffering in company.

We choose bows that are stiff but will not burst
And arrows that will bend the longest strings.
Shooting the foe, we shoot their horses first;
Capturing them, we center on their kings.
Yet there must be a limit to all things.
For countries there must be some boundaries.
When we repulse the threat invasion brings,
What is the good of further casualties?

The barbarian ruler dares attack our fort;
For miles the air thickens with rising dust.
We wave our shining swords as if in sport
And easily repulse their feeble thrust.
We seize this famous ruler and he must
Stand with stout cords about him and implore
Mercy. But soldiers know that it is just
To count one victory nothing in a war.

VISITING GENERAL HO'S COUNTRY VILLA

I never knew just where the South Pond lies;
You pass, I find, five bridges on the way.
Tall bamboo stalks shoot toward a brilliant sky.
A garden stands where water-shadows sway.

I love all pleasures solitude supplies.
How glad I am to be your guest today!
Whenever I'm where peace and friendship are
I never grudge that distances are far.

Beside the house I note the straight bamboo;
Flowers by the old fence glow as the sun sets.
A powerful horse can hardly stagger through
This puddle by the path. There snaky nets
Of wild wisteria weave their ambush, too.
In these secluded hills a poet neglects
Even his poetry! I'll sell every book
And buy a cottage in this rural nook!

That tall tree in the yard brushes a cloud;
Books in the room stack to the ceiling's height.
Disliking war, the general is proud
Of children who are studious and write.
I wake from wine. Far from the madding crowd
We listen to our poems until midnight.
Vine shadows dance upon my summer dress;
Outside, cool moonlight stipples quietness.

Our peaceful thoughts as suddenly are gone.
We should not tarry and we must turn back.
We follow as the water leads us on,
Leaving sublime clouds only in our track.
I laugh to think that dancing in the sun
Of greatness is to suffer on a wrack.
Who cares for drunken songs? My future ends
Will be to come here often with my friends.

◦§ CLIMBING THE PAGODA OF MERCY [28] ৡ৯

At this height, in the dizzy air,
Moaning storm-winds never cease.
Since we cannot be free from care
The climb disturbs the thought of peace.

But as religious counsel is
Resistance to what fear distorts,
Looking through dragon crevices
I marvel at the tower's supports.

I clearly see the Seven Stars.
I hear the River-in-the-Skies.[29]
The sun's now passed its Western bars;
The autumn moon's about to rise.
Suddenly, as cloud-masses stir,
Great streams and mountains are undone!
Below, I see a misty blur.
Where is our noble Empire gone?

I search where the sad grave is set
And shout for the great Shun to wake.
But the Queen Fairy at sunset
Drank at her feast by the Jade Lake.
Cranes sweep past and will not rest.
Pathetic, in their plaintive mood,
Wild geese fly to a darkening West,
Each seeking only for his food.

✑§ GIVEN TO COUSIN TU TSI ❧

I am an old man, lazy as can be
And you, my boy, can either walk or run
Beside me, as you choose. It pleases me
To ride my donkey in the morning sun.
My duty is to travel and inspect.
I'll go not to the mighty or the high
Because from them small profit can accrue.
My cousin is a person such as I
And at his cottage I shall win respect;
So this is what this morning I shall do.

"You are a simple person, unemployed;
Your homestead stands like a deserted town.
In autumn's frost your tall bamboos were spoiled;
Some of your lily-plants have fallen down.
Under such circumstances it is right
That, as an elder in our family,
I should keep your vicissitudes in mind.
I do not come for porridge, as you see,
But to place matters in a lucid light
And to say what is rational and kind.

Too many drawings make a muddy well,
So don't use too much water to wash rice.
When cutting your ripe sunflowers, do not fell
Plants with a broad-axe, or you'll pay the price
By injuring their taproots. Do not be
Lured by idle gossiping that serves
No useful purposes. Carefully scan
The counsel of outsiders; it deserves
Always to be viewed suspiciously;
The Ancients favor a united clan."

DRUNK

The statesmen are promoted up and up,
The scholar in cold rooms goes down and down.
Bureaucrats eat the best of all the crop,
The scholar has small rice and less renown.
A serious thinker to the Court's a clown
Though he write better than the ancient sages.
If he is disregarded by the town
Why should he leave a name to future ages?

I, a Tu-ling rustic, make men smile,
A fellow with worn clothes and thin, gray hair.
To get my dole of rice I stand in file
By the official granary, then repair

To old Cheng's hospitable quarters where,
When money's spent, we both guzzle our wine.
Drink must be had! We simply do not care
What popular opinion may opine.

We drop polite formalities of speech,
Esteem each other for our drinking might,
Always keep our cups in easy reach
And pour the spring brew late into the night.
Rain patters from the eaves while candlelight
Fades as the snuff drops and the low flame sputters.
Lusty singing keeps our spirits light.
Why worry of starvation in the gutters?

That literary light, Ssu-ma, washed dishes
Though learned Yang tried jumping off a tower.
A scholar should renounce excessive wishes
And live in some secluded, mossy bower.
After all, do not time and dust devour
Che, the bandit, and Confucius?
Why should sad talk consume a single hour?
Simply to live and drink suffices us.

✑ PARTING OF AN AGED COUPLE ✑

There is no peace. There's war on every side.
An aged man can only toss and moan.
All my sons and grandsons, too, have died.
What good is it for me to live alone?
Even my comrades when they see me groan,
Throwing away my cane, I leave my gate.
I have a few teeth left but every bone
Is stiff. I'm a utensil out of date.

Once a man has put on uniform
He must salute the sergeant and obey.
My old wife's clothes are thin and badly torn
Although the winter season's on its way.

We know too well this is the final day
Of mutual life together. I foretell
Her suffering from cold and hear her pray
That I may eat in plenty and keep well.

The rampart of T'u-men is hard to climb;
The ferry at Hsing-yüan is hard to spy.
This campaign is unlike the former time;
Though death be not immediate, I shall die.
I cannot help but draw a heavy sigh
When I recall long years of married life:
For young and old and all beneath the sky
Meeting and parting is the law of life.

The whole world is a martial expedition.
Battle-fires blaze forth on every hand.
Woods stink of corpses in decomposition.
Human blood encrimsons all the land.
No smallest thatch nor cottage can withstand
Such onslaughts, so I may as well depart.
The roof-tree and the ties of love disband.
I am dying of a broken heart.

ᴂ§ THE UNHAPPY PRINCE [30] §ᴂ

A white-crowned raven left the city wall
Alighting on the palace gate by night,
Sure augury the Dynasty would fall,
Then, rapping on the roof, caused instant fright.
Courtiers fled before the Tatars' might.
Strongest whips broke on the horses' hide.
Royalty scattered as it took to flight.
Many men and many horses died.

With precious jewels hidden in his vest
A young prince by the road weeps pitifully.
Though easily known, he stays anonymous, lest
His name be heard, but says he'd rather be

A slave. With lacerated body, he
Has lain in hiding in a thorny place
A hundred days. The Imperial family
Has from the first worn a distinguished face.

"Now royalty is low and treason proud.
Care for yourself and to yourself be true!
I dare not talk here in this busy crowd
Nor linger further on the road with you.
Last night in darkness the strong East wind blew
A bloody stench; we heard the camels moan.
Famous battalions are no longer true.
The Emperor has given up his throne.

But there is hope; you must wait patiently.
In this distress His Majesty relies
Chiefly upon the Uighur cavalry.
Don't say a word, for there are always spies.
Hope is dawning in the Northern skies.
Fierce Uighurs slash their faces with a knife,
Swearing to restore the Empire's prize.
There still is hope, hope at the roots of life."

⇜§ LAMENTATION BY THE RIVER [31] §⇝

I am an old rustic from Shao-ling
Crying vehemently but not loud.
By the meandering river in the spring
I shun attention of the busy crowd.
Here at the river's bank the thousand proud
Palace gates are locked and all the scene
Saddens under a nostalgic shroud:
For whom, then, do these willows wear their green?

Rainbow banners used to dance in air;
The whole Park burst with color, warmth, and glee.
The Mistress of the Palace would repair
Here in the Emperor's high company.

White horses pranced to golden minstrelsy.
The Imperial carriage came and in the sight
Of all a lady practiced archery
And one shot dropped a pair of birds in flight.

Where are those shining eyes and teeth today?
Even the wandering ghost is stained with blood
And never can return. The sparkling Wei
Flows East while the West Road is blocked for good.
Can heartless grass and flowers adorn the plain
Or dusty Tatar horsemen be withstood?
I search the North where hope may dawn again.

ᵛᶠ JADE FLOWER PALACE [32] ᶠᵛ

In this rude gully with its windy pines   5.5 ems
Gray rats scurry among broken tile.
Today the Prince's Palace leaves no signs
Of where it glittered in the dark defile.
Chambers are damp and dreary that erstwhile
Sounded with glee; flickering ghost-fires fill
A bluish haze and through the rocky aisle
The melancholy river hastes downhill.

Dead leaves mutter at each sobbing gust;
Colors of the autumn trees are grim;
All the brilliant women now are dust;
The powder and the rouge have long been dim.
A statue of a horse with broken limb
Is all the trace the Prince's chariot gives.
Musing, I chant my melancholy hymn:
Who cares how long a restless mortal lives?

You meet these dangerous times with youthful vigor,
Your wisdom grounded in heroic force.
The fortunes of our country call for rigor.
Who else but you could check rebellion's course?

In Feng-hsiang even the most exalted statesman
Is grateful to have horse, food and array.
Among the poorest of the green-robed placemen
A white-haired man plods on the footpath way.

True friendship among men has never given
Heed to rank or age in time of need.
Far off my wife and children cry to heaven!
Please lend me from your stud a flying steed!

⊷ CHANCE MEETING ⊱

A fierce wind whips the dust beside the stream,
Limbs hardly seen in this lugubrious place.
Peering through fog, I note, as if in dream,
A rider, and, behold! a well-known face,
Yün-ch'ing! His old horse with its stumbling pace
Is making for the hospitable door
Of Liu, who welcomes us with every grace.
With him we shun all topics that are sore,
Whispering no ominous word of this disastrous war.

The stove burns red with semblance of the dawn;
Like rippled silk the moon falls on the shade.
Now at Lo-yang our winter has withdrawn
With hopes of spring, once at Ch'ang-an betrayed.
Who would have ever thought, no more dismayed,
Our paths would cross and happily again
We'd feast together with a good friend's aid?
All watch the glad hours pass with mounting pain:
When the cocks crow our tears of parting fall like rain!

I am highly annoyed! We live at two ends of a row
So why haven't we seen each other for ten long days?
I gave up the horse that the government loaned me and so
I'm faced with the rough, rugged ground of the public ways.
I'm far too poor to hire a personal chaise
And, again, if I walked, my superiors wouldn't approve!
So a warm wish to see you suffers vexatious delays.
This is my problem, so please do not question my love!

This morning it rains; spring winds make house-walls tremble.
I was sleeping soundly so didn't hear the bell
And loud drum that summon courtiers to assemble.
To be sure, I have some kindly neighbors who dwell
To the East who would loan me a donkey. That's all very well,
But the mud is so slippery I dare not ride it to Court.
My troubles and trials are more than a man can tell.
I've petitioned to be excused as a last resort!

How can I bear the whole day with a longing heart
To hear your poems that impress me so movingly?
Youth fades as these early magnolia blooms depart
And the high price of wine is a frightful thing to see!
Inebriate sleep comes seldom to you and me.
Come quickly, please, and release the wine-keg's stoppers!
We'll empty a hearty gallon immediately,
For I happen to have precisely three hundred coppers.

◦§ THE FAIR LADY ℰ∾

She is the most beautiful woman of the age,
Living quietly in this mountain pass.
"Misfortune leaves me with the weeds and grass
Growing in long neglect while soldiers wage

War that has swept my brothers from life's stage.
High rank availed them nothing in these crass
And cruel times, lost in the anonymous mass
Of slain, ever obscure to history's page.

The world despises the unfortunate.
No love lasts longer than a candle's flame
Blown by the wind. My husband shuns my name.
He has already found another mate.
A pair of ducks share one another's fate;
With the mimosa blossoms it's the same,
Its petals join at night. But to my shame
He loves her laugh and mocks my tearful state."

High in these hills the water-springs are clear
Though streams run turbid with the mud and rain.
Her maid sells the few jewels that remain.
They mend their cottage thatch, grown thin and seer.
Some pleasant flowers she picks, but not to wear;
The constant cypress will her hands retain.
By tall bamboos she stands on a green plain,
Dress radiant, while the chilly night draws near.

✌§ THE HEAVENLY RIVER [34] ੪≈

The River-in-the-Sky is faint all year;
Yet though some clouds may further dim its light—
Except in autumn, when it's always clear—
It never fails to gleam throughout the night.

It glitters on the Central Capital
And on far cities at our border's rim;
Cowboy and Weaving Girl cross it each fall;
No wind or wave can trouble her or him.

POEM SENT TO TU TSO

Floating clouds must have darkened the afternoon hills
And I fear that bad roads have caused you some harm
And birds must have silenced their lyrical bills
When at last you re-entered your tree-shaded farm.
Uncle Tu Fu, who is lazy and calm
In disaster, stays here with his children and spouse.
They have traveled rough roads and now long for the balm
Of your aid to maintain this impoverished house.

The millet we gleaned in early September
You promised to share when it first should appear.
It must be ground fine, for I seem to remember
It's been over a month now in reaching me here.
We hardly need wait for the peak of the year
When the golden chrysanthemums come into flower.
I hold green-mallow soup with fresh millet most dear,
My mouth waters to taste it at this very hour.

What turbulent freshets of spring must have been
In your garden where so many eatables grow!
Those sturdy fall shrubs must by this time be thin;
You'll see more high clouds as the autumn leaves go.
Fragrant plants must be lush where the pond-waters flow
And the dodder vines rich in the neighboring wood.
Your frost-covered shallots are ripe now, I know.
Do send me some, please, if you will be so good!

SONGS OF A SOJOURNER

A sojourner named Tu Tzü-mei has stood
With wind-blown hair falling across his ears,
Compelled to search out acorns for his food
In cold and wintry hills as night-time nears.

No message from the Central Plain appears.
Covered with chapped, half-dead and shriveled skin,
Stiff limbs and frozen trunk are sadly thin.
    As the fierce gale blows on me, rude and rough,
    Just this first strophe should be sad enough!

This long ash-handled spade held at my side
Alone can save me from a mortal doom
And yet I cannot find the yams that hide
Securely in the snow as in a tomb.
My family shudder in a ghastly room.
I come home empty-handed with my spade,
No cloak to shield me and no soul to aid.
    This second strophe of my poem is strong
    To make all neighbors suffer at my wrong.

I have three brothers who live far away.
Which of you three is now the strongest one?
But since the long road lies in Tatar sway
We have small chance of a reunion.
Watching wild geese and cranes fly toward the sun,
I long to mount each one of them and ride
Until I safely reach your longed-for side!
    This third strophe thrice repeats my groans,
    Telling you where in death to find my bones.

There's my dear sister in the district of
Chüng-li, a widow and a mother, too,
Of young and feeble children whom I love.
How can I come after ten years to you?
The long Huai River with its tawny crew
Of monsters flows between. I have no boat.
Over all the land war-banners float.
    This fourth strophe shall be four times sighing
    Until fierce forest-monkeys answer crying.

ᴥ§ TWO SWALLOWS ᒃᴥ

A traveling family at dinner saw
Two swallows holding mud in tiny bills
Fly into their hut. They with due awe
Thought how one principle all nature fills:
Both sharing shelter in inclement weather,
Both passing time's inconstancies together.

Like us, you raise your young in wind and dust;
Like you, we toil across long, dreary space.
Both travel distances because they must.
You'll leave next autumn, granting heaven's grace.
We, too, if earth exists, shall leave this station,
Submitting to life's infinite mutation.

ᴥ§ TO PERFECT CHANG ᒃᴥ

Eminent guests dismounting from their horses
Are welcomed by fair women near the stream.
Broad fans are mirrored in the water-courses,
Loud songs re-echo as bright costumes gleam.
Robes sweep widely as they dance and whirl;
Wine pots refract each shimmering sunbeam.
Just note the face of each sweet-smiling girl,
Each bright glance glowing in keen competition,
Each coquettish eye betraying youth's ambition!

With song and dance the shining sun is downed;
Still loud flute-tones pierce the darkening sky;
Gleaming eyebrows move to choric sound;
Each headdress to its neighbor makes reply.
Horses are standing back to back in file.
At dusk far hills glow as the night is nigh;
Perfumed boats drift homeward mile on mile.—
My friend, you have a wife who waits and wakes;
Don't take a wrong example from wild ducks and drakes!

The peach-bamboo grows only in midstream,
Only in blue waves is it tall and fit.
The stem is purple jade in the sunbeam.
When peeled and cut, no goddess can keep it.

The Prefect of Tzü-chou displays a group
Of sticks before his guests, a marveling crowd;
Then, because I'm elderly and droop,
He gives me two that, struck, resound aloud.

They give metallic echoes when I wack them.
Since I am going East, I can't afford
That river-ghosts or dragons should attack them
Where I may have to guard them with my sword.

Let me tell you, sticks, each in its station
Grows sheer and straight; you are my best resort.
Beware of water and the grim temptation
To become dragons, you, my one support!

Ah, you would seal my doom and kill me then
If you should play any such knavish tricks!
Where wind and dust and tigers prey on men,
What would I do if I should lose these sticks?

ᣟ THE OLD CYPRESS [36] ᣟ

At K'ung-ming Temple stands an aged tree,
A cypress, trunk like bronze and roots like rock,
Offering the sky its spacious panoply,
Rain dripping forty yards around its stock.
A Minister once served a mighty Prince
Whose memory is treasured and increased
With years like this great tree and ever since
His honor is the brightest and the best
Whether in cloudfilled gorges of the East
Or moon-and-snow-white mountains in the West.

I recollect the Temple near Chin-t'ing,
Statues of K'ung-ming and his Prince enshrined.
Two aged cypresses stood wing to wing;
Paint on the doors and walls was much declined
But the trees signified his Ministry.
A firm grip on the precinct saved the state.
His the true symbol of austerity,
A noble figure above fortune's sport;
Since Creation had contrived it straight,
Providence provided its support.

Now the edifice demands repair;
Its timber like a mountain-mass must be
Too much for oxen in huge droves to bear
And has to come from an unflowering tree,
A marvel ripe to cut, measured for beams.
Alas, I find some ants have threatened rot.
The solid heart is flecked with cracks and seams
Which still must save our Phoenix from insult.
O good men in retirement, murmur not:
Remember, greatness makes it difficult.

◆§ THE BRIGHT CONCUBINE [37] §◆

Among the mountains in the long incline
Rising toward the region of Chiang-ling
The village lies where the Bright Concubine
Was born and where our sad reflections bring
To mind the Purple Palace where, unseen,
She lived in beauty. Now only the wide
Expanse of barren hills on every side
Lies in the yellowish dusk, through which is seen
Her lonely, desolate grave that keeps forever green.

In countless paintings I have seen her face
Bright with the colors of a glorious spring.
Her ghost emerges in this desert place.
I hear the pendants of her eardrops ring

Their silver tinklings chiming with the throngs
Of stars about the moon. Hark, from afar!
That heavenly music of her strange guitar,
Its melodies revealing with her songs
The many ills she suffered and her tragic wrongs!

✑ TWO EAGLES [38] ☙

Like white jade or a piece of cloud he stands
Throughout the clarity of autumn light.
This peerless, royal eagle countermands
All that the hunters do for his afright.
He mocks their nets; sharp arrows cannot bite
His sides; his proud and ever-dauntless soul
Scorns on the falconer's armlet to alight;
He frightens the huge roc, his royal goal,
Not the frail, timorous rabbit scurrying to a hole.

His mightier partner, a black eagle, flies.
I hardly believed there could be such a bird!
Perhaps he issues from the arctic skies?
Surely, no falconer has ever heard
Of such a one! At night his wings have stirred
The airs of the Sun Terrace. Geese and daws
Have fled in terror. His vast wings have whirred
High on the peaks of Wu. All birds must pause
Dreading his golden eyes and those white, fearful claws!

Ode To The Lute

HSI K'ANG

✑ In Chinese, as in Western poetry, a marked line is drawn between the lyrical and the nonlyrical. As ardent lovers of song, the Chinese developed a profound lyrical tradition; as practical men living in a physical world and accustomed to a down-to-earth view of life, they assiduously cultivated poetry of a descriptive or didactic character. Tu Fu and his associates perfected what may be called the verse epistle. Verse when combined with expository prose in a widely used form, the fu, led to what may be termed verse-essays. Hsi K'ang's Ode to the Lute may be designated an essay-poem. It gives a description, equally factual and enthusiastic, of the lute and the principles of lute-playing. The theme is expanded virtually into a praise of music itself. This led the poet to voice a philosophy of music, at once mystical and ethical and equally agreeable to two leading branches of Chinese thought, the Taoistic and the Confucian. Of primarily Taoistic inspiration is the belief that music assists the soul in merging with nature and with the infinite; of primarily Confucian inspiration is the thought that it stabilizes and confirms a life of order, social virtue, good conduct and good manners. Some passages are the quintessence of aestheticism, others even conspicuously didactic. The poem has long enjoyed popularity.

Hsi K'ang flourished in the third century A.D. It may be mentioned, however, that his authorship is questioned by some scholars and that the ode may possibly be the work of another hand writing at a later time. Vigorous as it is, one detects a touch of diffusiveness. This English rendering follows the structure closely but is slightly compressed, and a few obscure passages are omitted. Unlike all other poems in this volume, it is consciously rendered with a degree of license but not, I trust, license that is *illegitimate. The aim is to present the ode's essential value as clearly and fully as possible and to suggest how it might have been rendered into English in the time of the lute-playing Queen Elizabeth. For further comments, the reader is referred to the notes. Notwithstanding the high reputation of the ode in China, it has seldom been translated into the Western languages. Modern scholarship has done comparatively little to cast light on it. The reader is referred, however, to the translation into English prose and the extended commentary by P. H. van Gulik, to which work the following rendition is much indebted.*

⇜§ ONE §⇝

I have loved music since I was a youth
And practiced it intensely to this day,
For it appears an undisputed Truth
That joy in other savors dies away
Satiated by too long a stay,
While music lives, our solitude's support,
Ennobling life; we hum a tune, or play
An instrument, and then, should this fall short,
We further turn to words to implement our thought.

⇜§ TWO §⇝

Music has been the theme of many men
Writing of it from the first of time,
Lauding its virtues; and the poet's pen
Has decorated it in golden rhyme.
But, wearied of this repetitious chime
Praising its craft or grandeur, I refute
Their judgment of a subject so sublime.
Thus to praise music best beyond dispute
I have composed this ode in honor of the lute.

⇜§ THREE §⇝

The only trees that are the best to build
The lute grow where the mountains soar on high;
There, where the moistened soil is richly filled
With nutriment, and tapering to the sky

The branches drink pure influences that fly
Between the Earth and Heaven, far from earth's dust,
Neighbors of sun and moon, these tree-tops vie
In catching sunset's glow and dawn's red thrust;
A thousand years they wait, quiet, silent, and robust.[1]

⋙ FOUR ⋘

The scene, irregular, rugged, and rough,
Shows many a deep descent and rocky crest;
Here crags are steep; there looms a massive bluff;
There lies a gash on a huge mountain's breast;
A summit with dark-gathering clouds oppressed
Thunders half-hidden in its tragic pall.
Glorious the slopes in their green verdure dressed!
Glorious the rocky barrier and wall,
Where some stupendous peak rises above them all!

⋙ FIVE ⋘

Mysterious haze invests the mountain slopes
And clouds dissolve, as rain in torrents falls
Till in due course the furious water gropes
For passage down the jagged, roaring walls
With crashing speed that frightens and appalls.
At greatest depth the churning waters fill
With dragon forms whose frantic fury hauls
Whole cliffsides loose; but rage grows less, until
At last a placid sea embraces vale and hill.[2]

►§ SIX ?◄

But look more closely at each hill and glade
And precious products on their walls are seen:
Rarest forms of jasper and of jade,
Orchids glittering through darkest green;
Phoenixes in dazzling splendor preen
Rainbow wings, while over them a breeze
Blows gently; magisterial, serene,
They stand; bird, bloom, and lofty trees
Inspire warm love of music in such scenes as these.

►§ SEVEN ?◄

Hence is it that the wise men flee the world
To ascend the mountains in their holy calm;
Though the rocks be in rude fury hurled,
Solitude falls on them as a balm;
Saved from contamination and all harm,
Here in great quietness the sages learn
To look afar and to hear nature's psalm.
Girt with such noble sights, the soul may spurn
The world and so at last repudiate return.[3]

►§ EIGHT ?◄

Here their emotions become broad and even; [4]
They look afar, with eyes whose far-away
Gaze shows pure spirits that discover Heaven
And thus express the great Taoistic Way

Which the sage Yellow Emperor in his day
Embraced, and all musicians follow suit.
These with careful hands would cut and weigh
The young, fresh wood. Sipping their mystic fruit,
The noblest of mankind here made the elegant lute.

⊷§ NINE §⊷

Then a man comes with sharp and eager eye
Who shapes the lute according to the rule
Of ancient masters whose decrees defy
Change. For heirs of this great Singing-School
He chisels out the wood with his sharp tool,
Fits front to back, and on the wood finds room
For portraits of the masters and the cool
Forms of the phoenixes who spurn the tomb:
So from the noble mind new music comes to bloom

⊷§ TEN §⊷

It glows with jade, with ivory, and all five
Colors the painters love. Its silken strings
Are tuned with all the skill that arts contrive
Whereby the greatest modulation rings
Throughout the heights and depths that music sings.
Its tones, rising or falling, like the seas;
Loud, soft, swift, slow; whatever genius brings
To life, are set to magic melodies,
With sudden gusts and calms and dazzling harmonies.

⤳ ELEVEN ⤶

The opening bars of the lute's melody
Are strong like lofty mountains, or, again,
Like heaving waves, or, broad and generously,
Are like a smooth, majestic sunlit plain—
But, in a moment, stumbling upon pain,
Rugged, in rustling garments. Skill may gleam
Brightly, but not too brightly, with the sane
Modulation which all arts beseem.
The end must float in peace on the predestined theme.

⤳ TWELVE ⤶

One should play the lute on a high tower
Or lofty terrace. It is also right
To play it in a spacious, quiet bower,
Or on a limpid, clear and wintry night,
Clad in new rustling garments shining bright
And perfumed, with a tranquil heart, the whole
Cool instrument attuned to cool delight.
Then thought and fingers serve a single goal
And so the player's music amplifies his soul.[5]

⤳ THIRTEEN ⤶

First play 'The Limpid Water,' and then play
'The Composition in G-Sharp;' renew
The praise of Emperor Yao; lastly pray
To the arch-master of great songs, Wei-tzü.

Sing of the blest Isle floating in the blue,
Join the Gods who on the whirlwind ride,
Drink nectar with the blest, inebriate crew,[6]
Float calmly on the universal tide,
Abide in perfect bliss, having cast earth aside.

ᵛᵝ FOURTEEN ᶓᵈ

Songs cease and every instrument is still.—
Then, having tuned the lute, let new songs rise;
Make us think of dancing girls who fill
The soul with fresh delight, whose beauty lies
In serene poise whereat all passion dies,
Gestures oblique, long sleeves with fluttering hands,[7]
Low whisperings—then, suddenly, a rush
Of splendor, a pressing forward, fierce, shrill cries:
Now slow, now swift, as the winds fall or flush;
The end in unison, quiet, with a low heavenly hush.

ᵛᵝ FIFTEEN ᶓᵈ

For calm and tumult on the lute are one.
Sometimes its chords rise to a raucous scream,
Then, suddenly, this fierce debate is done
And tones run smoothly as a well-trained team
Gliding so its noble horses seem
To be not two but one. Notes pause or leap;
Jostle but never fall; like a poised beam
They are now up, now down, rejoice or weep,
Ornate yet elegant, imposing and yet deep.[8]

✒§ SIXTEEN ࠪ

Leisurely in refined expansiveness
The notes float smoothly forward in or out,
Sometimes with airs that gentle and caress,
Sometimes ascending to a perilous shout;
Like wild beasts rushing from a grim redoubt,
Or like mild geese with particolored back
Floating across the moon, all things about
To be or vanishing, for music's track
Is swift but never hasty, slow but never slack.

✒§ SEVENTEEN ࠪ

Fingers of the lute-player are like the wind
Across the waves; in distance like the cry
Of the phoenix in cloudy heaven; or are thinned
On nearer view to blossoms that we spy
Unfolding on their bough against the sky.—
Linger in fragrant gardens; climb low hills;
With April lay your heavier garments by;
Write verses; feel the calm the scene distills:
Then above other times learn how lute-music thrills.[9]

✒§ EIGHTEEN ࠪ

Such are the hours to play the stately pieces
Left by the Emperor Shun, of noble name,
When sadness in the lonely heart increases.—
Or, should we leap into the merry game

In halls with friendly mirth briskly aflame,
When wine has fired the throng, which is our root
Of warmest glee, when grief is put to shame,
And friend clasps friend? Whoever knows the lute
Must scorn the crude mouth-organ or the whining flute.

NINETEEN

Lute-melodies are Chi-hsi, Tung-wu, Kuang-ling,
With notes spontaneous, tender, bold, and clear,
K'un-chi, Yu-hsien, Fei-lung, and loved Lu-ming
Are also held by all lute-players dear.
Folksongs alike abundantly appear
With tunes of Ts'ai, Ch'u-fei, and Wang Chao.
Readily I might mention others here
Who in my happy rhymes would smoothly flow;
The lute's charms only quiet and noble persons know.

TWENTY

Its very structure is harmonious,
So that it answers music's every need;
Since strings are tight and long, its sonorous
Effects the more felicitously proceed.
Both hands may touch the strings with rapid speed
And far apart, for plucking or release.
If the player's life is true in word and deed,
Fixed to firm principles, all pains will cease
And the lute's blessed tones will grant him lasting peace.

TWENTY-ONE

If lumpish persons hear it, they will be
More sorrowful than they have been before;
Grief will gnaw their hearts persistently;
They know not what the gentle lute is for.
But when the strong and joyful hear, the more
They hear, the more resistless is their glee;
Their spirits to the empyrean soar;
Leaving all earthly cares, their hearts are free,
Serene and solemn men, one with antiquity.[10]

TWENTY-TWO

Therefore Po-i gained honor from his lute,
Pi-Kan his truth, Wan-shih his diligence,
Wei-sheng his faith; last and beyond dispute,
Yen Hui won from it his benevolence.
To each who sounds the lute-strings they dispense
A virtue that is specially his own.
Sometimes sweet charm, sometimes a moral sense [11]
Is gained, and so from earth to Heaven's throne
All persons praise the lute with its cool, healing tone.

TWENTY-THREE

Other instruments are no more heard
When lutes are played, and all the lesser sounds
Of gourd and bamboo fade. But like a bird
The Cloud-God comes, the God of Ocean bounds

Up from his depths, and all the dancing-grounds
Resound with flying feet in magic rings;
The Phoenix floats to earth; the air abounds
With shouts of glee; a fairy music sings
With the tumultuous joy that the lute's music brings.[12]

 TWENTY-FOUR

In admiration of the excellence
Of the lute's music I composed this song;
And thus I summarize my ode's contents:
Above philosophy its merits belong.—
But where at present is the classic throng
Of ancients who in olden time held sway?
Not to our age do the great masters belong;
Their skills were treasures of a happier day.
The noble soul alone can master it and play.

Book
Of
Songs

❧ Sometimes called the Confucian Book of Odes, the Book of Songs, or Shih Ching, is one of the most venerable Chinese classics. It must be recognized also as one of the most remarkable of poetry collections, having been known intimately to more persons than any other with the possible exception of the Psalms of David. The Book of Songs consists of slightly over three hundred lyrics, almost all anonymous. There are hymns, ballads, love songs, rhymes for dancers, and didactic pieces. The oldest may go back to nearly 1000 B.C. By a plausible tradition they were assembled at an emperor's command from all sections of China, thousands of songs being examined and only the moderate number finally admitted into the selection. Confucius held the anthology in the highest esteem, editing it, codifying the musical tradition which it enshrined, and giving it his canonical blessing. For nearly 2,500 years it stood high on the obligatory list of books to be studied and memorized by all scholars and official servants of the state. Only for a brief period, when Confucianism itself was temporarily challenged and its literature banned, did it fall out of official favor, but the poems, deeply rooted in the memories of the people, safely survived. They have never ceased to be so treasured. Countless millions have regarded them as the chief sourcebook of poetry, of imaginative literature, and of song. They have possessed a classless appeal, at once beloved as folksongs or popular lyrics and honored as refined works of art, dear alike to scholars and to the people.

The following versions are based on the literal English renderings of one of the most eminent authorities on Chinese linguistics, the Swedish scholar Bernhard Karlgren. Special effort has been made to represent the poems as songs and even as the folksongs which originally they were. In their subject matter they cover a wide range of experience. They were conceived as occasional poems, to be sung on appropriate occasions, much as people use proverbs or familiar quotations. To a supreme degree these are "poems for use."

As often in the case of books that enjoy such long and ardent veneration, the history of the Songs reveals curious vicissitudes. The dialect in which they were recorded became to a considerable measure obscured with the advancing centuries. Even in highly conservative China, the intellectual and spiritual climate drastically changed. It is probable that Confucius himself stood at a considerable distance from circumstances under which some of the poems were composed. How much more, then, with the scholars of a thousand or more years later! Almost all the poems were at one time viewed as containing allegorical significations. Here, again, is an analogy between them and the Hebrew Psalms as these came into the hands of the Christian fathers. It is true that schools of highly allusive and allegorical poetry flourished in China at an early date. Shamans recited seeming love poems that harbored hidden meanings, personal, political, or both. An esoteric poetry based on astrology was also well known. In general, however, the history of the odes as they were received in Chinese opinion shows that much that was in its original intention comparatively simple and open was later construed as a complex and esoteric lore.

There is admittedly much in the Songs that today remains dark and will always be so. In a few cases poems are by leading scholars translated so differently that even the original identity of a piece becomes uncertain. Yet, on the whole, these ancient Songs, rightly or wrongly, have to all appearances in recent years been clarified and not obscured. We believe that we see them today unencumbered by the accumulated dust of pedantic commentary. To be sure, the more disputable pieces are omitted from the following selection. But even so, the generalization holds that, in the long-run, time has been extraordinarily merciful to the Confucian odes. They have a freshness seldom encountered in the poetry of the twentieth century or in a current season. Few classics preserve a more youthful bloom.

The poems are here numbered as in the standard editions.

∽§ TWO §∾

Into the deepest valley
The vines extend and cling;
Yellow birds assemble
Fluttering on the wing,
Alight on the dense foliage
And resolutely sing.

Into the deepest valley
The vines extend and cling;
I cut the leaves and boil them
Until at length they bring
Cloth too smooth to irk me,
Fine clothes and covering.

I tell the watchful matron
That I shall shortly cease,
Quit scrubbing, rinse the garments
(I'll wash what clothes I please)
And then, returning homeward,
Wish both my parents peace.

∽§ THREE §∾

I gather herbs but fail to fill
My shallow basket with their load;
Sighing for one I dearly love,
I leave it by the valley road.

I climb the rugged mountainside,
Horses fatigued for many a mile;
From the bronze vase I fill a cup
Not to long for him all the while.

We scale the highest mountain pass,
My horses livid by the climb;
I pour a cup from the horn-vase
Not to long for him all the time.

Last, I ascend the beetling cliff,
My horses laboring and sick,
My driver desperately ill,
My own heart wounded to the quick.

⊰ NINETEEN [1] ⊱

Thunder resounds upon the Southern Peak.
Why, great prince, did you go so far away,
Not deigning to take leisure in my house?
Come back, come back to me, great prince, and stay!

The thunder roars upon the Southern Peak!
Why have you ventured on that perilous track,
Not deigning to repose in my poor house?
O, most majestic lord, come back, come back!

The thunder at the foot of the great mountain
Rumbles and roars! Why could you not remain
Here in my home? O, my majestic lord,
Pray you come back, come back to me again!

⊰ TWENTY ⊱

The plum-tree drops its fruits;
By summer seven are left:
Several young lads are wooers;
I shall not be bereft.

The plum-tree drops its fruits;
Autumn leaves only three:
Fewer men are wooers;
May one soon turn to me!

ANCIENT POETRY FROM CHINA/141

The plum-tree sheds its fruits;
In later fall I carry
My harvest-basket out,
Hoping I still shall marry!

⊸§ TWENTY-ONE ² §⊷

Pale are those minor stars,
Triad and Pleiades;
We hasten through the night
Early or late to please,
A harem of small lights
Who sparkle and then cease.

Pale are we, minor stars,
Who with the wife have striven,
Who hurry through the dark
From our lord-master riven,
With blanket and chemise,
Poor concubines of heaven!

⊸§ TWENTY-THREE ³ §⊷

White grass wraps the body;
The forest deer is dead.
Springtime betrayed a maiden;
Her gallant loved and fled.

The girl strayed with her lover
Deep in a forest glade.
White grass wrapped her body,
Delicate as jade.

"O lover, slowly, gently,
Do not disturb my dress
Or rouse the farmer's dog
To heighten our distress!"

◆§ THIRTY [4] §◆

High wind and rain descend!
Looking at me you smile.
Nevertheless I know
You laugh at me all the while.
My very heart's core
Is hurt by arrogant guile.

High wind and cloud and dust!
You promised to meet me here.
You have betrayed my trust.
I wait but you do not appear.
I brood on my wretched fate
While my heart grows heavy with fear.

High wind in the twilight sky!
Storm-dust whirls in a heap.
The day is howling and dark;
My sorrows are dark and deep.
I am chagrined at my longing,
Wretched, and cannot sleep.

Offspring of wind-blown skies,
Cloud-born lightning is burning;
Tempests crush the air;
The heavens above are churning;
Always longing for you
My heart is consumed with yearning.

❧ THIRTY-ONE ❧

HUSBAND

"Bang go the drums at home; men jump and bounce,
Whirling their weapons as their lord commands,
Build Ts'ao's wall with ramparts piled with earth,
While we alone march to the Southern lands.

Our general, Sun Tsi-chung, has led us on
To lay proud Ch'en and Sung beneath his sway.
He brought us South but does not bring us home;
Our hearts are heavy at the long delay.

Here we settle down and pitch our tents;
Here we remain draining our hardihood
Through aimless years. Our horses go astray;
Hunting for them, we find them in the wood."

WIFE

"Now through all time we two are separated;
We clasped our hands; you promised me your heart
Forever. Now no more can you support me.
We must live forever far apart."

❧ THIRTY-EIGHT ❧

Huzza! the dancers prepare to perform the ritual dance.
The sun rests at its zenith, at its point of farthest advance.

In the royal court, like a tiger, the tall dancer stands,
Reins of the royal chariot as silken threads in his hands.

Smeared red, a flute in his left hand, in his right a pheasant's plume,
He receives the ritual cup at the hands of the prince's groom.

On the West hill the hazel, in the swamp the low scrub-tree.
The man from the Western Mountain is the one who rejoices me!

↝§ THIRTY-NINE [5] §↜

Spring waters flow in amorous delay.
They rise in K'i, my thoughts fly on to Wei.
At every hour I yearn for you, my dear,
But on my family I must still rely.

Fair ladies, tell me, should I pass the night
At Tsi and take Ni for my drinking-place
To bid you all farewell? Leaving my clan,
I must consult you on all laws of grace.

Or possibly should I set out to pass
The night at Kan, drinking farewell at Yen?
You might return from there; since it is wrong
To hasten, I might oil my wagons then.

I brood on our spring waters, and I dream
Of Su and Ts'ao that I love so here.—
Now I shall go upon a pleasure drive
Delaying travel and allaying fear.

↝§ FORTY §↜

I leave by the North Gate,
Wretched and ill at heart.
Nobody knows my pain
Or how my bruises smart.
All is finished, Heaven has spoken,
Nothing is left, my life lies broken.

The king's affairs oppressed me,
Politics undid me;
At every door I knock
Now the folk forbid me.
All is finished, Heaven has spoken,
Nothing is left, my life lies broken.

The king's affairs obsessed me,
The premier removed me;
Wherever I have knocked
The people have reproved me.
All is finished, Heaven has spoken,
Nothing is left, my life lies broken.

◄§ FORTY-ONE §►

The Northern wind is chill,
Tumultuous the snow;
If you truly love me
Clasp my hand and go!—
Still you resist through modesty
And bitter is our urgency!

The Northern wind is wild,
Snow thick; we're far from home.
If you love me truly
Clasp my hand and come!
Still you resist through modesty
Though bitter is our urgency!

The fox is reddest red,
The raven blackest black.[6]
If you love me truly
You cannot now turn back.
Still you resist through modesty
And bitter is our urgency!

◄§ FORTY-TWO §►

Behind the corner of a wall
A girl waits who is kind and fair.
I love her; she is not in view;
I hesitate and scratch my hair.

This girl once plucked for me a reed
Glossy red and shining bright.
She is beautiful and kind,
The very sum of my delight.

She plucked the shoot on pasture ground;
The reed is lovely, that is true,
Yet my delight in it is not
For it, but that it came from you.

ᥰᥰ FORTY-THREE ᥱᥱ

The palace was painted bright,
The torrent poured down like slag.
She had sought a handsome lover
But drew a fulsome rag.

The palace was all washed clean
And its river as smooth as that.
She had sought a handsome lover
But drew a worn-out mat.

On pulling a net from the stream
A goose was its only load.
She had sought a handsome lover
But drew an ugly toad.

ᥰᥰ FORTY-FOUR ᥱᥱ

Two young men embarked upon a boat;
   Their ship sailed far to sea.
Thinking of them I become sorrowful,
   Troubled where they may be.

Two young men embarked upon a boat.
　My spirit takes alarm,
Fearing that they, daring such vast misfortune,
　Surely must come to harm.

⊰ FORTY-FIVE ⊱

A cypress boat of evil omen drifts
Mid-stream, capsized. Two tufts of youthful hair,
Swept by the tide, float from my lover's head.
O mother, O Heaven, what perfidy is there!

A cypress boat veers sidewise down the stream,
Drifting beside it tufts of youthful hair.
The drowned boy swore to be my faithful lover.
O mother, O Heaven, what perfidy was there!

⊰ FORTY-SIX ⊱

Vines on the wall must not be brushed away.
No harem secret bides the light of day.
If one is told, horror begets dismay.

Vines on the wall must not be brushed aside.
The harem's secrets must not be descried;
These are the bitter truths all men must hide.

Vines on the wall must not be brushed apart
Nor any whisper from the harem start.
All telling of such tales consumes the heart.

ᴠᴀ FORTY-SEVEN ᵬᴥ

The one who must grow old beside her lord
Must wear the wig and pins with the six gems,
Be gracious as a mountain or a stream,
Nature embroidered on her dress and hems,
So that the worst detractor may not call
The wife unworthy of her diadems.

Her pheasant robe is glittering and bright,
Her hair far darker than black ebony,
Her earrings carved out of serenest jade,
Her clear brow white, her comb-pin ivory.
Truly, she is a creature fit for heaven
Or is herself a stainless deity.

Newly embroidered is her ritual robe
Covering the plain undergowns that stand
Next to her lustrous body. O what splendor
Her forehead's form and dignity command!
Truly, a woman proper for a prince
Is paradigm of beauty for our land!

ᴠᴀ FIFTY ⁷ ᵬᴥ

The builder's constellation at its height,
He raised his stately home for avatars;
He planted fields with many sapling shoots,
Still following direction from the stars,
Catalpas, chestnuts, hazels, lacquer-trees,
To fashion lutes and sonorous guitars.

Climbing the venerable ruin-mound,
He overlooked the lands of T'ang and Ch'u,
Measuring hills and mountains by their shade,
Pondering on that prophetic view;
Descending, he inspected mulberry-trees
And questioned oracles, as wise men do.

After auspicious evening rains had fallen
He called his grooms at middle of the night.
When the sky cleared they yoked his ritual chariot
To bless the mulberry groves by the stars' light.—
Later, three thousand mares were given him.—
Truly, that man knew what is good and right!

✥ FIFTY-TWO ✥

Look at the rat,
Pale skin and sly.
A man without manners—
Why doesn't he die?

Look at the rat,
It has teeth to ply.
A man without morals—
Why doesn't he die?

Look at the rat,
Its limbs are spry.
A man without worth—
Why doesn't he die?

✥ FIFTY-FIVE ✥

Look at the great bend of the river K'i
And the rich pastures that its fields present!
Its lord is cut, pure, chiseled, freshly bright,
Polished, refined, conspicuous, eminent;
So excellent his features, I cannot
Ever forget a lord so elegant.

Look at the great bend of the river K'i,
The fertile pastures that its fields afford!
His eardrops precious stones, his leather cap
Shining, pure, chiseled, all to one accord.
So excellent his features, I cannot
Ever forget so elegant a lord.

Look, by the great bend of the spacious river
Luxuriant lands in which the flocks delight!
Their lord is elegant as bronze or jade,
Magnanimous, indulgent, most polite,
Gracefully bending on his chariot rail,
Clever in jests, yet never moved to spite.

⋖§ FIFTY-SIX [8] §⋗

We taste our joy in the river-valley.
What charms in that splendid man are met!
We may sometimes sleep or wake apart
But he swears that never will he forget.

We taste our joy on the friendly hill.
Apart we may sometimes sleep or wake,
But he loudly swears, this splendid man,
That his troth to me shall never break.

We taste our joy on the higher ground,
Where the stately mountain soars above;
Apart from me he may sometimes talk
But he swears he never will tell of our love.

⋖§ FIFTY-SEVEN §⋗

The regal lady is tall,
Clad in brocade, with a thin
Undergarment of silk,

Fair as few queens have been,
Ts'i's daughter with Wei for husband
And Prince Hing and T'an for kin.

Her skin is white as lard,
Her fingers tender reeds,
Her neck a shining moth,
Her teeth bright melon seeds,
Eyebrows bent as the silkworm,
Eyes flashing as diamond beads.

The stately lady is tall,
She drives to the town, admired
By the crowd; her stallions large,
With ruby bits, her car wired
With pheasant plumes. The court,
To ease her, is soon retired.

She is clef of all she sees:
The river profusely flowing,
Sturgeons with flashing tails,
Sedges and rushes growing,
Her ladies with high coiffures,
Her attendants, coming and going.

ᴥᔥ FIFTY-EIGHT ⁹ ᔐᴧ

Bartering cloth for silk, you came to town,
A traveling salesman, stocked with racy tales;
But me it was you sought, snatching me off,
Wading the river K'i, no thought for sales!
I never lagged behind and pledged myself
Careless of all rash matrimony entails.

To look for your return I clambered up
Precipitous, ruinous walls of Tun-k'iu;
My tears streamed down in a continuous flow,

Vainly keeping watch, longing for you.
At last you came to hustle me away,
With oracles—and more dowry than was due.

Before the mulberry tree has shed its leaves
How glossy are they with glowing tints diffused!
O dove, do not devour the mulberries!
O girl, resist or you will be abused!
Men may take license with women if they will
But a girl's loving cannot be excused.

When autumn comes these glossy mulberry leaves
Turn yellow and fall while waters of the K'i
Rise higher than the curtains of my cart.
I have at all times shown fidelity
While you have been licentious all your life,
Shameless and bold in your duplicity.

For three long years I was your loyal wife,
Unwearied in my household tasks; my chief
Devotion was to serve your daily needs;
Morning and evening brought me no relief.
My brothers turned their sullen backs to jeer.
Silently I brooded on my grief.

My wish was to grow old along with you.
The banks of K'i at least will not allow
The stream to flood the plain; but, surely, you
Recklessly revoked your marriage vow.
As children once we chatted innocently.
Those days have passed. It is all over now.

⋖§ SIXTY-TWO §⋗

Oh, my lord and soldier,
First hero of the land,
You are the king's proud rider,
Whirling lance in hand!

Since you rode to the East
My hair is tangled vine,
Not even worth the washing—
Why should I be fine?

The sun fiercely burns.
Ah, if it would only rain!
I yearn for you, my soldier,
My thoughts torn with pain!

How can I ever win
The herb Forgetfulness,
Always yearning for you
In soul's wretchedness?

⋘ SIXTY-THREE ⋙

The fox is slyly prowling
By the river: who can avert
The fate of a crying girl
Already lacking her skirt?

The fox is slyly prowling
By the river, while this so young
Girl is sadly crying
For her girdle, lost and gone.

The fox is slyly prowling
By the river, and who knows
The grief of this young girl
Stripped to her final clothes?

⋘ SIXTY-FOUR ⋙

She threw me a luscious quince,
I gave her a gem for her dress;
It was not that I gave her a gem
But a pledge for our happiness.

She threw me a rosy peach,
I gave her an emerald ring;
It was not that I gave her a gift
But my pledge for what time would bring.

She threw me a crimson plum,
I gave her a gem from the mine;
It was not that I gave her a gem
But our pledge to the end of time!

◦§ SIXTY-FIVE §◦

The early grain bears heavy ears;
The later grain is still in sprout:
I slowly walk, with shaken heart.
Those knowing me say I'm sad through doubt;
Those knowing me not think I have lost
A trifle and hunt that trifle out.
Ha, lover! you put my heart to rout!

The early grain bears heavy ears;
The later grain is still in sprout:
I walk slowly with troubled breast.
Those knowing me say I'm sad with doubt;
Those knowing me not believe I've lost
A trifle and search that trifle out.
Ha, lover! you put my heart to rout!

The early grain bears weighty ears;
The later grain is still in sprout:
I slowly walk with anxious soul.
Those knowing me say I'm laden with doubt,
Those not knowing believe I've lost
A trifle and hunt that trifle out.
Ha, lover! you put my soul to rout!

❧ SIXTY-SIX ❧

My lord and husband has gone off to war.
How long will he remain? When will he come?
Birds seek their nests; our oxen trudge to fold.
I dream about my lover coming home.

My lord and master has gone off to war.
Fowls come to roost; lambs in their fold are nursed.
My lord and master has gone off to war.
Pray that he may not die of hunger and thirst!

❧ SIXTY-SEVEN [10] ❧

My lord rejoices; his left hand holds a flute.
He enters the room and waves me to follow suit.
Ah, what joy!

My lord rejoices; his left hand waves a feather.
He beckons me out to the fields and the good clear weather.
Ah, what joy!

❧ SIXTY-NINE ❧

Down in the valley motherworts
Whose plants are scorched and dry:
A girl in trouble through a man,
No comfort but to sigh.

Down in the valley motherworts
Whose stems are seer and dry:
A girl in trouble through a man,
No aid except to cry.

Down in the valley motherworts
Whose leaves are pale and dry:
A girl in anguish through a man,
No ease except to die.

The cautious hare goes free while the poor pheasant
Is caught. Looking behind me I deplore
Rash acts that led to sorrow. How much I wish
That I could sleep in peace and move no more!

The timid hare is free while the bold pheasant
Is captured. Glancing backwards, I deplore
Bold deeds leading to sorrow. Now I pray
That I may sleep in peace and wake no more!

The wily hare is free while the brash pheasant
Is taken. Groping backwards, I deplore
Rash deeds ending in evil. Now I pray
That I may sleep in peace and hear no more!

&~§ SEVENTY-ONE &~

Cloth-plants throw out long creepers by the stream:
Far from my brothers and all my family
I call a stranger "father" but he does not
Even so much as deign to glance at me.

Cloth-plants extend long creepers by the stream:
Far from my brothers and all my family
I call a stranger "mother," who refuses
Ever to befriend or comfort me.

Cloth-plants project dense creepers by the stream:
Far from my brothers and all my family
I call a stranger "brother" but he does not
So much as make an inquiry for me!

ᕉ SEVENTY-TWO ᕀ

Plucking thin vine-stems,
When I fail to see
My lover makes one day
Three months for me.

Cutting thick southernwood,
Failing to see
My lover makes one day
Three falls for me.

Gathering harsh field grass
When I fail to see
My lover makes one day
Three years to me.

ᕉ SEVENTY-THREE [12] ᕀ

My splendid carriage rumbles as I come
To snatch you boldly from your parents' care;
My cloak is soft and bright as river-sedge.
I love you. Yet I fear you will not dare!

My gorgeous carriage groans! Well-dressed, I ride,
Robed in a bright-red garment, with the hope
That, since I truly love you, you will come;
And yet I fear that you may not elope!

For life you shall enjoy a separate chamber;
In death our splendid gravestone shall be one;
And if you tell me that you do not trust me,
I shall swear it by the sacred sun!

⊷§ SEVENTY-FIVE §⊶

How gracious this black robe!
When it is quite worn through,
Take me to your house
And let me weave one new,
Tending to your food
And ever serving you!

How lovely this black robe!
When it is all worn through,
Take me to your home
And let me make a new,
Preparing all your food,
Ever serving you!

⊷§ SEVENTY-SIX §⊶

Young Chung-tsi, I beg,
Don't leap the village wall
By night and do not break
The willows by your fall.—
Not that I mind the willows
But fear my father and mother
Even though I may love
You, Chung, above all other.

Young Chung-tsi, I pray,
Don't leap my parents' fence,
Breaking the mulberry-trees
And so be driven thence.—
Not that I mind the trees
But fear my father and mother,
Even though I may love
You, Chung, above all other.

You, Chung-tsi, I beseech,
Don't leap the garden gate,
Crushing the plants and shrubs;
Take better care, and wait.—
Not that I mind the shrubs
But dread what folks will say.
Even though I love you,
Dear Chung, keep well away!

⋄ஃ SEVENTY-SEVEN ஜ⋄

Shu has gone to the hunt; in the street
There is not one person to meet.—
Of course they are there
But cannot compare
With Shu, who is fair and discreet.

Shu has gone to the hunt and no sign
In the street of the drinkers of wine.—
Of course they are there
But cannot compare
With Shu, who is handsome and fine.

Shu has gone to the hunt, but, of course,
No one in our street rides a horse.—
Of course they are there
But cannot compare
With Shu, who has beauty and force.

◄§ SEVENTY-EIGHT §►

Shu in his chariot with four horses rides
To hunt, dangling their reins like silken strings.
The outer steeds advance in dancing paces.
Shu is on marshy ground where the fire flings
Great surges into the sky. Naked, he braves
A tiger whose corpse before the prince he brings.
Ah Shu, beware, beware, lest the dead tiger stings!

Shu in his chariot with four horses rides
To hunt; his two yoke-horses rear on high.
The outside chargers rush in random fashion.
Sparks from the hunting-fires fiercely fly.
Shu, the good archer, drives his chargers hard,
Beats a resounding gong; with a loud cry
Of triumph, shoots his prey; hordes of the wild game die!

Shu in his car with four gray horses rides
To hunt, his two yoke-horses with heads in row.
The two outside fan out like waves or wings.
Shu is on marshy ground. The fires now glow,
Then fade. At length he puts his quiver aside.
At last his gallant steeds are stepping slow.
The hunt now at an end, he lays aside his bow.

◄§ EIGHTY §►

With lambskin coat so glossy,
He is princely, straight and tall;
Truly, this man is steadfast,
A champion over all.

His lambskin coat is blazoned
With leopard-skins outside.
He is faithful guardian
For all the countryside.

Upon his lambskin coat
Three bright medallions stand;
So is he an adornment
Of his proud motherland!

⊸§ EIGHTY-ONE §⊷

If upon the highway
I give your sleeve a touch,
Deny no former friend
Nor blame him overmuch!

If upon the highway
I clasp your dear hand fast,
Do not reprimand me
But think of friendship past!

⊸§ EIGHTY-TWO [13] §⊷

She says, "The dawn-cock crows";
He says, "It still is night."
"Rise now, the stars depart."
"Still the dawn-star is bright."
"Go now, shoot the wild geese
Or water-fowl in flight!

After you have shot them
I shall dress them well,
We shall grow old together;
Lutes and guitars shall spell
Our joy in lusty feasting
More than our tongues can tell.

Could I be sure you loved me
And truly would come back,
I would make you jewels—
For I possess the knack—
And I would serve you truly
With whatso'ere you lack."

⋙ EIGHTY-THREE ⋘

A girl rides in my carriage,
The flower of womanhood,
Her face truly proclaiming
Kiang's royal brotherhood
Now I consort with her,
This lady, fair and good.

A girl rides in my carriage,
A bright hibiscus flower;
We shall stroll together
For many a happy hour—
Kiang's child, at whose great beauty
Time shall renounce his power!

⋙ EIGHTY-SEVEN ⋘

If you love me truly
I will lift my skirt and wade,
But if you do not love me
My love for you shall fade—
Why were such cowards made!

If you love me truly
I will wade the river Wei,
But if you do not love me
No such fool am I—
So great a fool should die!

ᵉ§ NINETY-FOUR [14] ᵌ≈

We met on open ground,
The grass with dew distilled,
Your forehead beautiful,
Heart warm, in love-game skilled;
Carefree and happy then,
Our love was all fulfilled.

We met on open ground;
Fresh dew lay on the grass;
The beauties of your brow
All other brows surpass.
We shall delight each other
Till life itself shall pass.

ᵉ§ NINETY-FIVE [15] ᵌ≈

The Chen and the Wei rivers
Flow past clear banks of sand;
Each knight and girl holds up
The first spring flowers in hand.
The girl says, "Have you looked?"
The knight, "Indeed have I."

"Then shall we look again
Beyond the banks of Wei?"—
Knight and girl are going
Joking happily;
One presents the other
A shining peony.

The Chen and the Wei rivers
Flow past clear banks of sand;
Knights and girls in crowds
Fill all the shining strand.
The girl says, "Have you looked?"
The knight, "Indeed have I."
"Then shall we look again
Beyond the banks of Wei?"—
Knight and girl are going
Joking happily;
One presents the other
A shining peony.

⤳ NINETY-SIX [16] ⤺

"The cock has crowed aloud,
The Court is summoned. Rise!"
"It was not the cock
But buzzing of green flies."

"The Eastern sky is bright,
The Court in full array."
"It was not the dawn
But the clear moon-ray."

"The insects fly in throngs."
"It's sweet to lie reclined."
"The Court will soon adjourn
And we shall be maligned!"

◄§ NINETY-SEVEN §►

What grace! I met you in the Nao Mountains.
We drove abreast; wild swine surged over us.
We struck at two; and then you bowed to me
And courteously called me dexterous.

What magnanimity! You met me once
Upon the Nao road; our horses ran
A gallant race; pursuing two male boars,
You said of me, "Ah, what a handsome man!"

What generosity! You met me once
On the South Nao road; our chariots went
In quest of two fierce wolves. You bowed and said,
"Truly, this friend of mine is excellent!"

◄§ NINETY-NINE §►

Ah! the sun in the East!
That fine man draws near!
He approaches my room,
He approaches my room,
He will soon be here!

Ah! the moon in the East!
That fine man has come!
He is with me here,
He is with me here,
He enters my room!

◄§ ONE HUNDRED §►

It is not yet bright in the East
But, called to the prince's feast
He behaves like a country clown,
Putting clothes on upside down!

Dawnlight still is dim;
The Court has summoned him;
He behaves like a lout,
Putting clothes on inside out!

He breaks the willow fence
Rushing madly hence.
Too early, too late, never right,
He cannot tell day from night!

◄§ ONE HUNDRED ONE [17] §►

The road to Lu is easy
Even where hills are high;
The bride travels upon it;
Her male fox is sly.
Since she has caught her lover,
Why do you yearn and sigh?

Five pair of wedding shoes
Were given, likewise a pair
Of cap-strings; that Lu road
Is open, smooth and fair.
The lady Ts'i is on it.
Why must you venture there?

How does one plant hemp?
Orderly, East to West
And North to South. In way
Of winning wives the best
Plan is to ask the parents.—
Why disturb your rest?

How does one split firewood?
An ax must strike the blow.
How do you win a bride?
Marriage brokers know
And they alone—so why
Perturb your spirits so?

They burst the fishing nets,
Those bream diving in whirls
Beneath the river-dam
Where the white water swirls:
Lady Ts'i goes to be married
With a cloud of dancing girls.

They burst the fishing nets,
Those bream with their slashing power:
The lady Ts'i rides forth
To her home, a fresh-blown flower,
Festive girls about her,
Bright as a summer shower.

They burst the fishing nets,
Those whirling trench and bream:
Lady Ts'i goes forth
To her home, her robes agleam,
Girls like clouds by her side
Fresh as the swirling stream!

ONE HUNDRED FOURTEEN

Crickets in hall! the year draws to its close.
If we do not feast the months will pass us by.
Grant that we may rejoice, but in rejoicing
With good decorum all our joys comply!

Crickets in hall! the seasons hasten past.
Though we were joyless, time would still move on.
May we rejoice, but in our most rejoicing
Remember what is seemly to be done!

Crickets in hall! war chariots at rest.
If we are joyless, months will slip away.
We should not be rash, but think and act
Decorously, even on a festive day!

On mountains thorn-elms, in the valleys white-bark:
You have robe and skirt but wear them not aright.
You do not swish them in becoming manner;
In wagons you are too timid and polite,
You do not gallop freely; others will have them
When you are dead and vanished out of sight.

On the mountains juniper, hawthorns in valleys:
Fine rooms you neither fumigate nor sweep.
You have bells and drums but do not sound them
Which on your death others will guard and keep.

On mountains lacquer-trees, in valleys chestnuts:
You have wine and food, with lutes you never play.
You should rejoice the live-long day with these:
Others will have them when you are cold in clay.

ONE HUNDRED TWENTY-ONE [20]

Buzzards flap great wings and light on oaks:
The service to the king must be sustained.
But if I cannot plant my crops of rice
How shall my father and mother be maintained?
O far blue Heaven, where is help obtained?

Buzzards flap great wings and light on thorns:
Service to the king must be complete.
But if I cannot plant my crops of rice
How shall my father and my mother eat?
O far blue Heaven, what justice will you mete?

Buzzards in flocks soar to the mulberry trees:
All orders from the king must be obeyed.
But if I cannot plant my crops of rice,
How shall my parents' hunger be allayed?
O far blue Heaven, when will you grant us aid?

I was just picking herbs
On Shou-yang hill.—
People gossip
However they will.
Never credit
Nor even view them;
Stop your hearing,
There's nothing to them!

I was just plucking licorice
On Shou-yang hill.—
People tell stories
However they will.
Never believe
Nor even view them;
Stop your ears,
There's nothing to them!

I was just picking parsley
On Shou-yang hill.
People tell lies
However they will.
Never trust
Nor even view them.
Cover your ears,
There's nothing to them.

ONE HUNDRED TWENTY-NINE

Thick grow the reeds and rushes.
The white dew turns to frost.
Beside the winding river
I call for one long lost.

I clamber north to find him
Where rapid waters gleam.
He still escapes my capture
By standing in mid-stream.

Dense grow the reeds and rushes.
The white dew still is frost.
Along the winding river
I seek my lover lost.
I clamber south to find him
Where rapid waters gleam.
Still he eludes my capture
By strolling in mid-stream.

Tall grow the reeds and rushes.
Hoarfrost has not yet ceased.
Still he escapes my capture,
My love for him increased.
I go about to find him,
Left-right, where waters gleam.
At last the man escapes me
On an island in mid-stream!

✑ ONE HUNDRED THIRTY-THREE [21] ✑

How can you say you have no clothes, for I
Will share mine with you always and be true.
The kingdom calls. We polish mace and lance.
I shall have the same enemies as you.

How can you say you have no clothes? I'll share
My cloak with you, suffering the same condition.
The kingdom calls. We sharpen sword and ax,
Leaving at once on the same expedition.

How can you say you have no clothes? I'll share
My shirts with you in fair or in foul weather.
We put our armor on, prepare our weapons;
You and I shall march to war together.

ᒧᔕ ONE HUNDRED THIRTY-FIVE ᘔᔍ

Deceptively, the stately house was grand.
In time scant food was served at any meal.
The end in no way answered the beginning.
Great is the disappointment that I feel.

Ah me! at first at every meal I had
Four vessels with four courses for my treat.
Now from each meal I walk away with hunger.
Great is the disappointment that I meet!

ᒧᔕ ONE HUNDRED THIRTY-SIX ᘔᔍ

Too much is much too much. In the feasting hall
You play your music with a zest above
Discretion. I admire your passionate zeal
But your extravagance I cannot love.

Winter or summer you beat your rattling drum;
Loud through the feasting hall its fierce beats boom.
Summer or winter by the public road
You wave aloft your egret's dancing plume.

Elms by the East Gate, oaks by Yün-k'iu meadow:
Ts'i-chung's daughter dances in their shadow.

On a gay morning Yüan's hemp-work gives place
To hilarious dancing in the market-place.

On a festive morning gaiety precedes
Labor. Dance-goddess, throw us pepper seeds! [22]

⋙ ONE HUNDRED THIRTY-EIGHT ⋘

Beside a cottage men find perfect rest;
In springtime fields their food refreshes best.

When fishing, must one fish for luscious bream?
When taking wives, must one select a queen?

Must one fish for carp to please the tongue
Or taking wives, have lady Ts'i from Sung? [23]

⋙ ONE HUNDRED FORTY ⋘

The poplar by the East Gate
Has foliage thick and fine.
Dusk was our hour for meeting—
Now the dawn-stars shine.

The poplar by the East Gate
Was made our trysting site.
Dusk was the hour agreed on—
The dawn-stars now are bright.

⋙ ONE HUNDRED FORTY-ONE ⋘

Thorns at the graveyard gate;
Axes hew them down:
That my man is wild
Is known to all the town.
Still he does not cease.
When shall I have peace?

Plums shade the graveyard gate;
There ominous owls are found.
I shall reprimand him
To all the country round.
Ruined he shall be.
Then he will think of me!

⋙ ONE HUNDRED FORTY-THREE ⋘

Moonrise and my lover,
My heart relieved.
How simple beauty is!—
Yet I am grieved.

The moon arises;
Dusk and love are best.
How tranquil is the night!—
How short my rest!

The moon ascends;
What beauty love has gained!
How simple beauty is!—
Yet I am pained!

⋙ ONE HUNDRED FORTY-EIGHT [24] ⋘

In valleys blackthorns gleam,
Their leaves trifoliate:
How glad I am that girl
Does not have a mate!

In swamps the blackthorns flower,
Burdening their boughs:
How glad I am that girl
Does not have a house!

In swamps the blackthorns grow,
Their fruits surpass their bloom:
How pleased I am that girl
Does not have a room!

~§ ONE HUNDRED FORTY-NINE [25] ℰ~

No, it is not the wind,
Not the departing cart.—
Turning my face toward Chou,
Home-longing fills my heart.

No, it is not the storm
And not the shaking cart.—
When I look toward Chou
Yearning fills my heart.

I'll gladly wash the pot
For him and cook the fish.
Who will drive me West
And so fulfill my wish?

~§ ONE HUNDRED FIFTY ℰ~

Wings of the summer moth,
How richly are you dressed!—
Ah, my grieving heart!—
Come home with me and rest!

Wings of the summer moth,
How richly are you clad!—
Ah, my pain at heart!—
Come home and make me glad!

Moths burst from their dark womb
To new life, white and free!—
O my aching heart!
Come, come and house with me!

ONE HUNDRED FIFTY-TWO [26]

The cuckoo is in the mulberry-tree,
Its seven young part company:
But my lord's conduct is stable,
My lord's conduct is stable,
My heart is full of glee.

The cuckoo is in the mulberry-tree
Its shiftless young on a far plum-tree:
But my lord is in proper array
With silk girdle and cap mottled gray,
My breast is full of glee!

The cuckoo is in the mulberry-tree
While its young stray off to a white-thorn tree:
But my lord's conduct is right,
Men mirror themselves in his light;
My heart is full of glee.

The cuckoo is in the mulberry-tree,
Its young drift off to a hazel tree:
But my lord's virtues are ample,
To all people a true example;
For ten thousand years may it be!

In the seventh month we clear the hearth;
In the ninth we commonly dispense
Fresh clothing. In the first the keen winds blow;
In the second cold weather grows intense.
(If we had no coarse garments how should we
See the hardships of the season through?)
In the third month we plow, and in the fourth
Good wives and children do as they should do,
Bringing our food afield. All men are eased.
The Inspector duly comes and is well pleased!

In the seventh month we clear the hearth;
In the ninth we share the clothing-dole.
Warmth descends during bright days of spring,
With singing of the golden oriole.
Girls take wicker baskets out to pluck
Fresh mulberry leaves while daylight hours grow long.
In crowds they gather the white southernwood.
The passions of young women then are strong,
Each in her fancy dreaming that she can
Take home as husband some young gentleman.

In the seventh month we clear the hearth.
In the eighth month we glean wild rush and sedges.
In Silkworm Month we tend the mulberry-trees,
Lopping with hatchets all outcropping edges.
(Shorter mulberry-trees shoot out profusely.)
In the seventh month the wild shrike cries;
In the eighth we spin both black and yellow,
Coloring the silk with varied dyes.
This eighth month calls for weaving cloth and then
We dye red robes for rich young gentlemen.

In the fourth month the flowering grasses rise;
In the fifth month grasshoppers softly call;
In the eighth month we reap and in the tenth,
With cool days, countless leaves of summer fall.
In the first month we hunt for fox and badgers

Or wild-cats in dense forest-lands, and when
The pelts are all assembled, we arrange them,
Cutting out clothes for the young noblemen.
In the second month we drill, we hunt, and bring
Young boars for home, the great boars to our king.

In the fifth month the locust stirs its legs;
In the sixth month the grasshopper its wings;
In the seventh it flits about the field,
But in the eighth the changing season brings
The hordes beneath the eaves; then, in the ninth,
Beside the door. The chirping cricket goes
Beneath the bed in the tenth month; and, next,
We smoke out rats, plug holes where the wind blows,
Plastering the door. Children and wife, take care,
This is your house, let New Year find you there!

In the sixth month we eat our plums and berries;
In the next month we have our beans and spice;
In the eighth we harvest all our dates.
In the tenth we reap our fields of rice,
Brewing the spring-wine to repair old age.
In the seventh we eat melons; the eighth month gives
Its crop of gourds; in the ninth we harvest hemp,
Gathering herbs, and so the farmer lives.
In forest lands we hack out firewood
With kindling for the fires to cook our food.

In the ninth month we hammer flat and hard
The vegetable-garden threshing-floor;
In the tenth we harvest early wheat
And later wheat, an ever-ripening store;
Barley, hemp and pulse are also ours.
Now business for the house has further scope.
By daytime in the fields we gather grass,
Evenings in the house we fashion rope.
Let us secure our house-thatch, firm and true,
And then prepare to sow our grain anew.

During the second month we cut the pond,
Klang, klang! Next, in the third, we haul the ice.
In the fourth month we offer up at dawn
Lamb and onions for our sacrifice.
In the ninth month the plants of summer wither,
Frost comes, and, with the tenth, our threshing floor
Is cleaned; we fill two vessels full with wine
For Heaven, offer lambs and sheep once more,
Then raise the great horn in the public hall,
With prayers for longevity to all.

◦§ ONE HUNDRED FIFTY-FIVE [27] ℈◦

Oh robber bird, O robber bird, you have taken
My loved ones from me whom I cherished so.
Why have you destroyed my nest and young?
You should have pity on them for their woe!

When heaven was free from rain and still unclouded
I twined the mulberry-shoots for window and door;
Now, wretched folk, how dare you cast me out
Offering insults till my heart is sore?

My claws went grasping for the grass and rushes;
Loaded with wisps of straw my beak would come;
I hoarded bundles till my mouth was raw!
Can you declare I have no house or home?

My wings are frayed, my tail all rent and ragged;
My nest stands high, tossed by harsh winds and rain.
Do not say I have no house or home!
Hear my cry of agony and pain!

We marched to the East Mountains and did not
Come back; now we return as cold rains start.
We talked of coming home and so prepared
Civilian clothes—sad toil that broke the heart—
(The caterpillars are on the mulberry leaves)
We pass the night, each curled beneath his cart.

We marched to the East Mountains and did not
Come back. Now that we start rain-clouds appear.
At home the gourds are reaching to the eaves;
Gardens are marred by footprints of the deer.
Spiders are at the door, ants in the chamber;
Glow-worms shine—to love and not to fear.

We marched in rags to Eastward and did not
Come back. Now that we start black clouds are massed.
Herons cry from the ant-hills; the old wife sighs,
Sprinkles and sweeps and plugs the wind-holes fast.
Gourds are bitter, chestnut-kindlings piled.—
Since last I saw this, three long years have passed.

We marched in rags to Eastward and did not
Come back; now that we come the rains are cold.
The oriole with brilliant feathers flies;
Wives seek out new husbands; manifold
Rituals for these new marriages are kept.
Such rites are well—but where now are the old?

"Yug, yug," the deer cry, cropping the wild herbs:
My guest and I take lute and reed and play;
The reed-pipes vibrate over our eager tongues;
Food baskets are laid out in fine array.
We take them and the man I dearly love
Shows what manners the men of Chou display.

"Yug, yug," the deer cry, eating the wild shrubs:
What joy to greet this brilliant friend of mine!
Although he never condescends to others
His conduct offers them a pure design
And mirror for themselves; they imitate him;
He feasts and jokes and drinks abundant wine.

"Yug, yug," the deer cry, eating the wild plants:
My guest and I play the guitar and lute.
We play again and yet again, enjoying
Happiness that is perfect and acute.
I have good wine to warm the friendly heart;
We feast and sing with pleasure absolute.

◆§ ONE HUNDRED SIXTY-TWO §◆

The four great stallions run unceasingly.
The ride to Chou is tedious and slow.
Along the winding route I dream of home
But there no soldier is allowed to go.
The service of the prince is absolute.
My heart is pained, my spirits depressed and low.

The four great stallions run incessantly.
Those horses with white body and dark mane
Are utterly exhausted. How I long
For home! But it is useless to complain.
The service of the prince is absolute.
I have no chance to sit and ease my pain.

Pigeons fly upon extended wing,
Flutter and soar in freedom and then, rather
Than fly, alight upon some bushy oak,
Later, at leisure, rise again and hover.
The service of the prince is absolute.
I have no leisure to support my father.

I yoke those four great stallions, white and black,
Racers, neck by neck, as brother by brother,
Rejoicing in their speed. I long for home
But, Heaven help me, I can do no other!
The service of the prince is absolute.
I have no leisure to support my mother!

⋞ ONE HUNDRED SIXTY-THREE ⋟

The plain is flashing with flowers,
The swamp is violet-lined:
The runners are racing past
In terror of falling behind.

My horses are eager colts,
The speed wets their reins like dews;
I gallop my horses, I race them,
I everywhere ask for news.

My horses are black and mottled,
Their reins are like silken wire;
I gallop my horses, I race them,
I everywhere ask and inquire.

My horses are white and dappled,
Their reins are glossy and wet.
I gallop my horses, I race them,
I pick up what news I can get.

My horses are piebald and spotted,
Their reins held poised in my hand.
I gallop my horses, I race them,
To gather the news of the land.

May Heaven guard and keep you in all things!
May you be well endowed! or if you lack
Abundance, may the Spirits see to it
That speedily your prosperity comes back!

May Heaven guard and keep you in all ways!
May you reap plenty, all good to the last grain!
May Heaven send you rich emoluments
Such as long years themselves scarcely contain!

May Heaven guard and keep you all your days!
Amassing riches like a mountain or hill,
A range, a river at its highest flood,
So that in all things you may have your fill!

Pure and auspicious be your sacrifice
Made at all seasons to each ancestor!
Those noble princes and those goodly kings
Shall say: "You have great happiness in store."

The Spirits are true and thus bestow upon you
Happiness. The folk enjoy their drink and food;
A hundred clans admire and imitate you,
Everywhere praising you as noble and good.

You are a moon new-rounded to the full,
A radiant sun new-risen into view,
A mountain clad in lofty fir and cypress.
May all life's blessedness devolve on you!

ONE HUNDRED SIXTY-SEVEN

We gather wild-fern that is now in sprout.
Oh to go home! The year will soon grow late.
It is because of the Hien-yun our army
Suffers unrest and knows this homeless state.

We gather wild-fern; now the plants are soft;
Summer returns, but, Oh, our hearts' deep pain!
We are hungry and thirsty, always keeping guard.
We shall not see our families again.

We gather wild-fern; oh for home! for home!
The tenth month without rest! The king shall lack
No service from us, but our hearts are sore.
We march away but we do not go back.

Four hardy stallions drag a festive car?
What is this ritual? Are these cherry-trees?
Whose chariot? Our lord's! We dare not pause.
Even in one month there were three victories!

We yoke four hardy chargers to the car,
Common soldiers trudging by its side.
There are ivory bow-ends and embroidered quivers!
Still the Hien-yun harrass from far and wide.

Long ago, when we marched, willows were green.
Now, as we return, cold snow falls thick.
We are thirsty and famished; our march is weary and slow.
Nobody knows! we are wounded to the quick!

◄§ ONE HUNDRED EIGHTY-ONE §►

Wild geese fly, beating their tragic wings;
Off to war our gallant men have gone.
But ah, what pathos in their expedition
For the widow and the solitary one!

Wild geese keep flying, then land on a rank marsh:
These raise huge bulwarks at their lord's behest;
Walls reaching forth a thousand leagues are built
By those who have no dwelling-place or rest.

Wild geese fly with tragic clamoring:
Wise men say we are pitiful and spent;
Fools suppose that for such sorry work
We are proud, haughty or arrogant.

~§ ONE HUNDRED EIGHTY-TWO §~

Can this be night! No, night has not yet ended.
It is torchlight in the courtyard which you see.
Our lord arrives with all his splendid train.
Hear his bit-bells tinkling merrily!

Can this be night! No, nighttime has not ended;
It is our master's torch that shines so clear;
Our lord arrives with all his splendid train.
That is the tinkling of his bells you hear.

Can this be night! No, but night nears the morning.
Our lord arrives; our court shines like the day.
See, his banners streaming at his portal!
What music and what glorious array!

~§ ONE HUNDRED EIGHTY-THREE §~

The rivers swell and drown in the salt sea.
The hawk is swift and deadly in its fall:
O friends and brothers, save our drowning state,
Our father and mother, parent of us all!

Floods are voluminous and overpowering;
The hawk is swift and mortal are its claws:
Thinking how reckless men possess the state,
I shudder at destruction of her laws.

Swift is the hawk that cries above the hill;
Slander and vituperation fill the air;
Politicians lie and none to stop them!
My brothers and friends are few, but ah! take care!

❧ ONE HUNDRED EIGHTY-FOUR [29] ❧

The wise crane cries in the great marshes,
Its voice carries to the far wilds;
The wise fish plunges in the still waters
By the lakeside island where winds are mild.[30]
The garden is planted in a still retreat
Where autumn oak-leaves are quietly piled.—
Leave all trees and stones here still;
Take your whetstones from another hill!

The wise crane cries in the nine marshes;
Its voice rises to the far skies;
The wise fish floats on the still waters
Where the lakeside island quietly lies.
The garden is planted in a quiet retreat
Where under oak-trees summer dies.—
This is the world of quiet shade;
On other hills hammer jade!

❧ ONE HUNDRED EIGHTY-FIVE ❧

Great Minister of War, you serve as fangs
And talons for the king; why have you pressed
Our sons into your service, throwing us
Into such misery, with no hope of rest?

Great Minister of War, you are the claws
And sharp teeth of the king; why have you willed
Such misery upon us, granting us
No refuge where our clamor may be stilled?

Great Secretary of War, you are imprudent;
Why have you crushed us in your cruel vice,
Wives and mothers of the men in service
Who tend at home their urns of sacrifice?

ONE HUNDRED EIGHTY-SIX

The light colt eats my garden shoots.
Tie him fast and keep him bound!
Prolong my morning with my true love,
Who makes my home our pleasure ground!

The white colt eats my garden shoots.
Bind the knot and keep it tight!
Prolong my morning with my dear love
Who passed with me this happy night!—

That white colt in the valley now
Is wholly free to eat or play.
His master is like purest gold or jade;
May he not be as rare and keep away!

ONE HUNDRED EIGHTY-NINE

The valley stream is pure, the southern hill
Dense like bamboo, luxuriant like pine:
Elder and younger brothers love each other,
Guarding the virtue of their house and line.

This prince well mirrors those who came before him;
He builds his house a hundred measures square.
Its doors are strictly stationed north and south;
He will live and laugh and flourish there.

Its building-frames are bound to one another;
Men pound the earth, tak, tak, to make it firm.
No rain nor wind seeps through, no birds nor rats
Molest it, safe from pests that fly or squirm.

Reverent as one who prays, swift as an arrow,
Soaring as the great phoenix that ascends
To heaven, straight as pillars, ample as temples,
Quiet as the home that serves its master's ends.

The rush mats are above, bamboo below;
There our master takes his sleep and rest.
He says, "My dreams are magic." What are they?
Of snakes and bears who auger men the best.

The priest divines them: "Bears mean many sons;
The snakes mean many daughters. Therefore he
Has sons to whom he gives becoming gifts,
Jade rings, red plaques, symbols of dignity.

Then he has daughters. They lay them on the ground,
Wrap them in dresses, give them spinning whorls;
They have nothing but simplicity, drink and food,
Loving their parents as obsequious girls.

ONE HUNDRED NINETY

Who says you have no sheep? You have three hundred.
Who says you have no cattle? There are ninety steers,
All seven feet high. Your sheep have curly horns,
Your cattle come with stately, flapping ears.

Some stray down hill to sip the valley pool;
Some sleep, some walk; your herdsmens' coats are straw;
They have bamboo hats and spacious carrying bags;
Your beasts accord with sacrificial law.

Your workmen bring in wood and forest game;
Your sheep are strong and handsome to behold;
When your herdsmen wave to them they come,
Obsequiously trotting into fold.

The herdsmen dream of locusts and of fishes,
Of tortoise-and-snake and falcon banners flying.
The diviner says: "Locusts and fish mean riches,
Snake-and-bird banners mean a race undying."

⊸§ TWO HUNDRED THREE §⊷

There the meal is plentiful; long, curved spoons
Serve ample portions on the smooth road to Chou,
Whetstone-smooth and arrow-straight; folk here
Eat little, but noblemen more than their due.

Here in the East shuttles and looms are empty;
We walk on frost with old shoes sadly worn.
Ah, nobles who ride along the smooth Chou road,
Coming and going, you fill my soul with scorn!

Our springs are cool that issue from the rock
But firewood here is damp from constant rain;
The exhausted people scarcely drag it home,
So overcome with poverty and pain.

Eastern men labor and they are not paid;
Western men have handsome homes and dress.
They wear the skins of black or mottled bears;
Their henchmen sit in all the offices.

They quaff pure wine; they have no use for gruel;
Their jeweled girdles hang with many a quirk.
They strut in boundless superfluity;
Like stars in heaven, they shine but do not work:

Though the Milky Way is seven times distant [31]
Its lady never wove her sparkling gown.
Although the Constellation of the Ox
Is mighty, it never dragged a load to town.

Though in the East, the Opener of Light,
The Morning Star, shines fair on Heaven's rim,
Though Hesperus, the Sovereign of the West,
Shines bright, there are tasks for neither her nor him.

Though the Celestial Fish curves through the sky
It never labored on a wheat plantation.
Though the Winnowing Basket shines on high
No grain is winnowed by that constellation.

North there stands a Ladle in the Heavens;
No ladling of gruel or wine disturbs its rest.
South, the Winnowing Basket lifts its handle;
The Ladle holds its handle toward the West.

⇜§ TWO HUNDRED SEVENTEEN §⇝

Your uniform caps are yellow with cleft bands.
What do they mean? You have good food and wine.
Are these for strangers? No! as mistletoe
And dodder-vine spread high over cypress and pine
Brother with brother must support their line.
Not having seen our lord our hearts are sad;
Having seen our lord our hearts are glad.

Your yellow caps are yellow with cleft bands.
What is the cause? You have good food and wine.
Are these for strangers? No! as mistletoe
And dodder-vine cleave close to cypress and pine

So we as one maintain our ancient line.
Not having seen our lord our breasts are sad
But having seen our lord our breasts are glad.

We have leather caps and cleft bands on our heads.
Our wine and food are good. Are they for others?
For strangers? No! for that could never be.
Surely, they are for nephews, uncles, brothers,
Offspring of like fathers and like mothers!
Death may come any day; life melts as snow.
Let us enjoy good wine before we go!

ৰ্পী TWO HUNDRED EIGHTEEN ইৎ

With linchpins in my wagon I am ready.
I think of that young girl, my lovely one.
It is not that I am hungry for her;
It is her reputation that has won
My heart and even if we have small company,
We shall feast there beneath a friendly sun.

Trees grow luxuriantly beside the meadow;
Only the doves and pheasants settle there.
The lady who is kind and gracious comes
To picnic with me in the open air.
Only her goodness leads me to that place.
I shall love her always and find her fair.

Our drink there will be temperate and good,
Even though we have no rare old wine.
Even though we lack luxurious viands
Our dishes will be elegant and fine.
Even though I bring no special bounty
We shall sing and dance in clear sunshine.

I shall climb the mountainside to split
Oaks for our campfire. Later I shall ride,
Happy at heart, driving my four tall stallions
Down the great highway with you at my side.
My reins will be the strings of a guitar!
Dear lady, you in time shall be my bride!

⋙ TWO HUNDRED NINETEEN ⋘

Green flies buzz, then settle on a fence.
Slanderers buzz, but, lord, reject their sense!

Green flies buzz, then settle on a thorn.
From them much discord in the State is born.

Green flies buzz, then seek the hazel tree.
Slanderers have entangled you and me.

⋙ TWO HUNDRED TWENTY ⋘

Guests first take their seats to left and right.
Vessels are full, viands and fruits displayed.
Wine is blended well and plentiful;
Many bells and drums are loudly played.
They toast the archers; targets are set up
And a well-ordered tournament assayed.

They dance to pipes and drums; musicians sound
In unison; high homage is expressed
To venerable ancestors who send us
Those favors that alone have made us blessed.
All drink. The guests choose partners for the dance.
Prizes are laid for the archery contest.

When our guests first take their seats they are quiet.
While sober, they are courteous and mild.
But when they are drunk they caper madly about,
Are loud and reckless, frivolous and wild.
Manners that were dignified and stately
Are in the twinkling of an eye defiled.

When our guests are drunk they bawl and shout,
Upset our sacred vessels and weirdly dance
Like the masked demon-actors, stumble about
And spilling slanted cups absurdly prance.
If they go home in time they have our blessing
But should they stay we look at them askance.

Not all who drink are drunkards; but for those
Who are we have an Inspector and one more
As censor. When the dancers misbehave
Embarrassingly, unsmiling, we deplore
Their license, being childish, hornless rams!
At three cups they forget and still drink more!

⊸§ TWO HUNDRED TWENTY-FOUR [32] §⊸

How I should rest under that willow tree!
There is great mobility in Heaven.
Do not intrude on it or be too active.—
Yet to the passive equal pains are given.

How I should rest under that willow tree!
Do not break your head against a jar!—
Yet persons who remain wholly inactive
Tempt fate and push passivity too far.

There was a bird that flew too high in heaven.
For what things are men competent and able?—
Why should I follow some insensate plan?
In the end I should be only pitiable.

Court officials wear fox-furs of saffron.
Their bearing is important and refined.
They come to Chou, the gaze of common people.
Such noblemen are greatly to my mind.

Court officials wear broad palm-shaped hats
Or tall black caps; their ladies wear a pad
Of long thick hair, most marvelous to see.
When I cannot see them I am sad.

Court officials wear ear-plugs of jade.
Men call their noble ladies fair and good.
When I am absent my poor heart is knit
In knots and sentiments ill understood.

Court officials flourish long thick sashes,
Like gorgeous trains; hair like a diadem
Or scorpion's tail is now the ladies' wear.—
They pass, and I walk swiftly after them.

It is not that the sash is really a train;
It is only that the sashes are so long.
It is not that ladies really curl their hair;
It naturally turns up: my thoughts were wrong! [33]

Delicate golden birds light on the hill:
The march is long and we have given up
All hope. You should instruct us, grant us wagons,
Feed us or give us even a water-cup!

Delicate golden birds light on the hill:,
They are free.—How dare we venture to give up?
We fear that we can neither march nor run.—
And you do not grant us even a water-cup!

Delicate golden birds light on the hill.
All those are free and happy and alive.
How dare we march! Not even a water-cup!
We are fearful that we never shall arrive.

◆§ TWO HUNDRED THIRTY-TWO §◆

The craggy rocks are, ah, so high!
Mountains and streams stretch far away.
How wearily the warriors march,
Having no respite, day on day!

The craggy rocks are, ah, so steep,
Mountains and rivers robed in mist.
How heavily the soldiers march,
Having no leisure to desist!

White swine in herds crash through the waves;
The moon is in the Hyades;
It rains; the warriors plod East,
With no thoughts save their miseries!

◆§ TWO HUNDRED THIRTY-THREE §◆

Proud bignonia-blooms glitter like gold.
Meanwhile the people languish in the cold.

Ah, those bignonia-blooms hold us to scorn.
Had I known this, I had better not been born!

Nobles are stars seen through a broken roof.
People starve while nobles hold aloof!

ANCIENT POETRY FROM CHINA/195

✑ TWO HUNDRED THIRTY-FOUR ✑

Is any grass not gold? or day not dark
When marching through these mountains, black and stark?

Is any grass not dark? Again, again
We soldiers march, leading lives less than men.

We are neither tigers nor rhinoceroses
But humans suffering daily miseries.

A warm-furred fox creeps from dark grass to view:
Frozen soldiers ride the road to Chou.

✑ TWO HUNDRED EIGHTY ✑

Blind men enter the courtyard of our Prince.[34]
Next we arrange the bell-frames, setting up,
With ornaments of ceremonial plumes,
The hanging drum, the small drum with its cup,

The bells, the musical stones, the sounding boxes.
Now, all complete, the symphony outpours;
Flutes sound, grave guests arrive; glad notes are blended,
Played to regale our sacred ancestors.

✑ TWO HUNDRED NINETY ✑

They clear the grass and trees on either hand,
Then with strong plows expose the fertile land.

Weeders work the fields in pairs by ranks
Of thousands, leading water from the dykes.[35]

The chief, his elder and his younger son
Grub on the grain-field till these tasks are done.

Loyal wives bring food to the strong men;
They double plow for the new plots, and then,

All being tilled, they sow the grain, set out
Rich seeds of life, young blade and tender sprout.

Men walk in rows and, see, in rows they keep
Strict order when, as harvesters, they reap.

Myriads on myriads of sheaves are laid,
Fragrant and aromatic, in the shade.

From these we make sweet wine and offer up
Sacrifices in the sacred cup

To ancestors whose mercy we engage
To grant tranquillity to ripening age.

Such is not for one day nor for one clime
But for unbounded space and timeless time!

ᵛᵍ TWO HUNDRED NINETY-ONE ᵍᵛ

Our plows are sharp, impelled with might and main;
We scatter seeds rich with the life of grain.

Traveling harvesters come to impound
The ripened crop in baskets, square or round.

First, for progress of the growing seed,
They clear away the thistle and the weed.

They have plaited bamboo hats and polished hoes.
Stroke upon stroke they reap with heavy blows.

Next, they comb the grain with rakes, till all
Is smooth; then stack it high as a great wall.

Finally, they store it to sustain the lives
Of myriad homes, with children, fathers, wives.

The horned bull is slaughtered for the good of man,
Continuing what the ancestors began.

Sturdy the stallions on the distant pastures:
White-breeched, light-yellow, glossy-black and bay.
All our glorious horses pulling chariots
Bang, bang, with zest unbounded, night or day.

Sturdy stallions race on distant pastures:
They are sometimes black and gray or brown and white,
Red and mottled, pulling mighty chariots,
Zip, zip, with boundless spirit, day or night.

Sturdy stallions race in distant pastures:
There are flecked ones, there are red with manes of black;
There are white ones with black manes and black with white,
Racing the chariots in the whirlwind's track.

Sturdy stallions run on distant pastures:
Some are dark-and-white, some white-and-red,
Some are fish-eyed, some are hairy-legged:
Swift and unswerved are those great chariots sped!

Robust, robust the gray stallions.
Morning and evening at Court they prance.
Then a flock of drunken men emerge,
Drums roar as they leap in the egret dance.

Robust, robust are the men like stallions.
Morning and evening the birds of a feather
Drink wine, leap into the egret dance,
Then all go home to rejoice together.

Robust, robust are the men and stallions.
Morning and evening those egret feathers
Wave, as they drink to the Prince's luck
And his sons and their sons—then go home together.

How rich, how ample the music is!
All is prepared by old tradition.
We set up our drums and loudly bang
For delight of our ancestors' audition.

Ghosts of the heroes of T'ang assemble,
Ancestors bless us with pure delight;
Hand drums din, flutes cry loudly,
Yet the music is peaceful, august and right.

Bells and gongs greet the great Wan dance.
Musical stones are harmonious.
Elegant guests are at ease and happy;
Majestic peace descends on us.

Reverently at dawn and twilight
We hold this rite from ancient times.
Pious, solemn men conceived it,
Ordering life by sacred chimes.

Our ancestors observe with favor
Such sacrifice in winter and fall;
Loyal descendants of T'ang maintain it,
Ever fortunate, one with all.

The
Manyōshū

ᴥᔓ The Manyōshū is the first and most celebrated collection of Japanese poetry, reflecting Japanese life and thought at approximately 800 A.D. It is comprised of some 4,500 poems, the larger number by known authors. Its title signifies a "Collection of a Myriad Leaves." Although the anthology bears witness to the strong influence of Chinese literature on the Japanese poets, it constitutes a truly remarkable image of the native taste and imaginative vigor of Japan.

More than nine-tenths of its poems are in an extremely popular verse form, the tanka, consisting of five lines of 5–7–5–7–7 syllables. The only type of longer poem highly prevalent is the chōka, with alternating lines of five and seven syllables, concluding with an additional line of seven syllables. There are approximately 260 of these poems, none being over 150 lines in length. Several stand among the most celebrated in Japanese literature. As a rule a chōka concludes with one or more short stanzas that may or may not be viewed independently. These repeat phrases taken from the preceding verses and serve virtually as summaries, much as do the "envoys" in European lyrics of the Middle Ages or the concluding quatrains of the French ballades. The form also suggests the coda in music. Throughout the Manyōshū poems are characterized by use of a rhetorical device known as the "pillow word." This signifies that a word is repeated or used in varying ways and forms throughout an extended passage. The poems abound in much conscious artifice.

Delicate artifice notwithstanding, the anthology has a singularly fresh, invigorating spirit, like cool, breezy air of a spring morning. It admirably voices the temper of a nation rising into new vitality, both material and spiritual. These are the vibrant songs of a people coming culturally of age. Some are personal, some patriotic. Warm love for the extreme beauty of the Japanese landscape is brilliantly expressed. The art is fastidious, as Japanese art traditionally is, but there is nothing excessively mannered, over-conscious or meretricious, as some Japanese art of a later date occasionally seems to its Western observers. It would be hard to mention three more joyous works than Kālidāsa's Sakuntalā, the Confucian Book of Songs, and the Manyōshū. The Japanese book approaches the first in artfulness and the second in vigor. The following selection is made with special stress on the optimistic character of the anthology as a whole.

It is natural to observe here that this oldest classic in Japanese poetry springs in large measure from the Chinese inasmuch as during the seventh and eighth centuries Japanese thought was fertilized by new and potent influences from abroad. China itself was undergoing a brilliant renaissance. During this period important embassies with profound cultural significance were sent from Japan to China while many persons of cultural distinction came from the continent to the island empire. All the Japanese arts were deeply affected. For the first time an adequate system of writing was introduced to Japan, where the Chinese characters were adjusted to the native language. Japan also underwent drastic social, political, and religious changes. The government was centralized to a degree hitherto unimagined; Confucian philosophy was introduced and, above all, Buddhism became the leading philosophical-religious system. These developments are all clearly reflected in the poetry.

A few of the Manyōshū poems are actually in Chinese, and several of the poets wrote in both languages. The earliest known manuscripts contain notations and extended commentaries invariably in Chinese. The Japanese poets studied the Chinese masters diligently, deriving much of their art from them. In short, the Manyōshū is not only one of the earliest important monuments of the native literature; it illustrates the all-important change between a provincial people and a people inheriting the vast riches of a continental culture.

These rhymed renderings have been made with constant reference to the translations prepared by the Japanese Committee for Classical Texts, issued in the United States by the Columbia University Press, 1964.

⋘ ONE [1] ⋙

I hear the roar of the great string
Of my Emperor's birchwood bow
Delighting his heart at the sun's rise
And when evening's sun sinks low.
I hear it now at the dawn's rise
And with fading light in the torchlit skies;
I hear the roar of the loud string
Of my peaceful Emperor's bow.

    At dawn with horses abreast
    Drawn up on either hand
    This morning he must be trampling
    His open, grass-grown land.

EMPRESS KŌGYOKU. I, 3–4.

⋘ TWO ⋙

O boatmen, rowing on this spacious lake,
Both those from far and from the nearer shore,
Do not disturb the birds my husband loved
Even with thoughtless splashing of an oar!

EMPRESS YAMATO-HIMÉ. II, 153.[2]

⋘ THREE ⋙

We lay in harbor waiting for the moon
While night was dark.
Now moon and tide have risen and at last
Let us embark!

PRINCESS NUKADA. I, 8.[3]

↜§ FOUR §↝

HUSBAND

I glean the beach of shells and shining stones
For my loved wife in our far-distant home.
O that these shining white-caps of the waves
Could bring them to her on their scurrying foam!

WIFE

But with his clothes damp from the morning mist,
Lacking my aid to dry them, night or day,
Laboriously over the mountain path
My husband with his gifts must make his way.

ANON. IX, 1665–6.[4]

↜§ FIVE §↝

In the great land the Empress rules are many
Provinces that are exquisite to view
But among all these regions are not any
So fair as the fair fields of Yoshinu.
For these are girdled by their lofty mountains,
Pure streams and orchards where the blossoms fall,
And she has built beside their crystal fountains
Her palace with its many-pillared hall.
At dawn and dusk the courtiers row under
The mountain shadows where the waters gleam
And I myself must also gaze in wonder
Upon the palace by the shining stream.

    I could look forever
    At those smooth rocks that lie
    In rapids of that river
    And never tire my eye.
    I can gaze forever
    At those bright palace halls
    And contemplate a splendor
    That never tires or palls.

KAKINOMOTO HITOMARO. I, 36–7.[5]

⋖§ SIX ⋗⋗

Our divine Sovereign rears her towering palace
Between the mountains and the river's strand
And there, surrounded by Yoshinu's rapids,
She climbs to contemplate her spacious land.
The folded mountains raise green walls of splendor
Above her as a tribute to her throne.
Springtime blossoms shower their beauty on her,
Succeeded by the autumn's crimson tone.
The river's god embellishes her table
From cormorant-fishing in its shallow bed
While on the deeper waters of its lower
Courses capacious fishing-nets are spread.
So equally the mountain and the river
Worship her and serve our Sovereign's shrine.
Surely, with such offerings laid before her,
She herself is honored as divine!

> The mountains and the waters
> Worship her and adore,
> While in her barge our goddess
> Sails where the rapids roar.

KAKINOMOTO HITOMARO. I, 38–9.

⋖§ SEVEN ⁶ ⋗⋗

Our noble Prince, child of the splendid Sun,
Holds his hunt, urging our horses on
Over the fields of Kariji, thick with reeds:
Ah! the delight of his light-footed steeds!
Boars and stags crouch and adore him;
Quails run to bend down low before him.
Like them we bow a blinded eye
Or see him sun-bright in our sky.
His freshness grows like grass in spring,
Our mighty lord, our sovereign king!

His hunt at end,
We gladly see
A captive moon
His canopy.

KAKINOMOTO HITOMARO. III, 239–40.

EIGHT

Though wide the Bay of Tsunu,
No harborage is there
Nor any port for shelter,
But why should travelers care?
We journey on the whale-path;
Gales of morning blow,
While tangled with the Ocean
The seaweed sways below.
And tangled like this seaweed
In waves of joyful strife
So did I cling and tangle
With my beloved wife.
I look back on my journey
The more I freely roam
By sea and hill and find me
The farther from my home.
My wife must weep and languish
As grass that droops and falls.
Ah! how I long to see her:
Bow down, you mountain walls!

Though mountain pines
Surround me here,
I wave my sleeve;
Do you see me, dear?

Though wind in bamboo
Woo my mind,
I think only of her
I left behind.

KAKINOMOTO HITOMARO. II, 131–3.

◄§ NINE §►

On heaven's sea the clouds emerge as waves
Whose coil of light and dark never debars
The moon-ship, voyaging on her constant path,
From harbor in the forest of the stars.

"HITOMARO COLLECTION," VII, 1068.

◄§ TEN §►

Quickly I shall reach my loved one's home
Though night obstruct my course
And deep in cloud her distant cottage stands—
Hasten, my good black horse!

"HITOMARO COLLECTION," VII, 1271.

◄§ ELEVEN §►

Over the distant mountain-crest appear
The sacred mists of evening.—Spring is here!

"HITOMARO COLLECTION," X, 1812.

⋖§ TWELVE[7] §⋗

Dancing girls tread ground for the new house,
Jeweled bracelets making merry din.
A youth who sparkles like their gems appears!
Let him come in!

"HITOMARO COLLECTION," XI, 2352.

⋖§ THIRTEEN §⋗

This morning you are up and out so soon
You wet your skirt's hem in the dewy grass,
And I, too, joining you in the fresh dawn,
Shall wet my lower garment as I pass.

"HITOMARO COLLECTION," XI, 2357.

⋖§ FOURTEEN §⋗

A man could easily dig in earth so long
That Nature would suspend
Her being and earth perish utterly:
Only love knows no end.

"HITOMARO COLLECTION," XI, 2442.

⋖§ FIFTEEN §⋗

I will tread the sharpness of keen swords;
My courage shall not quake;
Yes, I will lightly die with a glad heart
If only for your sake!

"HITOMARO COLLECTION," XI, 2498.

◄§ SIXTEEN §►

HE

Should thunder roar without end,
Clouds gather and rain descend,
You will have to stay with me.

SHE

Yet, should no thunder sound
And no rain fall to the ground,
I'll stay with you faithfully.

"HITOMARO COLLECTION," XI, 2513–4.

◄§ SEVENTEEN §►

Were my love a bracelet
On my left arm today
I would clasp her firmly
And start on my long way.

FURU TAMUKÉ. IX, 1766.

◄§ EIGHTEEN §►

Don't walk by the palace
In the new snow!
Such a thick fall
We seldom know
In our lowly valley,
For only on high
Mountains does such snow
Often lie.—
Don't tread on the snow;
Let it quietly lie!

Our Prince must see it
With his own eyes.
Don't walk by the palace
Where fresh snow lies!

MIKATA SHAMI.[8] XIX, 4227–8.

ᴥᰫ NINETEEN ᰫᴥ

As we walk through clover
In spring weather
Flowers stain your dress
Though faintly as a feather,
Token of the walk
We have taken together.

LADY FUKI. I, 57.

ᴥᰫ TWENTY [9] ᰫᴥ

Our peaceful Sovereign, offspring of the Sun,
Wills, as a deity in her domain,
To build a palace towering to the skies
On sacred earth of the Wisteria Plain.
So the gods of earth and sky unite
In floating many a sturdy cedar beam
From the far heights of Mount Tanakami
Down the swift rapids of the Uji stream.
And we, poor mortals, just as mallard ducks,
Splash in the water, never thinking of
Ourselves or of our homes but of the walls
Of the celestial palace that we love.
The sacred river also brings to hand
The tortoise whose shell-cryptograms presage
Eternal happiness for her demesne,

Brilliant beginning of a glorious age,
Foretelling also of the alien men
Who through the mountain passes shall descend
Presenting their obeisance to her throne
And to our Empire that shall never end.
So as we look upon these sturdy rafts,
Witness our laborious deeds and see
The logs we bind in poling down the stream,
We know all done for her divinity.

ANON. I, 50.

ৰঙ্গ TWENTY-ONE ৪৯

"Our peaceful Sovereign, offspring of the Sun,
Wills as a deity in her domain
To build a palace towering to the skies
On sacred ground of the Wisteria Plain."
From the Haniyasu dyke the Empress looks
First to the Eastern Gateway and perceives
The green hill of Kagu of Yamato
Luxuriant in its springtime robe of leaves.
Next, by the Western Gate, Mount Unebi
Arises, fragrant with its grassy ledges.
Then, to the North, lofty Miminashi,
Surrounded with its girdle of green sedges.
While, lastly, to the South, the Yoshinu
Lifts on the southern sky their lofty wedges.
Thus as shelter from the sun and heaven
The palace towers project their sacred spell
Over the everlasting Uji stream,
Its crystal waters and its holy well.

> I envy women who will serve
> Forevermore, reign after reign,
> Within its consecrated halls,
> The Palace on Wisteria Plain.

ANON. I, 52–3.

ᏧᏣ TWENTY-TWO ᏗᏧ

White water breaks against the rocks,
Then rushes past its banks, till soon
Look, in the mirror of a pool,
The image of the sliver moon!

ANON. IX, 1714. (218)

ᏧᏣ TWENTY-THREE ᏗᏧ

Even the ducks on Karu Pond
With water-cresses overgrown
Who skim beside its pleasant shores
Do not sleep alone!

PRINCESS KI. III, 390.

ᏧᏣ TWENTY-FOUR ᏗᏧ

Like the white cloud on this green hill
Which floating every day we see,
Although he greets us every day,
Our host is always new to me.

PRINCE YUHARA. III, 377.[10]

ᏧᏣ TWENTY-FIVE ᏗᏧ

Offerings I bring,
Clear moon on heaven's heights:
Make this one night as long
As full five hundred nights!

PRINCE YUHARA. VI, 985.

ANCIENT POETRY FROM JAPAN/213

⊰ TWENTY-SIX ⊱

Were white-caps flowers that sprang
On Isé's distant waves to life,
I'd gather them and bring them home
To my dear wife!

PRINCE AKI. III, 306.

⊰ TWENTY-SEVEN [11] ⊱

O solitary pine, how many men,
How many generations have you known?
Is it because of your great age the wind
Chants in your branches with so deep a tone?

PRINCE ICHIHARA. VI, 1042.

⊰ TWENTY-EIGHT ⊱

As countless yellow roses dot the plain
Infinite violets rise with the spring rain.

PRINCESS TAKATA. VII, 1444.

⊰ TWENTY-NINE ⊱

I thought there could not be
More love anywhere.
Whence, then, is this love come
That brings me to despair?

PRINCESS HIROKAWA. IV, 695.

◄§ THIRTY §►

When I behold Cape Kiyomi and rest
My eyes upon the boundless Miho Bay
Beside the waves of the Ioharian Sea,
My cares dissolve away.

TAGUCHI MASUHITO. III, 296.

◄§ THIRTY-ONE §►

Only one night I passed at Tago Bay
When one whole day can in no way afford
Time to view its beauty, but I had
To hasten, faithful to my Sovereign's word.

TAGUCHI MASUHITO. III, 297.

◄§ THIRTY-TWO §►

One city only blossoms like a flower,
Nara, glowing in its brightest hour.

ONO OYU. III, 328.

◄§ THIRTY-THREE §►

I met you by the roadside as I journeyed,
Stranger to me, as a cloud in heaven.
Words I could not speak strangled my breathing;
Silence possessed me; all my heart was riven.
Thanks to the mercy of the gods above us,
Each on each other's sleeve, when day is done
We lie together, for we now are wedded.
Oh that a hundred nights would melt in one!

From the moment that I saw you
My heart was freely given;
Body and soul lean toward you
As autumn clouds in heaven.

I cannot bear the thought
A night will soon be gone!
Oh that a thousand nights
Were molded into one!

KASA KANAMURA. IV, 546–8.[12]

৩ THIRTY-FOUR ৫

The mountain hangs over the waterfall
Where tall fir-trees in firm succession grow
Through endless ages, in luxuriance,
The Palace rising in the plain below.
The fir-trees that are firm, a firmament
Of permament succession, without change—
These comprise auspicious ornaments
For the pavilion where our Sovereign reigns.
Or stands it here because a god is here,
Gazing upon us with benevolent eyes,
Or from some ancient virtue of the place,
Its lucid streams, pure hills and crystal skies?

> Would I could feast my eyes
> Forever on this scene,
> The cascade foaming white,
> The valley clear and clean!

> I gaze in endless joy
> Where the pure river spills
> In rapids, silken white,
> Down from towering hills.

KASA KANAMURA. VI, 907–9.

◆§ THIRTY-FIVE ᠍᠍◆

Look, the unsullied river, Yoshinu,
Thunders in rapids down its mountain walls;
Below the heights the bull-frogs greet each other,
Above, issue the plovers' constant calls.
While palace lords and ladies throng its shores
I am enchanted by the joyful scene;
I pray the gods of heaven and of earth,
May it for countless ages rest serene!

How can I ever weary
Of that which never palls,
The gardens of the palace,
The river's waterfalls?

I wish that my own nature
And all whom time has bred
Were constant as the boulders
In that deep river-bed.

KASA KANAMURA. VI, 290–2.

◆§ THIRTY-SIX [13] ᠍᠍◆

Though all men held the wave-bright Naniwa
A ravaged and a ruinous estate,
A field no better than an old reed-fence,
Forgotten, unbefriended, desolate,
Now that our royal Sovereign deigns to dwell
In Nagara's high-pillared halls and plans
For new dominion over his estate
And over all his eighty princely clans
Who here have built their cots on Ajifu Field,
This city now becomes the citadel
Imperial and the heart of our demesne,
If only for the time of festival.

On hills bare as a moorland
Or place of no renown
There now blooms forth a city,
Our Lord's imperial town.

Fishing-girls in shallops
Row out along the shores;
From a wayfarer's couch I hear
Plashing of their oars.

KARA KANAMURA. VI, 298–30.

⚜ THIRTY-SEVEN ⚜

I sail along the coast
On a great ship full-oared
In full obedience to
Our Sovereign's will and word.

ISONOKAMI (OTOMARO). III, 368.

⚜ THIRTY-EIGHT ⚜

Tell me, you god who guard this island shore,
Even if a full account were reckoned of
These sands of beaches taking years to traverse,
Whether they could surpass my thoughts of love?

LADY KASA. IV, 596.

⚜ THIRTY-NINE ⚜

I love you always yet you awe me always,
I know not which is more:
So thunderous waves forever and forever
Lash the Isé shore.

LADY KASA. IV, 600.

✺§ FORTY ࣸ✺

I dreamed that I was clasping to my body
A two-edged sword. I asked what mystic rune
Or prophecy my dream contained, and knew
It held the omen I should meet you soon.

LADY KASA. IV, 604.

✺§ FORTY-ONE ࣸ✺

As one hears muttered thunder from a storm
Whose clouds both dark and distance veil from view,
So in reports upon my ravished ear
There fell the name of lovely Yoshinu.
But now I stand among its giant trees,
Marking the morning mists rise from below
Or, lingering on until the close of day,
Hear the frogs calling where calm waters flow.
Oh what a pity, being on a journey
And sleeping in my clothes as I do here,
Looking upon this clear and lovely shore,
I must perforce be without you, my dear!

    Standing beside the torrent
    Where mountains loom above,
    Never a day nor hour
    Do I forget my love!

KURAMOCHI CHITOSÉ. VI, 913–4.

✺§ FORTY-TWO ࣸ✺

The beach and bay are beautiful; beside them
Are sea-weeds dark and swaying, safe from harm,
Tossed by a thousand waves in morning wind,

Lapped by a hundred ripples in eve's calm.
O Suminoé Beach, where surf is racing,
White-crested in its splendor! more and more
I love you, and can never weary of you
Now or forever, watching by your shore.

Let me go now, my clothes stained
With yellow clay,
Part of your beach and white waves
With their rhythmic sway.

KARAMOCHI CHITOSÉ. VI, 931–2.

⤸ FORTY-THREE ⤷

Do not slight these flowers, for they enshrine
In every petal many words of mine!

FUJIWARA HIROTSUGU. VII, 1456.

⤸ FORTY-FOUR ⤷

These are new clothes; now take them as your own
Since, bowed in thought, your loving wife has sewn
Each part and parcel, keepsakes to remain
Close to your side till we shall meet again.

ANON. XV, 3753.

⤸ FORTY-FIVE ⤷

There is nothing more to fear;
Having yielded myself, my dear,
I have found my life's clue.
Have no more cares, for you know
You have me now, who would go
Through flood and fire for you.

LADY ABÉ. IV, 505–6.

ᵉ§ FORTY-SIX [14] ᵉ»

Yoshinu is fair and fair its palace,
Its mountains noble and its river clear;
As long as heaven and earth shall last, this valley
Shall flourish without change, year after year.

This tributary, Kisa,
Which long ago I knew,
Now seems to me much fairer,
More limpid, fresh and blue.

ŌTOMO TABITO. III, 315–6.

ᵉ§ FORTY-SEVEN [15] ᵉ»

Instead of squandered thoughts on trivial things,
Explore delight none but raw saké brings
Nor weaker drops assuage.
Confess how true the word of the great thinker
Who gave to saké and its noble drinker
The blessed name of "sage."
The Seven Wise Men in the olden days
Gave saké also the unstinted praise
Of gratified desire;
Far better, they declared, than pompous speech
Or solemn looks the joy our wine-cups teach
And drunken tears inspire!
I know not how to name it or to tell
The mystery of the transcendent spell
Of liquor so divine.
Ceasing to be as bloodstained mortals are,
I wish I were a brim-full saké jar
Soaked with its blessed wine!
Absurd indeed that wretch whom I despise
Who drinks no saké but who looks so wise;

He's like an ape, for sure!
Not the most precious treasure of a king
Can equal that inestimable thing,
A cup of saké pure!

ŌTOMO TABITO. III, 338–50.

₍₅ FORTY-EIGHT ₎₅

Where our Lord and Sovereign reigns in peace
Though to these farthest provinces I came,
I am as pleased as in the capital;
Contented where he rules, I feel the same.

ŌTOME TABITO. VI, 956.

₍₅ FORTY-NINE ₎₅

Do not smile to yourself too frankly
Nor betray what your thoughts are of;
Be a cloud that shades a green mountain,
Lest others suspect our love.

LADY ŌTOMO OF SAKANOÉ. IV, 688.[16]

₍₅ FIFTY ₎₅

My lover wears too thin a dress;   7 ems
O bitter East Wind, I implore
You not to blow with all your force
Till he is safe at home once more!

LADY ŌTOMO OF SAKANOÉ. VI, 979.

◄§ FIFTY-ONE §►

When we have drunk together, friends, and set
Plum-blossoms floating on our cups of wine,
I do not care if those on trees are gone,
Nor do I rate a later Spring with mine.

LADY ŌTOMO OF SAKANOÉ. VIII, 1656.

◄§ FIFTY-TWO §►

At home the autumn flowers are all abloom
In evening's glow after refreshing storm.
O for a precious hour when I might see,
Present before me here, your radiant form!

LADY ŌTOMO OF SAKANOÉ. VIII, 1622.

◄§ FIFTY-THREE §►

A fringed pink in the garden my love planted
In an auspicious hour
Now in this autumn-tide for her remembrance
Has risen into flower.

ŌTOMO YAKAMOCHI. III, 464.[17]

◄§ FIFTY-FOUR §►

Once I saw it through uncaring eyes,
With neither pain nor bliss.
Now that it becomes her sepulchre,
How dear this low hill is!

ŌTOMO YAKAMOCHI. III, 474.

✦ FIFTY-FIVE ✦

Across the river ford
Where frail sandpipers cry,
How can I ride back to you
Where clear shallows lie?
Yet once in fleeting dream
Your casual smile came
To light my burning heart
With love's unconquered flame.

ŌTOMO YAKAMOCHI. IV, 715 and 718.

✦ FIFTY-SIX [18] ✦

Soaring to heaven, Futagami's peaks,
Encircled by its river and its seas,
Are rich in splendor of its flowering spring
And rich in glory of its autumn trees.
Impregnated by a divinity,
Waves at its base at dawn are beautiful
Yet still more beautiful the flooding tide
On evenings which the quiet breezes lull.
This rocky promontory, skirting ridge,
And bi-forked summit where the lightning plays
Capture man's veneration for all time,
From the most ancient to the present days.

As resurgent waves
Crash on this promontory,
So do my own thoughts beat
On days of ancient story.

Hence I now suspend
All adulating words
To harken to the cries
Of wistful water-birds.

ŌTOMO YAKAMOCHI. XVII, 3985–7.

In lands as distant as the skies
Our Sovereign's summer palace lies,
With huge streams, snowy mountain passes,
Vast plains and valleys rich in grasses.
In summer, when the rivers run
With fish, cormorant's work is done;
Veteran fishers and their fellows
Toil among the river-shallows
Bearing torches by whose light
They ply their evil trade at night.
Then autumn comes with dew and frost
Bringing the days that I love most.
So with my noble friends I stalk
The birds, taking my great black hawk
Jingling his silver-coated band
Of bells, the best hawk in the land,
A daring hunter without fail,
Fierce beak and arrow-pointed tail.
He puts a hundred birds to flight
At dawn, a thousand at twilight.
This hawk, once my unfailing pride,
Not one his equal, far and wide!—
So, as I passed delicious days,
Happy in my falcon's praise,
My dull old servant thought it fit
To hunt without his lord's permit.
This idiot made the appalling
Error to hawk with the rain falling
And on returning wept and roared:
"He left Mishima's field and soared
Away into a storm-black cloud
Blotting the mountain in its shroud."—
I was at loss for what to do.
Where the hawk went no mortal knew.
My sighs and longing found no end.
I wept as I had lost a friend.
I set out watchmen, spread my foils
To take him in their subtle coils.

I beat both shoulders of the hill
To catch my darling if he still
Were there. And next, before a shrine
I prayed the gods to make him mine;
I prayed again and yet again
But found petitions all in vain.
I offered gifts of glass and cloth
But saw I only wasted both.
Then, as I slumbered fitfully,
A young girl came in dream to me
And said: "The lovely bird you seek
Has gone astray by Himi's creek,
Enticed to linger by his wish
To catch the tender, luscious fish
The villagers enjoy; and then
Has gone upon his way again,
Passed night at Matsudaé's Beach
And, wandering to the farthest reach
Of Tako's isle, is gone astray.—
On the day-before-yesterday
I saw your great hawk with a shock
At Furué falling on a flock
Of frightened mallards; and the same
Black hawk was at his cruel game
Yesterday. What I say is true!
In two days he'll return to you.
Take comfort! Wait him patiently."
She said this in a dream to me.

With my arrow-tailed bird
On Mishima Bay
I have not hawked
This many a day.

I have spread my nets
Between mountain and sea,
Yet a dream-girl says
To wait patiently!

ŌTOMO YAKAMOCHI. XVII, 4011–3.

226/ANCIENT POETRY FROM JAPAN

᦬ FIFTY-EIGHT ᦥ

When I look up and gaze at the young moon,
Lamp of the sky, of heaven the very core,
I think of eyebrows delicately painted
Of her I saw once only, and no more.

ŌTOMO YAKAMOCHI. VI, 994.

᦬ FIFTY-NINE ᦥ

Business took me from the hour of dawn
To sail till dusk on Nagahama Bay
Across wide Suzu Sea and there I saw
The waters shining in the moon's cool ray.

ŌTOMO YAKAMOCHI. XVII, 4029.

᦬ SIXTY ᦥ

These have been laws throughout Izumo province
Given men by paternal gods above them:
To see our parents means that we revere them;
To see our wives and children means to love them.
So has it been from the primeval days.
But you, who surely know the laws of life,
In the full-flowering time of dogwood trees,
Have you not promised falsely to your wife?
Morning and night you said bad days would cease
And by the mercy of celestial powers
Dearth and depression end, happy times come,
And winter cold be followed by spring flowers.
But now that your prosperity is here,
Your wife is waiting for you far away

In solitude and sorrow wondering
When you will tell her of this blessed day.
And all the while you court a girl of pleasure
Who has no settled place of house or home,
Who floats like waves upon a swelling tide
Or rather as mere shreds of scattered foam.
She melts like snowflakes when the south wind blows;
And yet you cling to her like tangled twine!
You pair like water-birds, plunging in gulfs
Bitter and bottomless as Ocean's brine.

How your wife must grieve!
While you are scorning her
She waits upon tip-toe
For your good messenger.

Meanwhile the townsfolk talk
On many a village bench
About that shameless man
And his more shameless wench!

Frail pink of blossoms fades
At time's remorseless stroke.
Old-fashioned clothes are best
Dyed from the sturdy oak.

ŌTOMO YAKAMOCHI. XVIII, 4106–9.

SIXTY-ONE

In the great age of the God-Emperor,
Awesome and still, a hero, lord of brutes,
Went on his journey to Eternity
And brought our "Trees of Timeless Fragrant Fruits."
He brought eight saplings for our nation's good,
So that glad praises of his exploits ring
Throughout our land, blessed with profusion of
These trees whose spreading branches flower in Spring.

Now in the month of May, when cuckoos call,
And blossoms glitter in the shiny leaves,
We pluck the blooms to give them to our girls,
Conveyed with care, wrapped in our cloaks or sleeves.
Sometimes we dry them for their rich perfumes
Or string the fallen fruits like colored beads
To hang them on our arms for lasting pleasure,
Sometimes we leave them till the autumn breeds
Cold showers and trees turn red first and then bare.
Yet the bright fruit still hangs alluringly,
Glittering in the clear September air.
Finally, when the winter snows arrive
The harvest still is lusty as the roots:
Hence, since the age of the God-Emperor
We name these, "Trees of Timeless Fragrant Fruits."

   This I have sometimes seen
   When flowers or fruits abound;
   But in my mind this tree
   Lives all its seasons round.

ŌTOMO YAKAMOCHI. XVIII, 4111–2.

⋐ SIXTY-TWO ⋑

Under every sky and in all places
Known to our great imperial realm below,
From our heart-lands where horses' hooves may clatter
To farthest isles where the ships' prows can go
Thousand on thousand blessings gods bestow
On men, of boundless worth and countless price,
But from the birth of time the chief by far is rice.

Now because no drop of rain has fallen
Our crops commence to droop and fall away,
Both in these lowland and those upland stations,
Scorched in the burning light of cloudless day.
The more and more I mark their disarray,
The more I watch clouds gathering in the West
And crave the rain as infants crave their mothers' breast.

But look! for on the breast of the great mountain
A mist is forming and a thin gray cloud
Gathers in its hollow, which, increasing,
Is covering all the summit in its shroud.
So with great vehemence I cry aloud:
"May it reach the Sea God's palace nor in vain
Darken the sky, as now, but grant us heavy rain!"

May the dark storm-clouds grow not to retain
Their wealth from our parched earth but once again
For our land's health grant us abundant rain!

ŌTOMO YAKAMOCHI. XVII, 4122–3.

ᵛᵉᵍ SIXTY-THREE ᵍᵉᵛ

In the garden in spring
Peach-blossoms glow;
On the flowery path
She walks to and fro.

Are those fallen petals
Where her feet go
On her morning walk
Or patches of snow?

ŌTOMO YAKAMOCHI. XIX, 4139–40.

ᵛᵉᵍ SIXTY-FOUR ᵍᵉᵛ

From my morning bed I listen
While hearing far from shore
The singing of a boatman,
The plashing of an oar.

ŌTOMO YAKAMOCHI. XIX, 4150.

⤚§ SIXTY-FIVE §⤙

Over hill and mountain I have come
To this provincial village, far from home.
Though believing to whatever place I came
The city and the country are the same,
Provided they are where my Sovereign reigns,
Yet irresistibly my heart complains
Because I am dissevered from my friends.
So, for solace, as the summer ends,
I give my horse the reign and blithely go
To moors where blossoming bush-clovers grow
And, near and far, set many wild-fowl free
To let my hawk pursue them ardently.
When his bells jingle on his lofty flight
All pressure on my heavy heart grows light.
I put an end to melancholy talk
And in my chamber keep my mottled hawk.

My arrow-tailed hawk
Delights to sit
In my room and be stroked:
Ah, the pleasure of it!

ŌTOMO YAKAMOCHI. XIX, 4154–5.

⤚§ SIXTY-SIX §⤙

Am I the craven one
To prove a thankless son
Living inglorious days
Bereft of fame and praise?
No, let my arrows fly
Deep into the sky;
Let my sword be bright!
I'll scale the mountain height
Keeping my Sovereign's trust,

Living because I must
To my proud name engage
Fame's voice from age to age.

A brave man should win fame
So that his valiant name
May ever sound the same.

ŌTOMO YAKAMOCHI. XIX, 4164–5.

◦§ SIXTY-SEVEN ?◦

New flowers bloom as seasons change; the trees
And shrubs in endless sequence reappear;
Varied also are the tunes of birds
Through all the livelong pageant of the year.
This endless alteration pleases us
Yet saddens; but the best of all, in May
The cuckoo comes, borrowing his neighbor's nest,
And with glad music chases care away.
He sings until young girls adorn themselves
With flags and orange-blossoms, from high noon
Till evening; then throughout the summer night
We see his wings darting against the moon.
His call is heard until the break of dawn
While even airy echoings prolong
His music; and as constant as his singing
Is my unwearied pleasure in his song.

As seasons change
New flowers resume
Processionals
In constant bloom.

The annual cuckoo
Eases my sad lot;
Too many the dull months
I hear him not.

ŌTOMO YAKAMOCHI. XIX, 4166–8.

ᵍᵍ SIXTY-EIGHT ᵍᵍ

Mirrored in the April lake
Wisteria blooms are clear;
Pebbles sunken in its depths
As precious stones appear.

ŌTOMO YAKAMOCHI. XIX, 4199.

ᵍᵍ SIXTY-NINE ᵍᵍ

On the shore road I travel to my home,
Riding mile on mile.
Since I would relish moonlight to the full,
I stay my horse awhile.

ŌTOMO YAKAMOCHI. XIX, 4206.

ᵍᵍ SEVENTY [19] ᵍᵍ

All successors to the Imperial Throne
Reign after reign have ruled our favored land
Since our ancestral gods surveyed all space,
Rowed their rock-built vessel, fully manned
By oarsmen laboring from stem to stern,
And, passing through dark clouds, at length inclined
To earth to pacify their world, where now
Our own Imperial goddess sits enshrined.
High on her heavenly throne she holds firm rule
Over her eighty clans, guiding the helm
Of order, blessing all her subject folk,
Bringing prosperity throughout her realm.
Good omens, such as only in old times
Were heard, are heard of her; good acts begun
Under her rule shall be retold forever,
Deathless as heaven and earth, or moon and sun.

Our Sovereign rules with folded arms, in peace,
Delighting in her varied autumn flowers,
Taking pleasure in her royal feasts.
Ah, what a glorious age is this of ours!

> While many kinds of flowers
> Make an autumn gay,
> She revels in them all.
> Ah, what a glorious day!

ŌTOMO YAKAMOCHI. XIX, 4254-5.

৺§ SEVENTY-ONE ৡ৵

Once in the long ago at wave-bright Naniwa
The father of all Emperors held his court
As here, in these auspicious later days,
Our Sovereign goddess makes her own resort.
She comes to us in early spring, when blossoms
Upon the tinted, swelling branches start,
When streams run clear, when mountain-peaks stand radiant,
When all things please the eye and warm the heart.
O palace of imperial Naniwa!
Here from all quarters of your commonweal
A host of tribute-bearing vessels comes
Much like a noisy flock of traveling teal.
During hours of early morning quiet
Up through the wide canals their oars are plied,
Or easily guiding their long boats with poles
They slip down stream on the calm evening's tide.
Far out beyond the beach the fishing boats
Appear, dotting the sea-plain as they sail
Among white waves breaking on one another,
Daring the white-caps and the sky-born gale.
These fishermen provide the royal table.
How wide and spacious is the view we see!
How free and open! The imperial House
One-time established by the Deity!

Cherry-trees are in full bloom
Here at the palace by the sea,
Where in wave-bright Naniwa
Our Empress reigns exaltedly.

In Naniwa of wind-blown reeds
I feel I might forget my home,
Gazing at the boundless sea
Through peaceful cycles yet to come.

ŌTOMO YAKAMOCHI. XX, 4398–400.

⊰ SEVENTY-TWO ⊱

Well I know my body
Transient as the foam,
Yet how much I wish
Death might never come!

ŌTOMO YAKAMOCHI. XX, 4470.

⊰ SEVENTY-THREE ⊱

Wind and wave diminish
Over a quiet sea.
Swiftly your ship will travel
And soon return to me.

ŌTOMO YAKAMOCHI. XX, 4514.

⊰ SEVENTY-FOUR ⊱

As this abundant snow
Comes with the New Year,
So may the Spring shower blessings
On all gathered here.

ŌTOMO YAKAMOCHI. XX, 4516.

SEVENTY-FIVE

In Koshi province famous regions lie,
Tall hills and rivers rushing to the sea;
Upon its mountain snow rests all the year
In honor of its high divinity.
Unlike pale mists that form and fade away
Each morning and each evening by the shore
Of the engirdling river Katakai,
Memory holds it fast forevermore.
Each year I look upon it from afar
Then sing of its strange beauty and great fame
For in the future all will wish to see it
Who have no more than merely heard its name.

Divine Mount Tachi's snows
Refresh me in the throes
Of summer's ardent heat.
Unfailing as the gleam
Upon the mountain's stream,
I'll worship at its feet.

ŌTOMO YAKAMOCHI AND ŌTOMO IKENUSHI. XVII, 4000–2.

SEVENTY-SIX

A god, Mount Tachi stands
Above low-lying lands,
Lifting aloft its proud
Forehead above the cloud.
Morn and eve proclaim
The honor of its name.
Crowned with eternal snow,
While summers come and go,
It stays forever cold
Just as in days of old,
Rugged its rockiness
Through ages numberless.

Deep are its mysteries:
On every hand one sees
Dark gorges, soaring peaks,
Swift rivers, dashing creeks,
While dawn and dusk with mist
Veil it in amethyst.

Grave as its cloudy veil
And constant without fail
As the torrents fall
Down the mountain wall
I shall chant forever
Of it and of its river.

Eternal snowdrifts lie
Where Tachi looms on high;
Its constant rivers flow,
As to them I shall go
Clad in the blessedness
Of so much sacredness.

ŌTOMO YAKAMOCHI AND ŌTOMO IKENUSHI. XVII, 4003–5.

◆§ SEVENTY-SEVEN §◆

What do I care if my name
Be upon every tongue?
My one concern is this:
That no man do you wrong.

LADY ŌTOMO OF SAKANOÉ'S ELDER SISTER. IV, 731.

◆§ SEVENTY-EIGHT §◆

Of all the famous places in the land
My heart dwells most upon the Capital
Where our Lord reigns; do you not think of it
When rich wisteria blossoms climb your wall?

ŌTOMO YOTSUNA. III, 329–30.

⊷§ SEVENTY-NINE §⊷

Beautiful on high the moonlit night
And clear the river-murmurs here below.
Come, let us all be merry as we can,
Both we who stay and even you who go!

ŌTOMO YOTSUNA. IV, 571.

⊷§ EIGHTY §⊷

My lady, it appears to me
You have lived in Eternity;
You, only, conquering time's flow,
Are younger than long years ago.

ŌTOME MIYORI. IV, 650.

⊷§ EIGHTY-ONE §⊷

Since chaos fell and heaven and earth arose
Fuji has towered aloft, noble, divine;
Sun and moon are both eclipsed behind it;
Clouds dread it, while its snows forever shine,
Tall Fuji, in whose praise all men combine!

When sailing out of Tago Bay I go
There gleams afar white Fuji's crest of snow.

YAMAMBÉ AKAHITO. III, 317–8.[20]

⊷§ EIGHTY-TWO §⊷

I would ever visit the tall trees
Men name the evergreens that ever grow
By the damp ruins of Asuka Palace
Upon the lofty slopes of Mimoro.

The river there is long, its cliffs are high,
Spring air is sweet, the rapid waters bright,
Limpid the light of autumn; great white cranes
Soar through cloud-banks on their morning flight.
Croaking of frogs sounds through the evening mist,
Elegant ruins molder with the years.
Whenever I have come to look upon them
Suddenly my eyes have filled with tears.

    As at Asuka's Pool the mists
    Drift always through the sky,
    Pensive longings rise in me
    That cannot ever die.

               YAMAMBÉ AKAHITO. III, 324–5.

⊰ EIGHTY-THREE ⊱

We serve our peaceful Sovereign at his palace
Upon the Plain of Saiga by the sea,
Where white waves glitter on the cleanly shore-lines
Whenever the sea breeze blows lustily.
Then, at ebb tide, men harvest dainty seaweed
Clinging to the island's gleaming hem,
Found here since ancient times when the Celestials
Fashioned for us our precious island gem.

    I fear to miss the seaweed
    Upon the rugged beach
    Since the flood tide hides it
    Away from sight and reach.

    At high tide cranes go crying
    Unto the reedy shore
    When their lagoons are flooded,
    Visible no more.

               YAMAMBÉ AKAHITO. VI, 917–9.

Here in the lovely valley Yoshinu
Stands the royal palace, built of old,
From which our peaceful Sovereign rules his people,
Guarded by green mountains, fold on fold.
Flowers load the boughs in spring while in the autumn
Mists cover all in clouds like floating foam;
Here, jostling as the clouds, brocaded courtiers,
Great lords and gracious ladies, press to come.

> By day bird-calls from tree-tops
> Continuously ring
> Breaking the valley silence
> Sweetly as they sing.

> Later as black night deepens
> From where the beaches lie
> We hear above the breakers
> The sanderlings' frail cry.

YAMAMBÉ AKAHITO. VI, 923–5.

In the Akitsu dale of Yoshinu
On his great morning hunt our Sovereign rides,
Placing game-trackers in the open fields,
Posting his bowmen on the mountain sides.
He rouses wild beasts for his morning's game,
Dislodges wild-fowl for his evening's chase;
So with brave horsemen dashing at his side
Through the lush grass he joins the lusty race.

> Look! our Sovereign's hunters
> With arrows by their side
> Over fields and rugged hills
> Scatter far and wide.

YAMAMBÉ AKAHITO. VI, 926–7.

⊷§ EIGHTY-SIX ⸱⸱

In Ōmi Field on the Inami Plain
Our Sovereign Emperor, whose peace is bliss,
Has reared a palace soaring to the sky
Fit for the heaven-sent ruler that he is.
Lagoons along the bay are thickly dotted
With fishing-boats hunting for albacore,
While all its crescent coast is thickly spotted
With salt-fires burning on the sandy shore.
His Majesty himself is pleased to visit
Plain boatmen and the toilers of his lands,
Viewing their various and useful labors,
Taking his pleasure in the pure white sands.

> The waves today are still
> Both near and far from land;
> Boats of many kinds
> Swarm on every hand.

> I have slept many nights
> Close to the ocean foam,
> My only bed the sedge,
> Longing for my home.

> Tomorrow I shall leave
> Akashi Bay and start
> For home, at length to greet
> My wife, with smiles at heart.

YAMAMBÉ AKAHITO. VI, 938–41.

⊷§ EIGHTY-SEVEN ⸱⸱

> Men of court ride out
> On hunting expeditions
> While women walk about
> According to traditions,
> Trailing robes of pink
> By the clear river-brink.

YAMAMBÉ AKAHITO. VI, 1001.

◄§ EIGHTY-EIGHT §►

I went to the spring field
To gather violets
But slept there all the night
With beauty none forgets.

YAMAMBÉ AKAHITO. VIII, 1424.

◄§ EIGHTY-NINE §►

There was snow yesterday; today it snowed;
All the bleak landscape bears a look of sorrow.
But I have marked the meadow where I plan
To walk and gather fresh spring herbs tomorrow.

YAMAMBÉ AKAHITO. VIII, 1427.

◄§ NINETY §►

Reverence rises from the sight of parents,
Love from that of children or of wives,
These are the fetters in which life has bound us,
This the way and manner of our lives.
We are not born of rocks or trees, and what man
Can drop these bonds as outworn shoes or clothes?
No man on earth can manage to escape them;
The way passed earth no mortal really knows.
When you come to heaven it is just possible
That you may do precisely as you please,
But where our Sovereign rules under the heavens
We live subjected to such laws as these.
To live beneath the sun and moon and practice
Strange ways is to behave with willfulness.

Such paths of life, being its contradiction,
Are ways that neither heaven nor earth will bless.

Heaven is far and duty none can shirk
Successfully. Go home and mind your work!

YAMANOÉ OKURA. V, 800–1.[21]

◄§ NINETY-ONE §►

Eating a melon I recall my children,
Eating a chestnut makes such thoughts increase.
From incidental things deep feelings rise,
Then linger, and we cannot rest in peace.

Why should gems, gold, silver be amassed?
My children are a treasure unsurpassed.

YAMANOÉ OKURA. V, 802–3.

◄§ NINETY-TWO §►

My tongue is awed; our pregnant Empress
Lifted from earth two stones to sooth her pain,
Clasped them to her, found their aid auspicious,
Then placed them reverently on Kofu's Plain.
She put them there to be a monument
That through all time men's grateful thoughts should start.
Seeing these stones I think of immortality;
Silence and reverence overwhelm my heart.

She left these healing stones that for all time
Man should be cognizant of the sublime.

YAMANOÉ OKURA. V, 813–4.

After gods left earth, our Sovereign ruled
One with the world-soul, answering every vow;
Not only was this said by word of mouth
But all of us must see and know it now.
Though many worthy courtiers exist,
Our lord, the Sun of Heaven, gives his command
That you, as scion of a noble house,
Should visit China, that far-distant land.
All gods who guard the coast and the wide seas
Will guide your prow, while the great spirits of
This land of Yamato, soaring to heaven,
Will look down on you with eternal love.
When you return, an envoy's duties done,
These gods again will guide your vessel's track
From Chika's cape to Mitsu's harbor here.
Be safe and well, my lord; quickly come back!

    I shall sweep the pine-wood
    For one we lack
    And stand waiting for you;
    O quickly come back!

    When I hear that your vessels
    At Naniwa ride,
    Scarcely tying my robe
    I shall rush to your side.

YAMANOÉ OKURA. V, 894–6.

When I count on my fingers
The flowers Autumn yields,
I find there are seven
    Dotting our fields.
    There is crisp blue-hemp
    And tall goldenrod,

Red-vine or swallow-tail
Close to the sod,
Bush-clover
Rich in grace,
Agrimony and pink
And gay "morning face."

YAMANOÉ OKURA. VIII, 1537–8.

ᴇ§ NINETY-FIVE §ᴡ

Now in the season when the clouded mountains
Begin to crimson with the frost and dew,
You cross them with five hundred of your followers,
Trudging along with all your retinue.
Your soldiers will protect our far-flung borders
From molestation by the enemy,
Subordinates inspect the promontories
As you yourself devise the strategy
Safe in the farthest place where echo sounds
Or the remotest nook where life can cling;
Yet when the springtime makes its next approach
You must fly back, quickly as bird on wing.
When on the steep slopes of the mountainsides
Crimson flowers of the azalea burn
And when our cherry-trees burst into bloom
How I shall greet you on your glad return!

I know, my noble lord,
You are a man to spurn
All needless words, to smite
The foe, and then return.

TAKAHASHI MUSHIMARO. VI, 971–2.

✑ NINETY-SIX ఇఒ

Look where the peak of Fuji towers
Between Suruga's waves and Kai,
No bird dare soar into its air,
No cloud conceal it in its sky.
No snow can quench its burning fire,
No fire consume its fallen snow;
Fuji is a mysterious god
Whose secret name no man may know!
Our sacred lake is by its side,
From which the roaring torrents run,
Here in the Land of Yamato,
The Empire of the Rising Sun.
This is our treasure and our god,
The one whom our petitions seek,
Whose sight can never tire our eye,
The lofty crest of Fuji's peak!

If snows that crown its crest
One June day be suppressed,
It snows again that night!
So awful is its summit
No cloud dare linger on it
But scatters into flight.

"MUSHIMARO COLLECTION," III, 319–21.

✑ NINETY-SEVEN ఇఒ

There was a girl named Tamana
At Sué that lies beside Awa,
Round-breasted and wasp-waisted, grace
Shining in her merry face.
When she stood glowing as a flower
All travelers felt resistless power
Drawing to her; one left his wife,
Giving her his keys for life.

Vanquished by her charms and airs,
Strong men were snared even in her hairs.

Should one stand at her gate
She would not let him wait
Nor felt the least fright
On the darkest night!

"MUSHIMARO COLLECTION," IX, 1738–9.

◆§ NINETY-EIGHT §◆

You, honored lord, have clambered all the way,
Breathless, perspiring, grasping roots of trees,
Scaling this twin-peaked mountain, Tsukuba,
For the unhampered view the climber sees.
Its god and goddess have so favored us
As to make every hill and valley plain,
Uncovering dark ridges to the sun
That hitherto were veiled in mist and rain.
Grateful and joyful, we unbind our clothes,
Make pinnacles our home, enjoy our ease,
Happy that we find no day of spring
So pleasant as such summer days as these.

Not since the Ancients passed this way
Has any day surpassed this day!

"MUSHIMARO COLLECTION," IX, 1738–9.

◆§ NINETY-NINE §◆

O cuckoo bird, your nest
Was stolen from another
And so you never sing
As father or as mother.
But when the may-flower blooms

You utter your shrill cry
And now in orange blooms
Continually fly.
Since you're so sweet to hear,
Receive this prayer of ours:
Please live beside our house
Among our orange flowers!

Through rain and darkness
Now are heard
Soft crying
Of the cuckoo bird.

"MUSHIMARO COLLECTION," IX, 1755–6.

⤳§ ONE HUNDRED §⤳

Climbing Tsukuba peaks
To ease my troubled heart,
Traveling, with grass for pillow,
I watch the wild ducks dart
Among tall water-reeds
Which cool winds ripple white,
Bowing them in a dance
Flecked with autumn light.
Later, the distant views
Seen from the mountain's tower
Relieve the heavy weight
Of many a weary hour.

As gift for a young girl
Reaping the autumn sheaves
On my descent I bring
This spray of tinted leaves.

"MUSHIMARO COLLECTION," IX, 1757–8.

On Mount Tsukuba eagles nest
By Mohakitsu's fountain,
Where men and girls maintain a feast
Of poetry on the mountain.
I shall associate with wives
Of other men and they,
As the mountain god decrees,
With mine may sport and play.
This freedom is bestowed
From the first birth of time;
Let no man now object
Or think such deed a crime!

Upon the phallic peak
Concealing clouds abide.—
Drenched in autumn showers,
How can I leave its side?

"MUSHIMARO COLLECTION," IX, 1759–60.

ONE HUNDRED TWO

When on spring hills
The cherry-tree flashes,
See how the young girls
Gather herbs in white sashes!

OWARI. VIII, 1421.

ONE HUNDRED THREE

Many a lovely province lies
Under Yashima's bright skies,
Over which our Sovereign reigns,

A god himself, as heaven ordains,
But here, where mountain air is sweet
And where two rippling rivers meet,
Has been decreed, at his command,
The palace where he rules the land.
Porch and pillars, row on row,
Rise by Mount Yamashiro.
Sound of running streams comes clear,
Lofty mountains cluster near,
On whose brocaded sides are heard
Clamorous calls of many a bird.
Here, when autumn days elate
His breast, the stag cries to his mate,
While all the colored forest thrills
With echoes sounding through the hills,
Until revolving seasons bring
The fragrant, bending flowers of spring.
Ah noble site and field of bliss!
Well did our Sovereign, learning this,
Finding all auspices complete,
Erect here his imperial seat!

    It must be for the beauty of
    These pleasant fields which all men love
    That the Imperial House is here.
    Forever let its palace stand,
    Hallowed throughout our blessed land,
    While hills are high and streams are clear!

TANABÉ SAKIMARO COLLECTION. VI, 1050–2.

ONE HUNDRED FOUR

Beside the shore of the whale-haunted sea,
Near great beaches where men gather shells,
There stands the palace of our peaceful lord
Within clear hearing of the Ocean swells.
Their clamor is obstreperous at dawn
But in the evening calm I note instead

Rhythmic, gentle plashing of the oars
Of fishers, while I linger in my bed.
Then, with the ebbing of the ocean-tide,
Plovers woo their mates in soft refrains
While from the sand-banks by the reedy shore
Issue the melancholy cries of cranes.
Whoever sees this palace sings its praise;
Whoever hears of it must yearn to be
Himself in the fair Halls of Naniwa,
The great imperial castle by the sea.

To Naniwa's palace here
Our Lord comes without fail
While near its walls we watch
Young fisher-women sail.

TANABÉ SAKIMARO COLLECTION. VI, 1062–4.

⋖§ ONE HUNDRED FIVE §⋗

The favorite mooring-place for ocean ships,
Since the God of the Eight Thousand Spears
Determined it, has been Minumé Strait,
Yashima's harborage for countless years.
Its breakers clamor in the morning wind,
Its seaweeds waver in the evening breeze.
O clean beach of white sand, how I rejoice
To roam unwearied by your echoing seas!
Travelers have been recommended well
To walk in joy beside this cleanly shore;
So has it been since the primeval time
And so is it decreed forevermore.

Shining Minumé Strait,
Pure mirror of the sky,
Never will any ship
Unheeding pass you by!

Clean shore and lovely bay,
A thousand ships come to you
And so will ever come
Joyously to view you.

TANABÉ SAKIMARO COLLECTION. VI, 1065–7.

ᴥᑫ ONE HUNDRED SIX ᑫᴥ

This quilted silk from Tsukushi,
Land of volcanic fires,
Though I have never worn it,
Comfort and warmth inspires.

MANZEI. III, 336.

ᴥᑫ ONE HUNDRED SEVEN ᑫᴥ

Wait till the moon comes over the defile!
Dark and dangerous now for many a mile
The pathway stretches. Only wait, my dear,
That I may see you, even a little while!

ŌYAKEMÉ. IV, 709.

ᴥᑫ ONE HUNDRED EIGHT ᑫᴥ

I saw him but once,
In the pale moonlight;
But now in my dreams
Night after night.

ATO TOBIRA. IV, 710.

⊷§ ONE HUNDRED NINE ࣺࣻ

Wild ducks float on the pond,
Dead leaves drift from the trees;
But my constant heart
Shall never float as these.

TANIHA ŌMÉ. IV, 711.

⊷§ ONE HUNDRED TEN ࣺࣻ

Do not forget your Eastern girl
Whose thoughts on you rely
While she cuts hemp-stalks in her yard,
Spreading them out to dry.

ANON. IV, 521.

⊷§ ONE HUNDRED ELEVEN ࣺࣻ

Now that I am here
Where is my old home gone?
I have crossed high mountains,
Cloud-covered, blizzard-blown.

If life be kind to me
I shall see once more
White waves breaking
Over Ōtsu shore.

LORD ISONOKAMI AMD HOZUMI OYU. III, 287–8.

ᵛᵉᶳ ONE HUNDRED TWELVE ᵉ∾

When I behold the brightness of the snow
That hovers over heaven and every part
Of earth, I am reduced to utter silence:
Purest veneration fills my heart.

KI KIYOHITO. XVII, 3923.

ᵛᵉᶳ ONE HUNDRED THIRTEEN ᵉ∾

There is gratitude on every hand
This New Year's Day; all pious persons keep
The promise of a fruitful harvest time,
Because today fresh snow on earth lies deep.

FUJII MOROAI. XVII, 3925.

ᵛᵉᶳ ONE HUNDRED FOURTEEN ᵉ∾

In and outside the palace court
Dazzling bright snowdrifts lie,
Yet the delight of seeing them
Never fatigues the eye.

ŌTOMO YAKAMOCHI. XVII, 3926.

ᵛᵉᶳ ONE HUNDRED FIFTEEN ᵉ∾

When at dawn of spring
Plum-blossoms weigh like sleet,
Breaking their loaded boughs,
Our joy will be complete.

KI, THE SECRETARY. V, 815.

≈§ ONE HUNDRED SIXTEEN ≥∾

When the plum-blossoms fall
Passing us swiftly by,
Are they not truly snowflakes
Whirling from the sky?

ANON. V, 822.

≈§ ONE HUNDRED SEVENTEEN ≥∾

When plum-blossoms fall
In Spring's relentless race,
Are not cherry-blooms
Prepared to take their place?

SAKIKO. V, 829.

≈§ ONE HUNDRED EIGHTEEN ≥∾

Once a plum-blossom spoke to me
As in a dream I picked it up:
"I count myself a gallant flower,
So float me in your saké cup!"

TABITO. V, 852.

≈§ ONE HUNDRED NINETEEN ≥∾

I traversed Ocean's vast brocade
On which a hundred isles are wrought
But never for a single hour
Has Nara vanished from my thought.

ANON. XV, 3613.

ONE HUNDRED TWENTY

My true love sighs for me
As faithful love persists;
See, from the far-off shore
Float the trailing mists.

ANON. XV, 3615.

ONE HUNDRED TWENTY-ONE

While the moon lights the mountain-ridge,
On the horizon furtively
Flicker the lights of fishing-flares
Far out upon a dark, wide sea.

When we suppose we are alone
Steering our ships in darkest night,
We hear the splashing of the oars
Of fishermen far out of sight.

ANON. XV, 3648.

ONE HUNDRED TWENTY-
TWO

Fishing-flares are far away
Where adventurous vessels go;
Oh make them brighter that I may
Sight far-off Yamato!

ANON. XV, 3648.

~§ ONE HUNDRED TWENTY-THREE §~

I know my wife at home thinks much of me
For on the surface of my well-spring here,
When I stoop down to take a cooling draught,
The shadow of her pallid face is clear.

WAKAYAMATOBÉ MUMARO. XX, 4332.

~§ ONE HUNDRED TWENTY-FOUR §~

I never shall forget the words
My father and my mother said:
"Good fortune go with you, my son"—
Laying calm hands upon my head.

HASETSUKABE INAMARO. XX, 4346.

~§ ONE HUNDRED TWENTY-FIVE §~

I shall cross over the steep mountain road
At Ashigara without glancing back.
Where bravest men may even fear to stand
I shall ascend breathtaking Fuwa's track.
I shall press on as far as horse can carry,
No matter if the path be sleek or stern,
For at the farthest shrine I shall petition:
"May those I love keep well till I return."

SHIDORIBÉ KARAMARO. XX, 4372.

❧ ONE HUNDRED TWENTY-SIX²⁴ ❧

If sleeping in your clothes, the grass for pillow,
You travel and your sash-string tears, demand
No other help but taking out this needle
Use it as at home you used my hand.

KURAHSHIBÉ OTOMÉ. XX, 4420.

❧ ONE HUNDRED TWENTY-SEVEN ❧

Obedient to our mighty Sovereign's word,
I rowed my boat through waves and dashing foam
Of the Hatsusé River and at each
Of eighty bends I glanced back toward my home!
At length I came to Nara. From my couch
I saw in lucid moonlight before dawn
The river bound by ice as hard as rock
And earth as frosted as white linen-lawn.
Often on freezing nights I paddled down
The stream to labor with the loyal throng
Of workmen building our Lord's glorious palace
Where may he reign and may I linger long!

I shall come to Nara Palace
For many ages yet
In ghostly visitation;
Think not I shall forget!

ANON. I, 79–80.

❧ ONE HUNDRED TWENTY-EIGHT ❧

A deer that seeks to mate with hagi flowers
Brings forth one fawn; now it has come to pass
That my one fawn, my only son, starts forth
On travels where his pillow must be grass.

I, dressed in mulberry cloth and purified,
Place in my shrine a sacred jar of wine,
Begging the gods to turn propitious eyes
On this endangered, roving child of mine.

Where the traveler shelters
Upon the frost-sheathed plains,
Cover my darling with your wings,
O flock of sacred cranes!

ANON. IX, 1790–1.

✑§ ONE HUNDRED TWENTY-NINE ౾❧

After travel from the Capital
To lovely Nara, pearl of Yamato,
Down to the port of wave-bright Naniwa,
On a still longer journey you must go,
Even to the Empire of the Setting Sun.
Therefore I pray the gods to guard your ship,
Watching at bow, at stern, and either hand,
To be at every port your constant guard
And guide you safely home to your own land.

May breakers on the shore
And waves in open sea
Spare you and grant your ship
Home passage happily!

ANON. XIX, 4245–6.

✑§ ONE HUNDRED THIRTY ౾❧

The pool beneath the sacred Mount Asaka
Is shallow, though it holds its image true;
I hold your image in my heart, my Prince,
But yet no shallow love have I for you.

ANON. XVI, 3897.

✑ ONE HUNDRED THIRTY-ONE ✑

When I started out upon my travels,
As limitless and boundless as the sea,
That lovely girl asked when I should return,
That loving girl, always so true to me!

ANON. XVII. 3897.

✑ ONE HUNDRED THIRTY-TWO ✑

Over Heaven's River
I throw a bridge of stars;
Across its upper shallows
I row a stately barge.
Over its lower shallows,
Even though rain is falling,
Whether the breeze is hushed
Or whether winds are brawling,
That no obstruction hinders,
Or no moisture mars
My lover's skirt in coming,
I throw this bridge of stars.

Though mist hides Heaven's River,
My faith is firm and fast.
Surely today my lover's
Ship will cross at last!

ANON. IX, 1764–5.

✑ ONE HUNDRED THIRTY-THREE ✑

Up from the Plain of Kasuga
Smoke-wreaths rise in a ring.
Do young girls boil starworts
Plucked from fields of spring?

ANON. X, 1879.

ONE HUNDRED THIRTY-FOUR

On the blue, surging sea
No island lies
Yet in the heavens on high
White clouds arise.

ANON. VII, 1089.

ONE HUNDRED THIRTY-FIVE

Our peaceful Sovereign, offspring of the Sun,
Holds the demesne of Isé by the sea.
Above it breathes the Deity of Wind,
Within is food to feast him royally.
When we survey this realm, its rivers swift
And clear, its mountains lofty and sublime,
Its spacious sea, its goodly harborage,
We know it famous to the end of time.
Because he prized these things whose lofty praise
I scarcely dare to speak, the deed was done;
His palace stands upon the Isé plain
Bright as the rising or the setting sun.
As long as heaven and earth, or sun and moon,
Shall last, shall courtiers serve him, and his hall
Be prosperous as spring hills loaded with blooms
And brilliant as their colored slopes in fall.

Near where the sacred spring wells forth
Foundations for his hall were laid;
Above it towers the mountain wall
Hung with Autumn's rich brocade.

ANON. XIII, 3234–5.

ONE HUNDRED THIRTY-SEVEN [25]

Although it be the night of sacrifice
When no man stays indoors and women fear
To let men enter, do not think that I
Would keep you standing at the door, my dear!
O for a horse to run on silent feet
That I might ride unknown to sound or sight
Across the wooden bridge at Katsushika
And come to you, my dear, night after night!

ANON. XIV, 3386–7.

ONE HUNDRED THIRTY-EIGHT [26]

My mother watches me as though fierce guardsmen
On each side of a mountain pass were set;
But whatsoever watch be placed upon us,
We know, beloved, that our souls have met.

ANON. XIV, 3393.

ONE HUNDRED THIRTY-NINE

Although the new-made road to Shinanu
Is cut so smoothly that it seems pure glass,
Please guard the feet I love so much securely;
Put on your silken sandals as you pass.
If you should walk upon the snow-white beach
At Shinanu, wherever you might tread
I should grasp the precious sands in handfuls
Believing them not sand but gems instead.

ANON. XIV, 3399–400.

✑ ONE HUNDRED FORTY ✑

If I should spend the night with you, my dear,
Our loves would be as clear as the bright bow
That glistens in the snow-white waterfall
At Yasaka on the Ikaho.
   A second air-drawn likeness comes to me:
Though I should never fear, may the god spare
His thunders crashing on Ikaho Mountain
Lest it harm the one for whom I care!
Finally, capricious winds upon the mountain
Sometimes blow fiercely over all its range
And sometimes fade to breathless quietness;
Only my love for you can never change.

ANON. XIV, 3414–6.

✑ ONE HUNDRED FORTY-ONE ✑

Swift across the boundless plains
And where the river-crossings wind,
Scarce touching earth, as if on air,
I came; now, dearest, speak your mind!

ANON. XIV, 3425.

✑ ONE HUNDRED FORTY-TWO ✑

Listen; great bells are ringing
Their loud and glad refrains;
The young lord must be hasting
To hawk upon his plains.

ANON. XIV, 3438.

◄§ ONE HUNDRED FORTY-THREE §►

Do not burn golden bracken,
So lovely to behold;
Let new ferns grow at will,
The new among the old.

ANON. XIV, 3452.

◄§ ONE HUNDRED FORTY-FOUR §►

When on a night of frost and cold
Bamboo leaves are crashing in harsh weather
The body of my darling wife is far
Better than seven coats worn all together.

ANON. XX, 4425.

◄§ ONE HUNDRED FORTY-FIVE §►

SHE
Had I foreknown my lord would come
I and my servant girls
Had cleared our garden, rank with weeds,
And strewn our house with pearls.

HE
Why should I wish a house with pearls?
Why should I care what grew
Though garden weeds might hide the house?
Enough to be with you!

ANON. XI, 2824–5.

I do not wish to think of you, but when
I look above to where the green hill looms,
The azalea flowers are you, my lovely girl,
And you, my dear one, are the cherry blooms.
Our parents and our friends would make us one;
Even the rugged hills, it seems, combine
To join us two together; so then, dearest,
Myself shall keep your heart and you keep mine.

Always I pray the gods
To give my spirit peace,
But heaven and earth conspire
To make my love increase.

ANON. XIII, 3305–6.

This is the truth, my lover:
My childhood could not last;
Since my long hair was clipped
Full eight long years have passed.
Blooming like a fruit tree,
I am a secret stream
Running beneath earth's surface
And you my constant dream.

I, too, have prayed the gods
To make my childhood stay,
But time must take its course
And love will have its way.

ANON. XIII, 3307–8.

SHE

Other husbands ride while only you
Trudge on the road until your footsoles ache;
Every time I see you there, I weep;
When I think of it my heartstrings break.
My husband, take my mother's shining mirror,
Also this colored scarf I love to wear,
Thin as a dragon's wing; so buy a horse.
Remember, dear, you are my only care!

> The ford is deep; your traveling clothes will soon
> Be drenched before you reach its farther side.
> What good for me to have a shining mirror
> When you toil on foot while others ride?

HE

If I bought a horse, dear,
Then you would stagger on
Afoot among sharp rocks;
We two must walk as one.

ANON. XIII, 3314–7.

SHE

My dearest lord has traveled far to gather
Wave-worn pearls beside the shore of Ki.
Once I stood by the roadside in the evening,
To learn by charms of his return to me.
Then came the oracle: "Lady, your husband
Does not return because he gathers pearls
Laboriously upon the distant beaches
Where the wave crashes and white water swirls.
He says, 'Seven days will be the most to take me,
Or two the very least after I start
Upon my homeward journey; do not languish,
My dearest one, but wait with a good heart.'"

I'd go with staff or none
But can't discern
By which of many roads
He may return.

By many crooked ways,
Sad and footsore
I journey to my love,
Treading a stony shore.

He passed one night with me,
Then took the mountain track,
Leaving my door ajar:
When shall I have him back?

HE

Although my love no longer
Wait at her door in pain,
Since in the past she waited,
I shall be there again.

ANON. XIII, 3318–22.

✑ ONE HUNDRED FIFTY ✑

Terrible is the Ocean,
Breeding black despair,
Yet shall we not dare it,
Lifting hands in prayer?

ANON. VII, 1232.

✑ ONE HUNDRED FIFTY-ONE ✑

Boatman, the wind is strong, great waves are high,
And day is gone;
Shall we float here like timid water-fowl,
Or still press on?

ANON. VII, 1235.

ONE HUNDRED FIFTY-TWO

Come to me, my dearest,
Bending blinds of frail bamboo!
If my mother ask me,
I'll say the night-wind blew.

ANON. XI, 2364.

ONE HUNDRED FIFTY-THREE

The sea is full of wonders. It may boast
The Island of Awaji as his crown.
He girdles Iyo Island with white waves
And if at dawn he leads his waters down
At sunset hour he guides his waters back.
We in port by night hear breakers brawl
Against the outer bar and wait for day,
Noting as undertone the waterfall
On the Asanu River, where the pheasants
Cry as the first beams of the sun increase.
Come, men, let us row out with a good will,
Now that the seas are calm and winds at peace!

Now that we have passed the rugged Cape
Of Minumé, where the fierce storm-winds blow,
And the wild cranes are calling us, I long
For the far-off port of Yamato.

ANON. III, 388–9.

ONE HUNDRED FIFTY-FOUR

As silently across the field of heaven
Marches the night,
I see the pebbles clearly through the water
Whenever moons are bright.

ANON. VII, 1082.

ONE HUNDRED FIFTY-FIVE

Let no rain fall to drench me, for I wear
Beneath my vest
The keepsakes that the girl has given me
Whom I like best.

ANON. VII, 1091.

ONE HUNDRED FIFTY-SIX

All through the fields
Grows the tall grass
On my way to my love:
Bow down as I pass!

ANON. VII, 1121.

ONE HUNDRED FIFTY-SEVEN

Like sails of fishing boats
Are the white waves that roar,
Rearing high and crashing
Against the Tomo shore.

ANON. VII, 1182.

ONE HUNDRED FIFTY-EIGHT

I know that by the mountain's jagged crest
The ship-like crescent of the moon must shine,
But here we revelers see it afloat
Mirrored in our uplifted cups of wine.

ANON. VII, 1295.

ONE HUNDRED FIFTY-NINE

There must be a white pearl beneath the sea,
Smooth and lustrous as the bright moonshine.
Although the gales blow and the waves run high,
I shall not rest till I have made it mine.

ANON. VII, 1317.

ONE HUNDRED SIXTY

How fortunate is he
And how should he rejoice
Who till his hair is gray
Can hear his wife's soft voice.

ANON. VII, 1411.

ONE HUNDRED SIXTY-ONE

When the spring mist drifts
Through willows by the creek
The warbler gayly sings,
A twig within his beak.

ANON. X, 1821.

ONE HUNDRED SIXTY-TWO

When spring comes the swallow,
Brushing frail bamboo tops
With flashing wing and tail,
Whistles and never stops.

ANON. X, 1803.

❧ ONE HUNDRED SIXTY-THREE ❧

Fluttering from plum-tree branch to branch
A warbler's singing there,
As white upon his wings keeps falling
Fresh snow through the air.

ANON. X, 1840.

❧ ONE HUNDRED SIXTY-FOUR ❧

Although your season has not passed,
Why, cherry flowers, do you alight
Upon the earth? Is it because
Our pleasure now has passed its height?

ANON. X, 1855.

❧ ONE HUNDRED SIXTY-FIVE ❧

When winter goes and spring comes, a new year
And month arrive, but a man's fire grows cold.
Mere things are best when new; yet it may be
Men are not truly good till they are old.

ANON. X, 1884–5.

❧ ONE HUNDRED SIXTY-SIX ❧

Could merely a spring rain have thoroughly soaked you
Though really only a slight shower fell?
If drenching storms should come for seven days
Would you not stay for seven nights as well?

ANON. X, 1917.

⊰ ONE HUNDRED SIXTY-SEVEN ⊱

Love thoughts come thick and lush
As grass upon the plain,
Which soon as cut and raked
Grows strong and wild again.

ANON. X, 1984.

⊰ ONE HUNDRED SIXTY-EIGHT ⊱

It may be that you like me not, though this
Makes my life hard.
Then why not come to see my orange tree
Blooming in my door-yard?

ANON. X, 1990.

⊰ ONE HUNDRED SIXTY-NINE [27] ⊱

Raindrops which tonight the wind and clouds
Down from the sky have driven
May possibly fall from the Oxherd's oars
Rowing his boat in Heaven.

ANON. X, 2052.

⊰ ONE HUNDRED SEVENTY ⊱

Tonight the Oxherd longing for his love
Makes annual crossing of the Heavenly River.
He can see her only once a year
And such is their hard destiny forever,
Just as it has been from the first of time.

But tonight, when autumn winds are high,
His gay red boat, trimmed with a thousand flags,
Propelled by many oars, will cross the sky.
Tonight, the seventh of the seventh moon,
He will embrace his love and gain his goal.
Lone star-man buffeting your starry river,
How your adventure overwhelms my soul!

This is the night celestial lovers meet
To undo in highest heaven for one another
Those girdles fashioned of the flashing stars
With joy incomparable to any other.

I think of the gay river-quay
To which he makes his vessel fast,
The Oxherd crossing Heaven's Stream,
Mooring his little boat at last.

ANON. X, 2089–91.

✎§ ONE HUNDRED SEVENTY-ONE ₹✍

Bright with new snow in blossom-time,
Next green in summer's shawl,
Then robed in dappled crimson,
O gorgeous hills of fall!

ANON. X, 2177.

✎§ ONE HUNDRED SEVENTY-TWO ₹✍

Do not go away, my dear,
In the cold night, so late!
See, frost has bent the stalks
Of bamboo with its freight.

ANON. X, 2336.

⊰§ ONE HUNDRED SEVENTY-THREE §⊱

When I come to her waiting
After a long while
She always beams upon me.—
I hasten to that smile.

ANON. XI, 2526.

⊰§ ONE HUNDRED SEVENTY-FOUR §⊱

When I come to her suddenly
She glows with her surprise;
Her eyebrows' gesture lingers
In my delighted eyes.

ANON. XI, 2546.

⊰§ ONE HUNDRED SEVENTY-FIVE §⊱

I shall not comb my hair
This morning when I wake;
Your loving arm, my pillow,
Spares it for your sake.

ANON. XI, 2578.

⊰§ ONE HUNDRED SEVENTY-SIX §⊱

Standing or sitting, gladness overcomes me
Through love's supreme surprise;
Though I tread only on the common earth
My heart walks in the skies.

ANON. XII, 2887.

~§ ONE HUNDRED SEVENTY-SEVEN §~

Were the Itada bridge itself to crumble
I should come to you here
By leaping on the cross-beams that had fallen—
Do not be troubled, dear!

ANON. XI, 2644.

~§ ONE HUNDRED SEVENTY-EIGHT §~

I long for you as those unresting workmen
Who drag huge logs over the forest floor
In the vast timber-woodlands of Izumi
To build the palace for the Emperor.

ANON. XI, 2645.

~§ ONE HUNDRED SEVENTY-NINE §~

Reluctant as I am to pass her gate,
I have bound knots of grasses by her door.
Do not disturb these knots, O western wind,
For I shall come to see them there once more!

ANON. XII, 3056.

~§ ONE HUNDRED EIGHTY §~

Though I am scolded like a thievish horse
That crops ripe barley grown across a fence,
It is predestined I must always love;
My thoughts of you cannot be driven hence.

ANON. XII, 3096.

ᥱ ONE HUNDRED EIGHTY-ONE ᕹ

In the stream's upper courses women wash
The tender herbs that, floating from above,
Descend into the valley; would I were
A leaf to reach the shallows near my love!

ANON. XI, 2838.

ᥱ ONE HUNDRED EIGHTY-TWO ᕹ

Fierce Autumn has arrived with clouded skies;
Thunder rolls; rain falls; and wild geese call.
Rising beside the dykes and hedge-bound fields
Elm trees are dappled by the tints of fall.
Then, with my tiny wrist-bells ringing clear,
I, a woman, delicately bred,
Stand on tip-toe breaking off the sprays
And hasten home to place them on your head.

I grieved for yellow leaves
Lonely upon their bough
And so broke some off
To place upon your brow.

ANON. XIII, 322304.

ᥱ ONE HUNDRED EIGHTY-THREE ᕹ

It is as men have told from mouth to mouth
Since the ten million gods lit on our lands—
These rice-abounding, green and fertile plains—
To quell the demons with their lusty hands.
Mount Mimoro is misted in the spring;
In autumn cold the maple leaves are red;
No mosses stain the rocky ledge that borders
Mad waters in the encircling river-bed.
And till these rocks in the fierce-flowing torrent

Gather green moss, may happiness be mine!
O let me in my dreams perceive the Way,
My God, who are a sword closed in a shrine!

Till mosses green the trunk
Of the most sacred tree
May this earnest prayer
Never part from me!

When the priest lifts his wand
To offer sacred wine,
How radiant on his brow
Glistens the berried vine!

ANON. XIII, 3227–9.

ONE HUNDRED EIGHTY-FOUR

Swinging my ax I built
A raft beside the shores
Of the swift Yoshinu,
Carving a pair of oars.
My wood was cypress wood
Upon the Mount of Niu,
My ax both sharp and bright,
Its cutting clean and true.
Then I rowed swiftly past
White beach and beetling rock,
Rejoicing in the spray,
Delighting in the shock
Of water as it dashed
Against the well-drenched shore
Or in the lusty voice
Of the great rapid's roar.

Roaring above the rapids
Rears the lashing spray:
I will show my wife
The same another day.

ANON. XII, 3232–3.

᭜ ONE HUNDRED EIGHTY-FIVE ᭥

The people in the village
Never cease to draw
Water from their spring,
Limpid, cool and pure.
The more they draw and drink,
The more their joys increase,
Just as I love you, lady,
With love that cannot cease.

ANON. XII, 3260–1.

᭜ ONE HUNDRED EIGHTY-SIX ᭥

My mother would have said: "What sort of girl
Is this you go each summer day to meet,
Crossing the length of the Miyaké Plain,
Treading its dew-drenched grass in your bare feet?"
"But mother," I would say, "you do not know her
And father has no slightest notion of
The boxwood comb, the fluttering sleeves, the hair,
Black as a snail, of this dear girl I love."

I never told my parents
Of her I seek to gain,
Pushing through summer grass
Green on Miyaké's plain.

ANON. XIII, 3295–6

Atsumori

⊷§ On Kyushu, the southernmost island of Japan, rice-growing farmers in a remote village annually perform a type of drama, the kōwaka, descended from medieval times and elsewhere unknown today as a performing art. References to plays so designated indicate that the species may have had its origins as early as the fourteenth century, but no manuscripts or printed books definitely establish the form until two centuries thereafter. Extensive collections have been published in Japan from time to time during the last two hundred years. Their literary or poetic value has been acknowledged by a handful of scholars, but even in their own country they have received relatively little attention and no substantial study appeared in any Western language until J. T. Araki's eminently notable work The Ballad-Drama of Medieval Japan in 1964. They must now be acknowledged a conspicuous ornament to Japanese poetry and one of the most important finds uncovered by modern scholarship in recent years. The plays are in many respects comparable to the great Noh drama. They occupy a fascinatingly ambiguous position between mature drama as a theatrical art and poetic recitation.

The presentation as seen on Kyushu is indeed frugal in terms of theatrical art, though impressive ceremony and decorum are introduced. The stage is approximately that of the Noh drama, but simpler. The participants are seen on a small bare platform, approximately square, to which an open passageway affords entrance. Music is continuous but confined to the barest accompaniment. There is no equivalent to the Noh chorus. There are three actors, if actors they may be called, who deal in very little that can be conceived as impersonation. All appear in elegant dress of a style that today recalls a bygone age. The leading figure performs a stately dance while reciting the major parts of the text, aided, however, by his two companions. The general manner may be described as a chant, at times rising to a unique form of singing and at times sinking into merely elevated recitation. The stories are as a rule taken from the heroic or epic narratives of the Japanese feudal age, although a small number are diverted to mythological themes or to the fantasies of folklore. Both prose and verse are used, though the poetic spirit incontestably prevails throughout. Many of the plays rely strongly on religious sentiment, especially upon Japanese cults of Buddhism. The performance is highly serious, closer, perhaps, to ritual than to acting as usually understood.

The play rendered here in English verse, Atsumori, most clearly illustrates several of the foregoing observations, especially the relation between the kōwaka and the Noh. Like the Noh plays, it deals with a traumatic experience, the conversion of a high-minded but worldly man from his worldly life to a life of religious blessedness. As in the Noh, violence is resolved into peace. Also as in the Noh and, to be sure, in other important forms of Japanese classical drama, it contains an imagined journey, poetically described. But there is more recitation than elsewhere, a firmer line of narrative poetry and less action or miming, less music, and less dancing. One of the most famous and beautiful Noh plays bears the same name, has the same major characters and incidents, but presents the subject in a more symbolic manner. The structure of the Noh play on Atsumori is more lyrical and less narrative. Although by no means more religious than the kōwaka, it makes more use of the supernatural.

Both plays are based on stories of a quasi-historical nature recounting the strife between two factions in feudal Japan, the Heike and Genji clans. The episode chosen relates to the latter part of the struggle, when the Genji in a surprise attack at dawn on the temporary Heike capital at Ichinotani force their rivals to take to their ships in flight. Atsumori, a young Heike warrior, is about to leave with his comrades when he observes that he has forgotten to take with him his flute, the most valued of his family treasures. During the interval of his return to the camp to recover the precious instrument, the Heike hurridly embark in their ships, leaving him isolated in the face of his foes. The veteran Genji warrior, Kumagae, overtakes him and challenges him to combat. The young man is readily defeated. On removing his helmet, the older sees him to be a noble youth of extraordinary beauty. He virtually falls in love with him. Nevertheless, his obligation to his own faction compels him to kill Atsumori, though only after he has promised to pray devoutly for the salvation of Atsumori's soul. He is so profoundly moved by this event that he eventually renounces his military career and becomes a Buddhist monk. He courteously sends Atsumori's body, still vested in its gorgeous armor, to the Heike camp. Later he takes down Atsumori's head from a pole where it has been rudely displayed in triumph, piously burns it, and, with the ashes in a bag about his shoulders, travels to one of the most famous of the Buddhist shrines, where he deposits them with the appropriate prayers.

Like the typical Noh drama, this play is in two parts, Part One is devoted to the militant scenes at Ichinotani, Part Two to the moving and pathetic incidents that follow. Incidentally, as in the instance of the hero in a typical Noh drama, there is a symbolic change in Kumagae's costume. In Part One he is seen clad as a feudal lord and leader on the field of battle, in Part Two in the dark and sober cloak of an ascetic priest.

The irony of this story is clearer in the kōwaka play than in its comparable Noh play, where a maximum of meaning is left to be inferred. Kumagae's attitude toward the war is suspected from the very beginning. It is further significant that the epic narrative on which both plays are based is considerably more ample and explicit. That Kumagae and Atsumori, for example, have family ties was certainly understood by the audience that first witnessed the performances but is left unstated. Asian art and poetry, to venture a familiar phrase in Western criticism, at all times leave much to the imagination.

This play is chosen for the present collection as affording a representative specimen of Japanese imagination in the fields of both poetry and drama. As in India, so in Japan, the very finest poetry is found in works for the stage. The kōwaka form is more readily accessible to readers, and especially to Western readers, than the Noh or the kabuki plays, the two other most widely recognized types of Japanese theater. A translation of the Noh drama on Atsumori may be found on the first pages of Arthur Waley's selections from the Noh. An eloquent prose rendering of the kōwaka play, to which the version given here is deeply indebted, is in Araki's book The Ballad-Drama of Medieval Japan, where a discerning commentary on the form is to be read. The verse-rendering aims to stress the poetic and literary qualities of the work, those inferred from Araki's term "ballad-drama." No effort is made to elucidate the nuances of the theatrical production as it is still to be seen on the island of Kyushu. But Japanese poetry would indeed be ill represented in any collection that failed to include a specimen of it in dramatic form.

✍ CAST OF CHARACTERS ❧

KUMAGAE	A Genji warrior
A CAPTAIN	One of the Heike faction
KAGEKIO	A Heike warrior
ATSUMORI	A young Heike prince
YOSHITSUNE	Leader of the Genji faction
AN ESCORT	One of the Genji force
TAIRA NO MUNEMORI	The Heike leader
MOTOKUNI	A Heike warrior
TSUNEMORI	A Heike warrior, father of Atsumori
NARRATOR	

✍ TIME AND PLACE ❧

The principal scenes, sufficiently explained by the dialogue, are imagined successively as on the beach near Ichinotani, on the bay at Yashima, and on the Sacred Mountain, Kōya. The action takes place in medieval Japan.

The play is produced as a dance-drama with three dancers who, following strict formulae, intone the lines, aided by musicians. It may be and may have been successfully produced in other ways.

⟨Part One⟩

NARRATOR

On the fatal field of Ichinotani
Sixteen high commanders of the Heike
Were lost, among them, pitiful to tell,
Tsunemori's son, young Atsumori.

This nephew of the Nation's Guardian gave
Sad thoughts in contradiction to the brave
Bright garments that he wore, that nonetheless
Could neither shelter him from death nor save.

His undergarment yields a plum-flower's scent
From crimson silk on which an artist spent
Great skill in picturing gay autumn flowers,
Symbols of death ever too imminent.

Bright greaves, gold-fitted sword and rich design
On purple armor make his costume fine;
Sixteen red-feathered arrows serve a bow
Wound with close sinews of wisteria vine.

He takes a gleaming saddle overlaid
With lacquer specked with gold, on which a braid
With silver circles shines; then leaps upon
His horse to join the princely cavalcade.

Even the horse he sits on has an air
Of splendor, gaily dappled, dark and fair,
With coin-shaped splotches blue and gray. He rides
This charger proudly down the thoroughfare.—

The fight has now been lost; the grim pursuit
Begun; he sadly takes the shoreward route
Riding at the Emperor's side, but then
Discovers he has left behind his flute.

This is the precious flute that he has played
That night before the Heike were betrayed,
Whose peaceful notes quivered in fateful air,
Heard by the foes in their dark ambuscade.

Little the noble warrior realized
Fatal forgetfulness of such a prized
Though frail-wrought object could bring on the event
Too little feared, previsioned or surmised!

This transverse Chinese bamboo flute had been
A guarded treasure by his clan and kin.
He reasons loss of such an heirloom must
In a young courtier be accounted sin.

He rides back to retrieve it but when he
Returns, all the great ships have pushed to sea.
Ah piteous Atsumori! he is left,
Lost and alone! He lets his horse run free.

Just at this moment great Kumagae bore
Down on him on the grim, surf-beaten shore,
Kumagae, banner-head of the Shi clan,
Whose sword that day thousands had felt before.

Although he had led the charge, Kumagae thought
His earlier deeds of glory rose to nought,
Since he had nowhere met a worthy foe;
Conquests of commen men small glory brought.

Now this old warrior, brooding on the fight,
As one deprived of fame through fortune's spite,
Nurses his anger as he rides along,
Muttering to himself, disgruntled with his plight:

KUMAGAE

How would my sullen heart rebound,
My recovered spirits thrive,
Could I now meet a worthy foe,
Grapple, and take the man alive!—

You there, riding by the shore,
I judge a leader of a band
Of Heike warriors. Turn and fight,
And if in courtesy you demand

To ascertain your foeman's name,
Kumagae, the Shi prince, am I,
A worthy foe, I trust, to meet,
Even though one of us shall die!

Do not flee along this beach,
Showing me a craven lack
Of courage! I'll not strike your rear.
Turn about! Come back! Come back!

NARRATOR

Ah, in what a grim and piteous plight
Is Atsumori, overmastered quite!
Knowing Kumagae holds him in pursuit,
He urges on his horse in headlong flight.

Just at this moment, glancing toward the sea,
He spies a stately ship of the Heike,
Pulls from his waist a crimson-checkered fan
And waves it for relief frantically.

The captain of the vessel has descried
Young Atsumori's back, vainly supplied
With a cushioned guard to ward pursuers' darts,
And to Kagekiyo, that old warrior, cried:

CAPTAIN

What youth is this ashore who waves
Our vessel with his crimson fan?
Is it Yukimori, lord of horse,
Or Atsumori, that young man?

NARRATOR

Then Kagekiyo, that old chief removed
His giant helmet and with spear-hand grooved
Into the wave-washed gunwale, sadly stares
Upon the figure of a youth he loved.

KAGEKIYO

Ah, noble captain, there is no mistake
In this unhappy warrior that we see.
The armor that he wears, his horse's coat—
Pitiful Atsumori, it is he!

NARRATOR

The captain then issues a loud command
To draw the vessel closer to the land
For Atsumori's rescue, but the waves
Erupt too violently upon the strand.

For two days past the wind had blown a gale
With mounting waves too fierce for oar or sail;
Swells coil as serpents, foam appears as snow,
Sand blows, salt spray beats on the deck like hail.

Lesser boats in those vast swells are lost;
Efforts of the larger ships are crossed
To reach the shore, where they are all the more
Buffeted by waves and roughly tempest-tossed.

Seeing the vessel cannot come to him,
Wretched Atsumori tries to swim
His horse to it but the brave steed sinks down
Low in the waves, struggling for life and limb.

He rises high above the saddle-bow;
This haughty soldier is too young to know
That he might reach even that far-off ship
Should he only hold his body low.

Too brave but innocent, he thinks of course
Not to be separated from his horse
A point of honor; but the noble steed
Labors in vain under the breaker's force.

He grabs the horse's mane and rashly flouts
The billows, battered by their cuffs and clouts;
Kumagae sees their strongest efforts fail
And from the shore in high defiance shouts:

KUMAGAE
Foolhardly Heike, see the ship
Driven further by the undertow.
Come back, come back and let us fight!—
I fit a coarse shaft to my bow.

NARRATOR
When Atsumori marked Kumagae draw
A vulgar arrow to his bow and saw
What ignominy it were thus to be killed,
He turned, obedient to samurai law.

He pulls the reins, turning his steed around;
At last in shallows, the horse's hoofs strike ground;

He prances wildly, kicking storms of spray,
Gaining the headland with a lusty bound.

Then Atsumori places on his bow
A red-winged arrow of his own and so,
Now eager to engage his enemy,
Declaims a poem that all true warriors know:

ATSUMORI

When lifting the catalpa bow
To notch the shaft and draw it back,
Do you comprehend, my lord,
How to leave your bow-string slack?

NARRATOR

Kumagae, from no courtesy adverse,
Knowing how noble warriors converse,
Knocks aside the stirrups of his mount
And answers Atsumori with this verse:

KUMAGAE

Often in target-practice men
Fancying their shots have missed,
Hear their umpire call "a hit,"—
So let our arrows be dismissed.

NARRATOR

Atsumori throws his bow aside
To draw his sword. "Take this," Kumagae cried
And lightly parries Atsumori's stroke.
Now a long contest with their swords is tried.

But this in turn is inconclusive, so
Casting aside their swords, with blow on blow
They tug and grapple each about the neck,
Groveling fiercely on the ground below.

Though the young Atsumori's heart is bold,
He is no match at all for such an old
And seasoned warrior as Kumagae is,
Who easily brings him to relax his hold.

He tears his helmet off, flings it aside
And, wondering his resistance is so mild,

Looks downward at the piteous, youthful face
Of one scarcely more powerful than a child.

His face is lightly powdered, teeth dyed black,
Dark eyebrows thickly lined. There is no lack
Of courtly breeding; he is perhaps fifteen.—
Saddened at the sight, Kumagae's arm falls slack.

KUMAGAE

Who are you, my young courtier,
Child of what Heike known to fame?
Though breathing in great agony,
Tell me at least your princely name!

ATSUMORI

I know, Kumagae, you are praised
Alike in learning and in war.
Then why speak words that violate
All rules of the samurai lore? [1]

I am a high courtier, versed
In music and in poetry;
I was familiar with our lord
In time of his prosperity.

Now in three tempestuous years
Wherein our fortunes have expired,
I have learned the hero's code
And what of warriors is required.

I have learned that in the thick
Of battle, as their quivers came
Empty and sword-guards hacked, men paused,
Shouting their province and their name.

I have never heard it said
One fallen and pinioned by his foe,
As I am now, should tell his name,
Lying in agony below.

Kumagae, I perceive too well,
You wish me to reveal my name
Only that you may show my head
To Yoshitsune, for your fame.

All this is well and good and known,
Leaving upon your fame no blot.
Show it to your master, then;
He may know or may know it not.

If he does not, let it be shown
To his lordly elder brother;
And if he knows it not, in turn
Then display it to some other!

If none among your men can tell
Who I am, then show it to
The captives in your rebel camp;
Ask them, for they are not a few!

And if at last you find that none
Has ever known my face before,
Think me of no renown and throw
Me forth! Trouble yourself no more!

KUMAGAE

Young courtier, you know too well
The true samurai's battle code.
We are the sad ones of this world,
Bowed by our stern and cruel load.

In answering our lord's demands
Or furthering our own estate
We wrong our parents and our sons;
Such is the samurai's fate.

Guest for an hour among the flowers,
Friend for a night to view the moon,
A passing breeze, a cloudscape view:
All leaves and blossoms fall too soon.

Though many thousand soldiers fought
Upon this field of mortal strife,
That I, Kumagae, met you here,
Was ordered by some former life.

Accept your fate and speak your name!
Though I behead you, I shall pray

For your soul in the afterworld
And this I swear to you today!

ATSUMORI

I did not think to tell my name
But with this promise that you give
To pray for my departed soul
I'll speak my name here while I live.

Whom truly do you take me for?
Who do you think that I should be?
Know, then, that I am the third son
Of Kadowaki no Tsunemori.

The title of "Novitiate,"
Still is mine. I am Grandee
Atsumori, age sixteen,
Scion of noble ancestry.

Today is my first time in war,
Profession of the samurai.
This is all you need to know.—
Take my head quickly, Kumagae!

KUMAGAE

Then, courtier, you are direct heir
Of the Buddhist Emperor, Kammu.
So you are sixteen years of age!
My son is the same age as you.

This worthless son of mine is foul,
Dark-skinned and of a barbarous mind;
But when I think he is my own
I pity him and still am kind.

Ah, how remorseless I have been!
Today at dawn he came to harm.
An arrow from the enemy
Pierced him in the upper arm.

Then he turned to me and said:
"Pull the arrow out for me!"

I wished to ask him if the wound
Was slight or hurt him painfully.

I, as an archer of renown,
Dared not let friend or foe perceive
I should inquire so tenderly
Or in so small a matter grieve,

So I glared at him and replied:
"What an unworthy son you are!
If the wound be poisonous, pull
The arrow out and thrust it far

Into your belly and so die!
But if the wound be only slight,
Pull it out yourself and hunt
The foe to kill you in the fight.

Do not disgrace our family name!
This field's the pillow for your head.
Hunt death!" He gave one glance at me,
Then turned, well knowing what I said.

I do not know his fate since then.
But if I should be allowed
To live on, to go home, and meet
His mother there, gray-haired and bowed,

And tell her that her son was killed,
How she would grieve! Then how much more
Tsunemori must to learn
His fair child dead on this far shore!

NARRATOR

If the two wretched fathers' thoughts should be
Compared with common objects that we see
In nature, these would be the restless waves
Or tides that shift and moan incessantly.

In pity brave Kumagae looks again
At Atsumori lying there half-slain,
His hair as elegant as cicada wings
In fall, his eyebrows fluttering in pain

As faintly as the moon on distant hills.
Somehow the pale sight of him instills

In Kumagae memory of old poems
To which the soul of a great warrior thrills.

He thinks of Narihira who long years
Ago, when in deep love, brushed off the tears
That gathered on his hunting-shirt one night
Of snow and cold among rude mountaineers.

He sees the likeness of a painted face,
Shadowed with blue, possessed of every grace,
Garments of rich embroidery and brocade:
Beauty that no artist's brush could trace.

KUMAGAE

Though with this head I win a prize,
What profit can that prize afford?
How long would that head last, or I?
All passes. I shall spare this lord!—

Go, young man! Our fight is over.
Go, tell the Heike clan who won
Our duel! Say Kumagae spared you
Since you recalled his own dear son!

NARRATOR

He helps him to his feet, brushing away
Blood-stained sand on armor and array.
He lifts him tenderly upon his horse.
Now both men ride beside the ocean spray.

But they have scarcely gone beside that sea
A league or more before Iba, Mitsui,
Mekada, Mabuchi and many others
Appeared, with an ensuing company,

Grim commanders of the Genji force,
Riding there abreast, five hundred horse,
Flying the banner with the four-eyed crest,
Defiant in pursuit without remorse.

Kumagae looks over his saddle-bow
And gazing from the sea-washed shore below
Sees, watching from the hill-top, Yoshitsune
With Benkei and fierce generals row on row.

All knew Kumagae fought an enemy
Yet spared him. They suspect some treachery.
Next say it could be treason; and then vie
With one another to kill him instantly.

He is a bird for whom the snare is set,
A wretched fish caught in the barrier-net.
There is no possible escape, he thinks,
For either of them when so hard beset.

KUMAGAE

Young hero, rather than this vast
Band of our foes beyond control
Kill us, I shall with my own hand
Kill you and pray for your loved soul.

NARRATOR

He seizes Atsumori fast; he leaps
To earth with him; then with one blow he sweeps
The head from body, holds it up aloft.—
Although a demon, proud Kumagae weeps.—

Kumagae checks his tears.—On searching through
Folds of the dead man's garments brings to view
A transverse flute in classical design,
Artfully fashioned of Chinese bamboo.

Then on the steed-hand side he finds a scroll.
What can it be? He hastens to unroll
The silk. Ah, pitiful young Atsumori,
So brief his years, so great his joy and dole!

Its poems were written when this lord was still
A courtier near the throne. The Emperor's will
Was that each month a contest should be heard
Where the young lord might show his noble skill.

The councillor's daughter who was then thirteen,
Fairer in face and form than any queen,
Played the koto; Atsumori loved her
Even the very instant she was seen.

He sent her poems and letters for three days;
Then fate descended; they went separate ways,

She dwelling in the city rich with flowers,
He enslaved to war that wounds and slays.

He crossed the cruel seas. How sad was then
A heart that was the city's denizen
While by Ichinotani's lonely coast
He found the world no freer than a den.

Here he composed these songs amidst the crowd
Of soldiers, with his heart in sorrow bowed.—
Kumagae's tears fell on the sacred scroll,
Reading its tragic lines of verse aloud:

KUMAGAE
First comes spring dawn whose azure skies
Resound to the bush-warbler's trill,
Elegance permeates the wilds,
Flowing from his tiny bill.

Mist wraps the paths, yet perfume flows
From blossoms that no eye can see.
How exquisite in hue and form
Those unseen, fragrant blooms must be!

Then summer skies descend and light
Fronds of a wisteria vine.
A cuckoo calls. Nocturnal flames
Compel the insects to resign

Their wars to vex us; and as they
Unhappily are conscious of
The heat of these consuming flames,
So am I wounded by my love.

Autumn must then descend on us;
Many chrysanthemums, red or gold,
Orchids, asters. Forest deer
Call across the mountains cold.

Maples beside Tatsuta River
Are red; bush-clover comes to bloom.
The pensive cricket by my pillow
Murmurs through the twilight's gloom.

Last, winter evenings come and dark
Frozen nights, whitened with snow.
Even the stream must then be white
Where glistening water once would flow.

The path is white, with not a sign
Of footsteps in that lonely place.
That white itself, they say, must go,
Leaving behind no mark nor trace.—

Behind the tree-tops on the hill
I saw my homestead disappear;
Now by this moss-covered road
I lie at Ichinotani here.

I sleep forgotten, who was once
The youngest child of Tsunemori,
A youthful Grandee-Without-Post,
The faithful warrior, Atsumori.

NARRATOR
This Atsumori wrote, Kumagae read.
Giving his men the sad remains, he shed
Warm tears and now to the lord Yoshitsune
Carries the bamboo flute, the scroll, the head.

YOSHITSUNE
Kumagae, it is strange indeed,
This trophy that you hand to me!
The Saeda and Semiore flutes
Were Prince Takakura's property.

During the stress of war he gave
The latter flute to those steadfast
Monks of Buddha's shrine at Mii.
He kept the Saeda to the last.

When killed where Mount Kōmyō lies,
This flute passed to the Heike's hands.
They held a trial to decide
Who played it best in all their bands.

Then in that most rigorous trial
Prince Atsumori played the best;

Although the youngest of them all
Who came, he outshone all the rest.

Far music on a flute was played
Today before our armies stirred.
So it was he who in the palace
Played notes more rich then thought or word!

Whether we knew this youth or not,
Tears for such a one must flow;
Yet lord Kumagae acted well
In compassing his overthrow.

Go, my lord, and henceforth be
Lord of the keep at Musashi.
Hasten there, accepting this
Reward for your fidelity.

NARRATOR

So Yoshitsune speaks, but Kumagae
Receives new honors with a tragic sigh.
His henchmen are delighted but not he.
With the order given he cannot comply.

KUMAGAE

I strove for a samurai's fame
But now my battle-pride has ceased.
It is not now as once it was:
I'll wear the black robe of a priest.

I must not leave these sad remains
Of Atsumori on rough ground,
For horse-hoofs of the rioters
In Genji cavalry to pound.

Perhaps if I now rescue it
From lying here in alien dust
I shall be thought a traitor, yet
Bring it to his home we must!

I'll choose good soldiers, two or three,
Who, sailing in a swift, small boat,
Will take his limbs to Yashima
And with his body bring my note.

Part Two

The Heike fled from Ichinotani Bay
The second month, first year and seventh day
Of the most tragic time of Genryaku,
Then on the leeward waters took their way,

Leaping from isle to isle along that shore
Till eight days after their sad vessels bore
Full sail into the haven Yashima,
Arriving but a little time before

Kumagae's vessel draws into their ken.
And thereupon Kumagae's faithful men
Stop their vessel at a prudent distance,
Since these were deadly enemies till then.

ESCORT
We're sailing from the Genji's camp
With private words from Kumagae
Which we desire to lay before
Noble lord Motokuni's eye.

NARRATOR
Heike have fled from fatal Ichinotani,
Scurrying across a wide and hostile sea,
Yet the forces of the Genji clan
Seem to pursue them still relentlessly!

Their recent grief, travel by land and wave,
Life's uncertainties that haunt the brave,
Dreams broken by loud winds that sweep the pines
Have held their meditations dark and grave.

So much the more these warriors are forlorn
To hear the cry, "a Genji vessel," born
Across wild water; so they ply their oars
More fiercely, to escape the Genji's scorn.

Taira-no-Munemori sees their flight
Their senseless terror, their ignoble fright,

And, shamed at the indignity he sees,
Issues his command to them forthright:

TAIRA

How unbecoming is your fear!
Must Buddha's precepts pass away?
What peril from so small a craft?
Motokuni, go, hear what they say!

NARRATOR

Taira's reproof is instantly confessed.
Motokuni, hastening to his cabin, dressed
In his most gorgeous costume, reappears:
All white beneath under a dark-blue vest;

Arm-guards of peach, plum and arbutus hues;
Cape where lions and peonies interfuse;
Armor shining fresh, red-serpent scaled;
His great sword such as only princes use;

His sash of crimson grips his dagger tight;
Metallic rings about his legs shine bright;
Embroidered chin-bands fasten his tall hat;
His staff a halberd gleaming ivory-white.

MOTOKUNI

You say that from the Genji camp
You come with words from Kumagae,
Peaceful and private. What are these?
The lord you seek so far am I.

ESCORT

Young Atsumori at the hand
Of Kumagae has died and he
Thought best to send these arms to you.
Lift them aboard there speedily!

MOTOKUNI

How strange! I clearly understood
That death passed Atsumori by,
Taken by ship to Naruto!
Your report must be a lie!

You have good cause, my lord, to doubt
My story of that gallant youth,
But only peer into our ship!
Too quickly will you learn the truth!

NARRATOR

Now Motokuni fears that it is true
And brings his craft along for closer view.
Leaning on his halberd he discovers
What well his own foreboding spirit knew.

He sees bright greaves, a sword of strange design,
Purple armor, undergarments fine,
Red-feathered arrows eager for a bow
Wound close with sinews of wisteria vine.

There is no doubt what Motokuni sees!
There are no other arms or robes like these.
Throwing his staff away, he madly leaps
Upon the corpse in sorrow's ecstacies.

Tears will not come, although he longs to weep;
Cries will not come from any source so deep.
It is long till Motokuni speaks,
Faintly, as one roused from haunted sleep:

MOTOKUNI

How pitiful! I gave him this
Armor to protect his life
The day he sailed to Ichinotani,
There to lose all in feudal strife.

So like an adult he appeared
When he took the arms from me,
Saying that if the war's fierce gale
Would cease to vex life's tortured sea

He would reward me with some fief
From those his clan in plenty had
And that holding this estate
Would surely make my spirit glad.

Now I know things as they are.
O that ever it should be so!

I truly thought that you escaped
Safely by ship to Naruto.

How harsh and sudden is my pain!
How much deceived a heart can be!
O to hear you say again,
"Is that you, Motokuni?"

ESCORT

We are entrusted with a task
And may not let a moment slip.
Take up the ruinous remains
And place them in your captain's ship!

MOTOKUNI

Pardon! I have been lost in thought
And so in action much remiss.—
Lift the body in your arms!
When was a tragic day like this!

NARRATOR

Then with much lamentation they arose
Carrying out the body with its clothes
To where the father, Tsunemori, stands
Bringing the heavy journey to its close.

TSUNEMORI

How wrongly winds had given news
Of rescue, so that we inferred
With joy, he was in Naruto!
Now we see how much we erred!

NARRATOR

Now comes into the ship the Emperor's mother
With her imperial train and all those other
Hundred and sixty women of the court
Crying in grief their courage cannot smother.

They groan, "Is this reality or dream?
Is it true, or does it merely seem?"
So Buddha when he entered in Nirvana
Was mourned but held our world in no esteem.

It is only after a long stay
That Tsunemori's silence ebbs away.

Then with tears down-pouring from his eyes
These are the words he comes at length to say:

TSUNEMORI

When we were leaving our old home
You stood forlorn there, Atsumori!
Looking back and loath to leave
The fatal walls of Ichinotani.

Just to encourage you, I spoke
Harshly and said: "How wrong of you
To cling to your ancestral land,
Not giving life where death is due!

In battle-death your fame will rise
As clouds that leave the earth below.
You should be ashamed to let
Your loyal henchmen see you so!"

You came down to the water's edge
And finding you had left your flute
You scarcely seemed disturbed but went
Back to your house. I followed suit

But tumult separated us.
I was to see you nevermore!
Compassionate Kumagae sends
Your trophies to this far-off shore.

All such memorials are shells
Left vacant, spiritless and cold.
Tomorrow none will share my grief
Nor I shall ever be consoled.

NARRATOR

The moaning father writhes in his lament
While all the Heike warriors augment
His bitter cries until at length he asks
To hear the message lord Kumagae sent.

Tsunemori knows the warriors' code
By which he believes that Yoshitsune owed
A letter to him coming with the corpse
But such is not the address upon the fold.

The letter bears lord Taira's name and by
His oath the messenger, bound to comply,
Hands it to the Minister, who declaims it,
Kneels on the deck, holding the missive high:

MOTOKUNI
"I, Kumagae, write to you
In deep respect.—I met this lord
Thinking promptly to conclude
Our fight, as fortune might afford.

Then I suddenly forgot
He was a hateful enemy,
My daring and my martial skill
Vanished from me utterly.

I had offered him my aid,
When suddenly there came in view
From East and West a host of men:
There were too many, we too few.

Even the strongest warrior
May be reduced to helplessness
Unless the subtlest orator
Rescue him from that distress.

Unfortunately I was born
To life in war, with bow and horse,
Endless scurrying East and West,
Charging against a hostile force.

I gained more praise than I deserved;
Yet in this case won only grief:
On that day this young lord and I
Were yoked in bonds beyond relief.

If we might only be relieved
From that love contracted there,
If that friendship were dissolved,
We could be rescued from despair.

This only holds us both apart
In pain where nothing may atone

Till merciful Buddha places us
Together on one lotus throne.

I shall in time report to all
The place where I shall spend the whole
Span of my mortal life to pray
For the deliverance of his soul.

May the years to come support
This promise given today to you!
Proclaim this among all your clan!
Tell them, I swear these words are true!—

To the Minister of the esteemed
Lord Taira, this is my reply:
In Genryaku, the seventh day,
The second month: Lord Kumagae."

NARRATOR

Truly, all nobles of the Heike clan
Proclaim Kumagae a barbarian,
Or rather Naraka, the fiend of hell,
A torturing demon rather than a man!

But what compassion and what skill in prose!
What benignity of spirit flows
From his calligraphy! Hence a reply
From Tsunemori's personal hand now goes.

So to Kumagae's envoy is assigned
This letter which the Minister has signed,
Who, rowing back in haste to Ichinotani,
Gives it to Kumagae, as designed:

KUMAGAE

Without the fortune of the bow
I had never seen the hand
Of Tsunemori, lifted it
Aloft to read and understand:

"We have received the mortal limbs
Of Atsumori and some small
Remembrances; 'the town of flowers'
May now remain beyond recall!

The ephemeral world passes like mist;
Those who meet must quickly part;
In this defiled and transient place
There is no harbor for the heart.

Buddha Sakyamuni lost
Rāhula, his beloved son.
Seven days since Ichinotani's fall
I had not seen the much loved one.

Only swallows through the skies
Seemed prattling messages of him.
The wild geese flying wing to wing
Brought solemn words as day grew dim.

I could not hear his much-loved voice;
I searched the cruel skies in vain;
I threw myself upon the earth;
Still no words relieved my pain.

I prayed that Buddha look on me,
Petitioning the Radiant One.
After seven long days had passed
I found the deed of mercy done.

Within, my soul was cleared by faith
Although my eyes grew dim with tears.
Hence I have once again beheld
My son to calm my mortal fears.

Had I not praised the High Serene
Lord of all Felicities,
I had not in mercy reaped
Compensations such as these.

My gratitude to you is such
No utterance can repay; far too
Shallow would be the gray-green sea,
And low, snow-crested Sumeru:

The past were too remote; the years
To come too infinite for me
To treat details in this reply
To Kumagae at Musachi."

Kumagae reads these words while his remorse
Evokes the sacred and eternal force
Within him; now the Buddha wins the heart
And so he muses on his future course:

KUMAGAE

I hear we shall attack the foe
At Yashima on the sixteenth day
In Genryaku, this very month,
And that we leave without delay.

Now if I, Kumagae, go
Into the warring world again,
It follows that I shall once more
Experience the world of pain.

But since I now have grown aware
That all things in this vain life pass,
Even like moonlight on the waves
Or drops of dew on leaves or grass,

And that the praise of April flowers
Extols what first is swept away,
And men who praised the Autumn moon
Themselves have failed to live till day,

Can one of fifty years retire
From life's illusion with regret?
I'll win salvation by these thoughts,
Saving my soul. My mind is set!

NARRATOR

He hastened to the capital and stole
Atsumori's head high on a prison-pole
For all to see. In grief he carries it
To his house and there sings requiems for the soul.

He sees the head's cremation make a fleck
Of ash, soon cool and white without a speck;
Then gathers up this handful in a bag
Hanging it reverently about his neck.

KUMAGAE

To what use shall I put this bow
Which till the present nursed my pride
Only to conceal from men
That fraility has been my guide?

I'll cut it up into three parts
Having three stupas then in hand [2]
As timbers for a blessed bridge
To bring me into the Pure Land.[3]

NARRATOR

He leaves his palace, living on the crest
Of Eastern Mountain, where resides the blest
Priest Honen, founder of the Pure Land faith.
He cuts his hair, casting it toward the West;

He changes his proud name of Kumagae
To that of Renshobo, to signify
The soil from which the lotus comes to flower.
He studies arts that bless and purify.

KUMAGAE

In place of flowering sleeves I wear
Only a common, jet-black cloak
Such as we find in far-away
Hamlets worn by village folk.

I wear this cloak though it afford
No aid to spare me from my doom;
This is the being I've become
Through mad devotion. And for whom?

For one whose body fades away,
A tear of morning dew that wets
Fresh leaves, when spring winds bow the plants.
I suffer, yet have no regrets.

NARRATOR

Here Renshobo practices devotion,
But one day feels at heart a strong emotion
Urging him to view the sacred mountain
Of Kōya, distant as the farthest ocean.[4]

He bids his guardian-sage a short farewell;
He passes many a monastery, wherein dwell [5]
True devotees of Buddha, where each priest
Has within its walls his simple cell.

He sees the establishments of Seikanji,
Imakumano, Yasaka, Chōrakuji,
And at Kiyomizu, the most sacred shrine
Which the blest Emperor Saga caused to be.

Its architect was wise Sumitomo,
Its engineer, skilled Tamuramaro;
He prays to Buddha of the Thousand Arms:

KUMAGAE

May Atsumori's soul to heaven go!

NARRATOR

During the progress of his pilgrimage
He scans the ruins of those shrines which rage
Of fire destroyed, but at the Four Tombs cries:

KUMAGAE

Though years pass by, these only do not age.

NARRATOR

He views the Mutsuda River with its fair
Temples and cloisters and Yahata, where
The Imperial hunt is held; he meditates:

KUMAGAE

Let the old pheasants guard their young with care!

NARRATOR

He passes by Udono inns and sees
High fences densely worked from twigs of trees.
He worships the child-king at Kubotsu:

KUMAGAE

May the child I love enjoy your mysteries! [6]

NARRATOR

At Tennōji, the nearer to his goal,
He kneels beside the spring's clear-flowing bowl,
Then prays the Luminous Deity of Mount Kōya:

KUMAGAE

May your Sacred Mountain guard his soul!

NARRATOR

The venerated Mountain Kōya is
A hundred leagues from towns and villages;
Its eightfold summits rise symbolic of
The eightfold petals of blest lotuses.

Its vales fall to the depths; its cliffs soar high;
Among its lower woods the warm winds sigh;
The glow of evening, captured in these vales,
Falls as a benediction from the sky.

The temple-path to left is emblem for
Deities of the Realm of the Womb-Store; [7]
The temple-path to right serves thirty-seven
Gods in the Cloister Tower's Interior.

The principal deities of the Golden Hall,
Ratnasa, Aksobhya, Amitābha,[8] all
Were carved by the Great Teacher; the Main Tower
Is jewel-covered, a hundred cubits tall!

The Iron Tower is modeled on the sky
Of the Southern Heavens; its upper halls supply
A thousand images of Amitābha;
In the midmost tower-chamber lie

Twenty-eight followers of Avalokitesvara;
Then, in the lowest hall, sits bodhisattva [9]
Bhasisajyaguru with twelve emanations,
In whose blest hands all arts of healing are.

The multitude, even of those elsewhere
Fallen through sin into profound despair,
May here by these Three Buddhas be redeemed:

KUMAGAE

Ah, Marvelous Ones, I bow to You in prayer!

NARRATOR

Thence passing through the entrance-corridor,
Where buried in the sand an endless store

Of human bones are strewn, at last he lays
Atsumori's ashes on its floor.

Then in the Valley of Pale Lotus Flowers
He builds a hermitage with pleasant bowers
He calls Chishiki Cloister; he plucks blooms
Offered in reverence to celestial powers.

He cups spring-waters flowing from the side
Of the steep mountain-wall towering beside
His hermitage to give as sacrifice.—
There, at the age of eighty-three, he died.

Strong both in virtue and iniquity,
Famed for deep learning and high chivalry,
We know of no comparisons elsewhere,
But in our land, no hero such as he! [10]

The
Rigveda

The poets of India have maintained through the centuries a remarkable line of continuity. The Rigveda, most ancient of collections of Sanskrit hymns, dating from approximately 1,000 B.C., exhibits qualities still prominent in Indian poetry written today. The great antiquity of Indian epics, most impressively seen in the Mahābhārata, also helps to establish the Sanskrit as one of the oldest and most persistent of literary traditions.

This poetry is both religious and sensuous, strongly metaphysical, and frequently erotic. Above all, it is incomparably rich in symbol and metaphor, in the rhetoric of its much-elaborated imagery and profuse figures of speech. When placed beside it, most baroque poetry of Europe seems simple and limpid. There is a warmth of tropical emotion, an intoxication of spiritual idealism, a grandiloquence of expression that may well be distasteful to a Western reader until he becomes acclimatized to this unique idiom. Moreover, these qualities appear in virtually all forms of Indian poetry, whether epic, lyric, or dramatic. Such luxuriance in style is in some respects Elizabethan. The uninitiated reader is likely at first to see in it an excess of decoration, yet with a moderate degree of effort he may find that these impediments disappear and that its nobility and elegance gain his admiration.

Translation of such a literature obviously presents special difficulty. Only a few translations have been moderately successful and very few brilliantly so. Something like a triumph has recently been achieved by Daniel H. H. Ingalls in An Anthology of Sanskrit Court Poetry. For the even more remarkable poetry of Sanskrit drama, the happiest English rendering is possibly that of Sūdraka's The Little Clay Cart, in a prose translation by Revilo Pendleton Oliver.

The poems in the Rigveda are generally described as hymns. There are over a thousand. A few are charms. Many deal with rituals whose meanings are today open to considerable conjecture. Most bear witness to the luxuriant jungle that is Hindu mythology. The meaning of even the simplest poems is seldom perspicuous. But where a translation is even remotely loyal to the eloquence of its source, the presence of an inspired poetry should be evident.

So, too, is the basic meaning, even where the mythology, strictly considered, seems at best remote to us and at worst wholly foreign. A few extended treatises on the lore of the Rigveda exist, as that by A. B. Keith, but even among leading scholars much remains in the realm of doubtful speculation. The ordinary reader, whether in India or the West, is left in a virtual jungle, which he is on the whole indisposed to explore. The great poetic power still remaining in the hymns is all the more impressive since it indubitably exists, any gulf between the ancient and modern worlds notwithstanding. This is largely owing to the universal cogency of the images, the references to dawn, fire, night, the sun, water, vegetation, rain, lightning, and the elemental themes of life, death, human welfare, and misery. Unlike the Hebrew Psalms, the poems are never intimate nor personal. But they speak not only for one or another of the Aryan tribes invading India but for the human race as a whole. Their symbolic overtones, frequently sexual, are unmistakable. The hymns are poetry in its primal magnificence. Commentary can in fact add remarkably little to what a reasonably sensitive and imaginative reading is sure to yield. A few notes are given at the back of this book, chiefly describing the basic significance of the deities invoked. Such aids must remain, however, of minor value. Almost certainly the greatest Sanskrit poetry is that of the dramatists, as Bhāsa, Kālidāsa, Sūdraka, and Bhavabhūti. But the Sanskrit hymns still stand as a major contribution to the world's heritage in poetry.

ᜒᜈ DAWN [1] ᜒᜈ

The singers welcome you with gracious hymns,
Goddess of Morning, bringer of the light,
Sublime, by Law true to eternal Order,
Red-tinted, far-refulgent, shining bright.

Dawn comes with fairest face and form to make
Roads clear for travelers hastening on their way;
From her high chariot she commands all earth,
Ushering in the splendors of the day.

Her car is harnessed with two purple oxen;
She injures none, answering every call
For aid; this Goddess of perpetual riches
Enters with joy and is proclaimed by all.

She glows with changing tints and double glory
Eastward, and then, reflected in the west,
Her lustrous body gleams; she treads the path
Of perfect Order, which she knows the best.

The radiant child of heaven walks erect,
Conscious that her limbs are shining clear,
New-bathed in dew; she stands for all to see,
Driving away malignant grief and fear.

This daughter of the sky, like some chaste woman,
Bends her forehead down to the earth's floor,
This Virgin, granting boons to all who worship,
Having brought them blesséd day once more!

v, 80

ᜒᜈ THE FROGS [2] ᜒᜈ

As honest Brahmans who fulfill their vows
Through long dry months these sullen frogs remain
In silence but at last they burst in song
As Brahmans do to the great God of Rain.

For months their skins are dry as the parched pool
Upon whose bed they lie; but from a cloud
Fierce torrents fall; then the frogs' calls resound
As cows who low to calves, lusty and loud.

When on their thirsty throats these spring floods fall,
The time of loneliness and yearning done,
Frogs seek each other with ecstatic cries
As when a father greets a long-lost son.

Each receives the other with glad talk,
Reveling in the dampness and the wet;
The Green Frog and the Spotted Frog embrace
Lifting voices in a mad duet.

The endless repetition of their music
Is like a neophyte learning a song;
While their watery eloquence increases
Their very limbs seem to grow large and long.

One sect is green, another sect is mottled,
One moos like cattle and one bleats like goats;
They bear a common name yet their talk varies,
Modulating through distended throats.

Brahmans around their eucharistic vessel
Dispute the meaning of its sacrament;
Frogs assemble at their pool in springtime
Arguing their bliss with vast content.

Brahmans celebrate with pious unction
Their soma juice, lifting their chant together;
All sectarian frogs disport themselves
After roasting through the parching weather.

Those keep their god-appointed calendar
With rituals in grim determination;
These, when the blessed days of rain return,
Are free from bleaching and extreme vexation.

Cow-Bellow and Goat-Bleat are glorified;
Green Frog and Spotted are worth more than gold;
In their most rich and fertilizing season
Our herds are multiplied a thousand-fold.

VII, 103

In the beginning was the Golden Germ!
This Sovereign God and Lord of all Creation
Established and upheld the heavens and earth.
What god should we adore with our oblation?

Giver of vital breath, of power and vigor,
Whom all gods honor in his lofty station,
The Lord of Death, whose shadow is immortal!
What god should we adore with our oblation?

He with his grandeur has become sole ruler
Of all that breathes, in sorrow or elation;
He is both Lord of men and Lord of cattle.
What god shall we adore with our oblation?

His hands alone have reared the snowy mountains
And still uphold the world; his commands ration
The laws and boundaries of the sea and sky;
What god shall we adore with our oblation?

By him the heavens are strong and the earth steadfast;
His power decrees the fate of every nation;
The sea and heavens are strong by his decree.
What god shall we adore with our oblation?

It is by his will that two fierce armies
Combat at dawn, fired to extreme vexation;
When over them the self-same sun arises
What god shall we adore with our oblation?

Since the first rain-cloud came and from its germ
The god of flame burst forth in exaltation
And thence the gods themselves sprang into being,
What god shall we now serve with our oblation?

He first released the floods from which all things
In heaven or earth have flowed without cessation;
He is the God of Gods, none else but he;
Whom, then, shall we adore with our oblation?

Surely, he will not harm us from whose hand
All things have come in orderly gradation
As issuing from one river's primal source.
Which one shall we adore with our oblation?

Prajapáti! you who only rule
All things and who shall rule forevermore,
Who comprehend the longing of all hearts,
Grant our hearts' wishes in abundant store!

X, 121

◢§ THE MARUTS[4] §◣

Youthful Spirits, Maruts, angels of cloud and storm,
We glorify your cohorts thundering through the sky,
Riding on rapid chargers, Lords of life-giving showers,
Glittering band, whose windblown bracelets clang on high.

You ride on wings of lightning, as thunder echoes and roars;
You are the water-bringers, Oh, hasten to us again!
Our fires on our altars kindle to meet your fires above,
Descend, most youthful of sages, in fierce outpourings of rain!

Your auspices have raised our kings supreme in battle,
Whose armies on foot or in chariots rush like your water-courses;
You send our soldiers forth adorned in their glittering armor,
Fierce against every foe, mounted on gallant horses.

You leap forth higher and higher, Maruts, strong in glory,
Like spokes of rapid wheels whirling in blinding fires;
You are the mightiest sons of Prisni, greatest mother!
Firm in all intentions, ardent in all desires!

You hasten on with mottled deer to your chariots,
With rims of wheels heaven's god has hammered fast;
Waters are struck with madness; tallest woods are shattered;
The Red Steer of Thunder releases his vivid blast!

Earth herself has spread her thighs before your coming;
As husbands you enter her there in the rain and wet;
You have yoked the winds themselves to your wagon poles;
The hurricane itself is lashed with your streaming sweat!

Ho! Maruts! Heroes skilled in Law, immortal,
Be gracious to us here from overflowing fountains,
You, hearers of truth, you sage and youthful Spirits,
Resting upon green shoulders of your lofty mountains!

v, 58

❧ THE MARUTS ❧

When will you take us by both hands, as fathers
Clasp sons, the gods for whom blest grass is cut?
Why do you, Spirits, roam the skies, not earth?
In what glad pinfold are your cattle shut?

Where are your newest favors strewn and when,
Great Angels, will you end our miseries?
Why, gods of rain and lightning, do you hold
Secret all your high felicities?

If, Maruts, sons of Prisni, you were mortal
And we praised you with your immortal breath,
Your faithful servants would not then, as now,
Tread like wild beasts their loathsome road to death.

Do not allow the plague to strike us down
And let no drought wither our parching plain!
May these forever leave and in their stead,
Maruts, shower down from heaven windless rain!

Like cows the lightning lows and, mother-like,
The rains and thunder follow in their place;
Darkness descends in daytime from its cloud,
Laden with cool waters' healing grace.

Maruts, at your voice the whole world trembles
While all men shudder on the reeling ground.
Against the green banks of your swollen streams
The hoofbeats of your frantic steeds resound.

Rims of your flying chariot wheels, be strong,
Your horses, cars and reins all function well!
Our hymns, moreover, call the gods of fire
To cast upon us all your magic spell.

Form, singers, in your mouths the chant of praise,
Invoking in your song the rain-clouds thus!
Shout, laud and glory to the Marut host
And may the tuneful, Strong Ones, dwell with us!

I, 38

‌⊸§ DAWN §⊸

Greet us with favor, Daughter of the Sky,
Dawn, goddess of the light, rich, bounteous one!
Come with steeds and cattle, bringing wealth,
O Morning, rouse us with your joyful sun!

Your car awakens other chariots
Glorious by land and sea; our Kānva sings
With all his royal sons the lusty praise
Of heroes, wealth and gifts of liberal kings.

Like a good matron, Dawn herself appears
Rousing all life to action; birds are done
Brooding at rest; all creatures having feet
Gather to where her chariot hastens on.

Men and beasts all bend before her glance,
Excellent One, Daughter of Sky and Day,
Beaming felicity and solemn rites,
Chasing foes and enmity away.

From you each living being takes his breath,
Lady of Light, whose chariot flashes flame.
O Dawn, with strength itself so wonderful,
Your priests and worshipers extol your name!

Bring from the skies the gods to drink the juice
Of sacrifice, and, being what you are,
Grant health to steeds and cattle and decree
That heroes' fame may glitter from afar.

May Morning's rays grant riches which light toil
Amasses, such as sages of old time
Evoked; graciously hear our songs of praise
And answer us with bounty, bright, sublime!

Dawn, as you have opened heaven's doors
Today, grant us safe dwelling, food and kine,
Bring us abundant wealth, O splendid one!
You, plentiful, strong, radiant, divine!

I, 48

৺৪ SŪRYA, THE SUN GOD⁵ ৪৯

Your rays lift you aloft, all-seeing God,
First to appear on the horizon-rim;
Before your all-beholding, radiant eye
The stars slink off like thieves, faded and dim.

Your herald torch, refulgent from afar,
Lights all beings with its burning blaze;
Swift and all-beautiful, Lord Sūrya,
Sole illuminator of our days!

You stride forth with the host of heavenly gods,
Averting evil from all men on earth,
Measuring all things from your noon-day sky,
Bringing all living creatures to their birth.

Seven white steeds harnessed to your car
Bear you, great Sūrya, god of radiant hair!
Prime light, the god of gods, most excellent,
Conqueror of darkness, sovereign of the air!

Remove all callow sickness from my limbs;
To flowers and parrots give my yellow hue;
Your virile deity ascends the sky!
Grant that I owe my mastery to you!

I, 50

⤳ INDRA [6] ⤶

To the most liberal, lofty Lord of Wealth,
Indra, the strong, we bring our present hymn;
Bounty of waters pouring down a slope,
Spreading abroad, we owe alone to him.

All the world pours a libation out
Like ocean's flood, abundant, manifold,
To him whose thunder-cloud above the hill
Shatters in livid lightning, streaked with gold.

To the most terrible, exalted god,
Radiant as dawn, we bring our sacred rite,
Who moves in ardor with his flying steeds,
Indra, power of fierce, incarnate light!

To this all-seeing deity we belong
Who shelters every living thing from harm,
And as all creatures owe their lives to him,
To him we chant this sacramental psalm.

Lover of praise, we lift this hymn to you,
Only to you, bidding you hear our prayer;
To you our parent earth has bowed herself
And you have measured out the spacious air.

You own the thunder as your mighty weapon;
You send down floods to the land's parching floor;
Your bolt has shattered this broad, massive cloud;
You reign in earth and heaven forevermore!

I, 57

◆§ AGNI, GOD OF FIRE ⁷ §◆

The immortal Son of Strength is never faint;
He is the Herald of all sacrifice;
Striding the air, he greedily consumes
Oblations on our altars in a trice.

Through the dry wood his tireless spirit runs;
His back, when sprinkled, glistens as a horse.
He instantly devours his proper food;
He roars and shouts to heaven without remorse.

The god descends, granting his gifts to men;
With tongues for sickles and a mighty cry,
Impelled by wind and the dry wood, he fells
Whole mountains where their forests tower on high.

Like a black bull roaring among the herd
He roars among the trees, howling aloud
Much as his thunderbolts and lightnings rage
Against a dark and heavy-laden cloud.

Both fixed and moving things, living and dead,
His bare teeth grind. All priests delight to bring
His service to their sacrificial fires
Where seven-fold tongues leap at their offering.

Grant, Son of Strength, your aid, as sure as iron
To those who love you; give a present boon:
Bright, bounteous Lord, the singers' chief delight,
Preserve us, Agni, and befriend us soon!

I, 58

⊸§ AGNI §⊷

Like the sun's glare, like varied wealth,
Like life-breath, like one's own son,
Like a swift bird, like a milch cow,
Like pure flame, his work is done.

Though he burn the wood, he is home's safety,
Like ripe corn, famed among folk;
Like a chanting seer, like a conquering hero,
Like a friendly steed, like a firm yoke.

Caring for people, like a dame at home,
Flaming insatiate, like eternal might,
Shining brightly, like a polished car,
Gold-bedecked, thundering to fight.

Like a keen dagger, he strikes with terror,
Like an archer's arrow or a flaming sword,
Master of present and of future life,
Like a maiden's lover or a matron's lord.

All ways lead to him: we reach his rest
As cows at evening to their homes are driven;
He flames beneath as the floods swell
Or darts his rays to the peak of heaven.

I, 66

⊸§ AGNI §⊷

Victor of the forest, friend of man,
Ever he claims obedience as king,
Gracious as peace, blessed as mental power,
Priest who receives the gifts his servants bring.

Crouched in a cavern, he strikes gods with fear,
Bearing in his hand his potent light;
Men blessed with understanding find him there
And offer prayers there to his manly might.

Undying Sun, he rules both earth and sky,
Agni, guard of spots the cattle love;
Life of all, he strides from lair to lair,
Through land and water and the sky above.

All who know him, meeting him aright,
Performing sacrifice, obtain great wealth.
He is the nest of life in herbs and man,
To mothers and to sages perfect health.

I, 67

ᘓ DAWN ᘚ

The Dawn has come, the fairest form of radiance,
Our brilliant and expansive Day is born;
Night has left us for the Sun's emergence,
Yielding up a birthplace to the Morn.

The Bright, the Fair, has come with her white offspring,
The Black One has resigned her dwelling-place;
Immortal Sisters, following each other,
Both move with changing hue and altered face.

Familiar, endless are these Sisters' pathways,
Taught by the Gods, alternately they move;
Formed fair, of various tints but single-hearted,
Night and Dawn neither clash nor stay, but love.

Our eyes behold the leader of glad music
Whose splendid colors have unclosed the portal;
Stirring up the world, she leads to riches;
Dawn has aroused all creatures who are mortal.

Rich Dawn has set afoot the coiled-up sleeper,
This one to pleasure, that to prayer or wealth,
One to know little not beneath his nostril;
Dawn wakes all creatures to new life and health.

We see her here, manifest Child of Heaven,
Girl-like, blushing at her morning dressing,
Our Sovereign Lady Dawn herself appears
Modest, auspicious, granting us her blessing.

She is the first of endless dawns to come,
The last of countless mornings that have been,
That decorously usher in the living
But wake no dead, for these are not their kin.

Since you, Dawn, cause Divine Fire to be kindled
And through the Sun's eye have revealed creation,
Inciting men to offer pious worship,
You have performed your sacred obligation.

How long, how long they follow in procession,
Dawns that have been and future dawns, like brothers;
She yearns for former dawns with serious longing
But steps forth shining gladly with the others.

All men are gone who in the earlier seasons
Looked on a sunrise and an earlier morn;
We, who are living now, perceive her brightness;
Others soon follow who are still unborn.

Daughter of Law, foe-chaser, Order's guardian,
Joy-giver, tutor to all pleasant voices,
You bring delicious food for gods' enjoyment
And are the first in whom man's soul rejoices.

From the Eternal Sessions Dawn has risen,
To glitter brightly on the present day,
She will shine for mornings long hereafter
With strength that shall not slacken or decay.

On the horizon she has walked in splendor;
The goddess has thrown off her veil of darkness,
Astonishing the world with purple horses,
And with the glory of her naked starkness,

Bringing with her life-sustaining blessings,
Lustrous herself and freeing light from prison,
Last of innumerable mornings vanished,
First of bright dawns that come, she has arisen.

Arise! the breath of life again has reached us!
The shades have fled afar at light's persistence.
She has shown the Sun his path to travel
And we arrived where men explore existence.

Singing the praises of reflugent mornings,
With his hymn's web, the priest and poet arises.
Shine, then, today, goddess, on those who hymn you,
Granting the gift of sons, that each man prizes.

Dawn, pregnant, giving sons and kine and horses,
Glows upon the man who brings oblations.
Now let the priest and poet be well rewarded
Whose voice is loud as the wind's protestations!

Mother of gods, Āditi, child of glory,
Ensign of sacrifice, shine out exalted!
Rise up, bestowing grace on our devotions
And make the progress of our land unhalted!

Whatever store of wealth the Dawn possesses
To bless the man by whom her praise is given
Now be it granted by the hierarchy
Of Earth, Sky, Sun, Stars, Light and Hosts of Heaven!

I, 113

DAWN

The rising Sun with the refulgent Dawn
Appears in heaven. While a rosy red
Covers the sky and sacrificial fires
Are lit, out steps each man and quadruped.

Great God guides all; and yet the bright Dawn serves
The least one's need no less than heaven's decree;
The last of endless Dawns and first of those
To come emerges for all men to see.

There in the Eastern regions of her sphere
See Heaven's Daughter, clad in robes of light!
Truly, she knows the path of sacred Order,
Measuring the quarters of her arc aright.

The Bright One steps down to us and as if
A young street-singer opens up her breast.
Naturally as a household fly she comes
Or faithful wife to terminate our rest.

Look! In the east half of the watery region,
With ensign of the Mother of Cows unfurled,
She fills the laps of Earth and Sky, her parents,
Showering incessant favors on our world.

Her pride is in her pure and spotless form;
She knows no rich or poor, no low or high;
No one is stranger to her, none her kin;
Her vision vast and boundless as the sky.

Mounting her car as though to gather riches,
Dawn views mankind as if she had no brothers;
Smiling, richly attired, she shows her beauty
As a good wife to her husband and no other.

Night, her elder Sister, looks on her
And, having seen, resigns her citadel;
Thereupon Dawn enters, decked with sunbeams,
As women going to a festival.

All earlier Sisters of the Dawn have vanished;
Each day another Sister enters thus;
So, as in former days of happy fortune,
May Dawn with riches ever shine for us!

Come, Dawn, arouse for us all liberal givers,
Leaving all niggard souls in deepest rest;
Shine, wealthy ones, on us who pay her honor—
On us, her priests and poets, who serve Dawn best.

This young girl from the East has shone upon us,
Her car harnessed with oxen, red and chrome;
The splendor of new day rushes upon us;
Hearth-fires now are lit in every home.

Wise men stay indoors to eat their breakfast;
Wild birds leave their nest in search of food;
Dawn is gracious to all liberal persons
Who rest in pious homes and find it good.

My prayers honor those who should be lauded;
Our wealth is magnified by Dawns that love us;
Great Goddesses, may we deserve your favors
A thousand-fold, praising the Powers above us!

I, 124

ᴥ§ MARUTS §ᴥ

I come to you with fervent adoration,
Laying my prayer before the Strong Ones' path,
And if my pious hymn attains your favor,
Unyoke your horses, mollify your wrath!

Maruts, to you out of a contrite heart
Our prayers and our petitions have been given;
Come to us, who rejoice in your support,
For you alone present our prayers to heaven!

You, Maruts, whom we praise, should grant us grace
Saving us from forces dire and vicious,
That all our sequent days to come hereafter
May be triumphant, happy and propitious.

We fled in terror from the might of Indra;
Oblations meant for you we could not give.
But we who set these offerings aside
Turn now to you to shield us and forgive.

Indra, by whom the spirits know their dawnings
And to whose strength the endless mornings belong,
Favor us and the Maruts with your glory!
May we reconcile you by our song!

Indra, we pray you, guard our conquering heroes
And spare the Maruts from your indignation—
Those wise, victorious and gracious angels—
And grant rich food and honor to our nation!

I, 171

₰ AGNI ₰

Agni, accept this flaming brand,
This waiting with my prayer on you!
Hear kindly where this song is due!

Let us praise you with a hymn,
Seeker of horses, Son of Power,
Born in an auspicious hour.

Wealth-lover, giver of our wealth,
Song-lover, you to whom our song
Is sung devoutly, loud and long,

Be a liberal Prince to us;
Grant us your precious gifts today,
Driving our enemies away!

Being as you are, pour rain from heaven;
No man or plant resists the rain;
Give food again and yet again!

Whoever lauds you, asking help,
Herald of Gods, hearing his hymn
Most youthful one, come near to him!

Between divinities and men
Your friendly footsteps, Agni, wind,
A genial envoy to mankind.

Befriend us, for you know us all,
Laud the deities as you pass,
Yet sit down on our sacred grass!

II, 6

✧§ INDRA §✧

He who, just born, is the chief god,
By lofty spirit, power and might
Protector of gods, before whose breath
The two worlds tremble in afright,
    He, O men, is Indra.

He who set flaming hills to rest,
Who, when the earth quaked, gave it calm,
Who measured air and all the earth,
Upholding heaven on his arm,
    He, O men, is Indra.

He who made the universe
And chased the demon's brood away,
Who, as a gambler, takes in gains,
Makes losses of his foes his prey,
    He, O men, is Indra.

He, when the bold ask, where is he?
Or even brag that he is not,
Swoops like a hawk on his foes' wealth,
Leaves them, we see, not even a jot,
    He, O men, is Indra.

He who uplifts the poor and low,
His priests and him who breathes a prayer,
Who favors those who pour his drink
And hold his altars in repair,
    He, O men, is Indra.

Who holds all horses, chariots,
Cattle and towns in his command,
Who gave the Sun and Morning birth
And leads the waters by his hand,
    He, O men, is Indra.

He when two rival armies clash,
Dire enemies, one strong, one weak,
Whose favor those in chariots
Each for himself is bound to seek,
    He, O men, is Indra.

Without whose help no people win,
Whom they invoke in every fray,
Whose mere reflection is the world,
Who drives the immovable away,
    He, O men, is Indra.

He who deals the fatal stroke
Before the sinner is aware,
Who slays the Demon at a blow,
Leaves proud provokers in despair,
    He, O men, is Indra.

He who found after forty years
Sambra in his mountain den,
Who braved the dragon with his force,
Slaying that enemy of men,
    He, O men, is Indra.

Who reined the Bull with seven reins,
Who set the Seven Rivers free,
Who, thunder-armed, rent Rauhina,[8]
Whose rape of heaven was not to be,
    He, O men, is Indra.

Even Earth and Heaven bow down to him,
Mountains shudder at his breath,
The Soma-Drinker, thunder-girt,
Wields the certain bolt of death.
    He, O men, is Indra.

He favors him who pours his brew,
Chanting the sacramental song,
Who gives him ample sacrifice
And keeps his praise upon his tongue,
    He, O men, is Indra.

Surely, you are true to those
Who pour libations wave on wave;
We laud you now and evermore
Here in the synod of the brave.

II, 12

ᥲᥩ MARUTS ᥤᥲ

Maruts, who bring life to its highest power,
With gleaming lances, breasts adorned with gold,
Rush onward through the sky, lords of the clouds,
Your swiftest chariots readily controlled.

You are the only masters of such strength,
The Mighty Ones, angelic forms on high,
Riding the storm-winds, flashing far and wide,
Measuring out the quarters of the sky
Your cars fly forward to the victory.

Strong, born together and together great,
Holding the heavens in majestic sway,
This majesty and might grows more and more,
Resplendent as the sun's far-darting ray.
Your cars fly forward to the victory.

Your potency deserves to be adored,
Your shape and motion glorious to see
And longed for at the rising of the day.—
Usher us to immortality!
Your cars fly forward to the victory.

You lift the waters from the Ocean floor
Where their rich blessings in abundance lie,
Pouring them down for us in blessed showers.
Never, magicians, are your milch-cows dry.
Your cars fly forward to the victory.

When you have put your golden mantles on,
Boarded your chariots, yoked your spotted deer,
Rushing across the wide expanse of heaven,
All your enemies disperse in fear.
Your cars fly forward to the victory.

Where you have resolved to go, you go;
No mountains and no rivers hold you back.
Your flights encompass the celestial sphere;
Onward you travel on your heavenly track.
Your cars fly forward to the victory.

Whatever has been said in ancient times,
Whatever has occurred or shall befall,
All deeds of mortals under the wide sky—
You have observed and comprehended all.
Your cars fly forward to the victory.

Be gracious to us, Maruts, do not kill us;
Protect us through our brevity of days;
Shower over us your great and many blessings,
Taking warm satisfaction in our praise!
Your cars fly forward to the victory.

You, Maruts, are our friends; lead us to fortune,
Harken to the many hymns we sing you,
Deliver us from all of our afflictions,
Accept, most Holy Ones, the gifts we bring you!

v, 55

MARUTS

You, Maruts, stand beside the throne of Indra;
To you our sacrificial singing brings
This poem of praise, offered with zeal of one
Thirsting for waters of the heavenly springs.

You are armed with wisdom, armed with daggers,
With spears and arrows and with good strong bows;
You have large horses and good chariots,
Fit to deal enemies decisive blows.

In terror of your coming woods bow down;
You shake wealth from the mountains and the stars;
You only make the firm-set earth to tremble,
Yoking your spotted deer to your swift cars.

Like twins of noble countenance you come
Bright with the wind-blast, wrapped in robes of rain;
Spotless, with tawny deer, dappled with red,
You climb heaven's hill again and yet again.

Richly clad, moist and munificent,
On the parched earth your blessed raindrops came;
Noble in birth, adorned with golden armor,
These singers in the sky win endless fame.

Within your arms lie energy and strength;
Across your shoulders rest the lightning's spears;
Bold thoughts are in your minds, weapons beside you;
Majesty in all your form appears.

Vouchsafe to us, dear Maruts, splendid cattle,
Heroes with chariots and heroic steeds;
Children of heaven, as our last distinction,
Let us enjoy your aid in noble deeds!

Ha! Maruts, skilled in law, immortal, gracious,
You in whose care reside the heavenly fountains,
Hearers of wisdom, sage, though ever youthful,
Resting on rain-drenched slopes of lofty mountains!

v, 57

ᴇᴣ PŪSHAN ˁ ᴣᴇ

You are like heaven; one form is bright, one holy;
Like Day and Night, dissimilar in tone;
You aid all magic powers, self-independent;
You rule auspicious, Pūshan, and alone.

Goat-borne, the guard of cattle, lord of strength,
Inspirer of our hymn heard South or North,
Brandishing here and there your sinewy goad,
Witnessing all, Pūshan, the God, goes forth.

Good Pūshan, with your cloudy ships that travel
Golden across the oceans and the air,
You go, an envoy, to the Lord of Heaven,
Subdued by love and find your glory there.

Pūshan, who drives the goats for steeds, is called
His sister's lover, suitor to his mother;
He who loves is ever dear to us,
More lauded and more hymned than any other.

May he who loves his sister hear, and he,
Brother of Indra, always be my friend!
May the sure-footed goats bring Pūshan to us,
May this God visit man, days without end!

VI, 58

◄§ DAWN §►

The radiant Dawn has risen up in glory,
Like the white splendor of the Ocean's waves;
She smooths the pathways for the human traveler,
Both rich and friendly, blesses man and saves.

We see that you are good; your luster shines;
Over heaven's walls your splendor streams;
You deck yourself but leave your bosom bare;
You rise majestic on the morning's beams.

Goddess, your step falls lightly on the hills;
You pass invincible, self-luminous;
So, fair one, with wide pathways through the waters,
Daughter of Heaven, bring wealth and joy to us!

Dawn, give me riches! With untroubled oxen
You bear at will your inexhaustible treasure.
You, a goddess and a child of heaven,
Early praised, have dowered us beyond measure.

At dawn birds issue from their resting-places;
So men rise at the break of day for food;
On liberal mortals who remain at home
The Goddess Dawn confers her greatest good.

VI, 64

Forth from the middle of the flood of Waters—
Their chief the Sea—flow, cleansing, never sleeping;
Indra, the thundering Bull, once delved their channels;
Now let those Waters place me in their keeping!

Waters which flow from heaven or those streams,
Dug from the earth or by their nature free,
Bright, purifying, hurrying to the Ocean,
May their Goddesses be friends to me!

Those mirrors by which Varuna, the gods' Sovereign,
Distinguishes the truth from perfidy,
Distilling wines, the bright, the purifying,
May their Goddesses be friends to me!

They from whom King Varuna with Lord Soma
And all the noble deities that be
Drink their utmost fill of strength and vigor,
May these Goddesses be friends to me!

VII, 49

≈§ VARIOUS DEITIES [11] §≈

Mitra and Varuna, guard and protect me,
Save me from worms that nest within and swell,
Brush off the scorpion hateful to the eye—
Drive off the snake that wounds the foot as well!

Push off the genii that assault the thighs,
The knees and ankles, and all those that dwell
In double joints! Agni, brush them away!—
Drive off the snake that wounds the foot as well!

The poison that engenders on the leaves
Of water-plants is fatal, so dispel
Its charms; all these the gods may put away.—
Drive off the snake that wounds the foot as well!

Save me from gorges and from dizzy heights,
From shallows and from depths no tongue can tell;
May watery swellings in the body cease!—
Drive off the snake that bites the foot as well!

VII, 50

✍ VARUNA [12] ➤

Spare me, Varuna, from the house of clay!
Have mercy, save me, Mighty Lord!

When thunder roars I shudder as reeds sway.
Have mercy, save me, Mighty Lord!

Ah Bright and Powerful God, I went astray.
Have mercy, save me, Mighty Lord!

Thirst found me though the floods washed me away.
Have mercy, save me, Mighty Lord!

Varuna, what my great offenses may
Have been, forgive! have pity upon me!

We broke your laws in open light of day!
Punish us not for our iniquity!

VII, 89

✍ PARJANYA [13] ➤

Praise the great Parjanya, Son of Heaven, who sends us rain!
May he give rich pasturages!

Parjanya lays in kine, mares, plants and womankind
The germ that birth presages.

Pour into his mouth those rich and savory juices!
May he find us in all ages!

VII, 102

ᴀ᷄ ĀDITYAS [14] ᴁ᷄

You give your worshiper great help, Varuna.
Mitra, the Mighty One, your lusty arms
Afford immeasurable aid and succor,
Shielding your devotees from threatened harms.

O Gods, Ādityas, well you know our troubles;
With your incomparable help spread over
Your worshipers your strong and sheltering wings
Resembling birds who keep their young in cover!

May we rest under Indra's favoring grace
And yours, who hold your friends in rich supply
And spare them ills, as prudent charioteers
Know the rough roads and shrewdly pass them by.

Men sink and faint to lose your given wealth
But on men whom you love no danger falls;
Those whom the Ādityas guard and shelter
No loss of courage frustrates or appalls.

Resting on you, we fight like men in armor;
You guard us from all peril and offense;
As a guide from a river bank directs
The traveler, shield us, grant us confidence!

May it be unlucky for the fiend who haunts us
As wolves hunt cows! Come, drive him farther on!
Spare us from evils, hidden or manifest,
Casting them all into Oblivion!

Daughter of Heaven, drive evil Thoughts away
Into Oblivion! To Oblivion's lap
We here consign all such; even if a chain
Of gold were dreamt, the end were a mishap!

If any friend of yours has evil Dreams,
Cast them into Oblivion, drive them off!
Oblivion is their one and rightful cell.
What Night engenders may the Daylight scoff!

Now we have conquered and attained our will;
The evil Dream departs and leaves us peace.
Shine, Dawn, and drive malignancy away!
You are our aid and you are our release.

VIII, 47

✍§ INDRA §✎

I send forth my song of praise for Indra,
The hero-gladdener, precious beyond price;
With this hymn and plenty he invites you
To consummate and complete the sacrifice.

You wish your kine to have a noble bull
To gratify their longing and their will.
Lord of your cows, no one shall turn from him,
No man molest him or none dare to kill.

The dappled kine stream with their holy milk
By means of which the sacrament is given
To hosts inhabiting the seats of gods
In the three luminous theaters of heaven.

Praise, even as he is known, the mighty Indra,
Guardian of cows, Truth's Son, Lord of the Brave!
To him and his Bay Steeds on sacred grass
We lift our chanting in a mighty wave.

Our cows once yielded Indra, armed with thunder,
Milk mixed with honey, when he leaped on high
In seven vaults; we, too, have drunk the soma
And so will reach his palace in the sky.

Chant, chant your hymn of laud, you choristers,
Let children sing his praise, as a strong fort,
Let the shrill viols and lutes send out their voices,
Praise him as our impregnable resort! . . .

VIII, 58

Sacrament flowing on your course, lift us renowned on high
And make us stronger than we are!

Sacrament, shine on us with light, exalt us to the sky
And make us stronger than we are!

Sacrament, with your strength and skill drive away our foes
And make us stronger than we are.

Give us a portion of your sun through which all learning flows
And make us stronger than we are!

Well-weaponed Sacrament, come, pour your wealth upon us
And make us stronger than we are!

As one victorious in battle, pour your riches on us
And make us stronger than we are!

By worship, men have strengthened you to prop the Law,
Making us stronger than we are.

Sacrament, bring us quickening seeds and awe,
Making us stronger than we are!

IX, 4

⚜ AGNI ⚜

The Mighty One arisen before Dawn
Saves us with light from dark and tribulations,
Fair-shapen Agni in white-shining splendor,
Fills at his birth all human habitations.

You are eternal Child of Heaven and Earth,
Flower superior to any other,
You, Burning Babe, subdue the gloom of Night,
Bursting forth roaring loudly from your Mother.

You are, in truth, the Sun-God here on earth,
Nourished by Vishnu with his keenest rays;
When friends have offered sweet milk to his mouth
They sing with one accord his fervent praise.

Then, bearing food, Plant Mothers come to meet you,
With food for you who make food for us then.
Because you give our food its altered form
You are the votive Priest in homes of men.

Embannered in your own refulgent glory,
Sharing with every god yet far the best,
Come, Priest of holy rites, in glittering chariot,
Agni, I summon you to be our guest!

Over earth and heaven and your parents
You have spread, Agni, with your sovereign light.
Come, youngest god, to those who long to meet you,
Bringing all gods through your victorious might!

X, 1

⊷§ AGNI §⊷

Our king, the potent, terrifying envoy,
Kindled by strength, the beauty of pure light,
You shine, all-knowing in your lofty splendor
With white-rayed Morning chasing off dark Night.

Vanquishing the glimmering black with beauty,
Ushering Dawn, the Daughter of the Sky,
You hold aloft the radiant torch of sunlight,
Our messenger from Heaven, lifted high.

The lover follows after as a suitor,
Attendent on the blest whom all men bless,
Agni, beaming forth his stainless luster,
Robes Night in his whitely-shining dress.

His emergence kindles lofty voices,
Which only the true friends of Agni hear,
Resounding through all heaven and audible
As the clear morning-call of the great Steer.

Your splendors rise aloft like choirs of music,
Ringing and roaring as a crackling comet,
Searching heaven with their brightest radiance,
Sporting and piercing to the highest summit.

His team roars loudly on the roads of heaven;
His chariot-fellies gleam and glitter brightly;
As the most god-like, far-extending envoy,
His ancient flames are resonant, shining whitely.

So bring us ample wealth, come as the envoy
Of the two youthful matrons, Earth and Heaven;
Impetuous one with the impetuous horses
By whom the pathways of the clouds are riven!

X, 3

◄§ AGNI §►

He is the one unfathomable ocean,
Born many times within, when hearts are blest;
The Bird dwells in the center of the fountain;
The God hides in the secret couples' breast.

Inhabiting one dwelling-place in common,
Strongest stallions and their mares are bred;
The Sages guard the seats of Holy Order,
Leaving the highest names sealed and unsaid.

At the unmoving point of all life's motion
The Child of Fire is born; fire-sticks produced him;
With magic power the Holy Pair has coupled,
The God has come; his altar priests induced him.

Sticks carefully laid give the Child cheering viands;
Order's chains are woven, link by link;
Earth and Heaven wear them like a mantle,
Growing strong through pleasant food and drink.

Fire calls loudly to the Seven Red Sisters
As tongues that in the radiant rainbow shone;
He, born long ago in air, has halted,
Sought and attained the garment of the Sun.

The pathways which the wise have found are seven,
One for each pilgrim, glad or heavyhearted;
Agni stands a pillar on high ground,
The point from which these human paths have parted.

Being and not being in the heavens
In Matter and Creation's bosom meet;
The Fire-God is the first-born of this union,
The Milch-Cow's birth under the mad Bull's feet.

x, 5

⊰ WATERS ⊱

You, Waters, are beneficent; so help us
To energy and joy males discourse of;
Give us a portion of that noble sap
That mothers know in longing and in love!

We come to you to come to the abode
To which you gladly send us on at length.
You, Water-Goddesses, who give us bliss,
Stream upon us with new health and strength.

You are the Queens who rule all precious things
With deluges of joy and healing balms,
Who hold supreme control of mortal men
And with your coming shield us from all harms.

Within the Waters, as wise priests have told me,
Dwell those virtues by which bliss is won;
Good Waters, medicine my mortal body,
Make me desire to live and view the Sun!

Waters, come! With your calm, healthful motion
Wash away my crimes; banish them hence!
Come, Agni, rich in milk! Through your pure moisture
Cover me with your magnificence!

x, 9

❧ INDRA ☙

Twin messengers speed forth to bring to us
The meditating God and thus induce
Indra to accept auspiciously
Our offerings of sacred soma juice.

You wander far, great Indra, through the realms
Of heaven and earth upon your spacious ways;
You bless your faithful bringing solemn rites
And scorn mere babblers without gifts or praise.

More beautiful than beauty seems to me
When pious thoughts are in a son instilled,
When a wife lures her husband and with shouts
Of joy the auspicious marriage is fulfilled.

I have seen the lovely meeting-places
Where, as the milch-cows glow with sacred fire,
The Mother of the Herd ranks best of all,
Encircled by the seven-toned peoples' choir.

One moves victorious through the Maruts' band.
Pious Agni comes at length to rest.
Through the priest who pours the sacrament
The offerings of his servitors are blest.

The sage who knew the laws of Gods informed me
That fire lay hidden in the cloud-bank's shroud;
Indra had himself informed the sage
That Agni rode the splendor of the cloud.

The stranger asks the way of him who knows it;
He travels on, taught by a skillful guide;
Truth springs from the blessings of instruction,
The tried companion always at our side.

At length he breathes again, dry days remembered.
He sucked in secret at his Mother's breast;
In youth itself old age had come upon him,
He had grown gracious, anger laid to rest.

Good priest, these blessings you will give the people
Who bring such presents as they may afford;
May Agni, satisfied with your petitions,
Pour for you his most bountiful award!

X, 32

ᴈ§ DICE [16] ᴈ⊷

Sprung from tall trees upon their windy heights,
These dice transport me, rolling on their table;
Gambling gives me my supremest joy,
Making the sacramental wine a fable.

Dice never vexed me nor were angry with me;
They have been friendly to me all my life;
For the dice's sake, whose single word is final,
I alienated my devoted wife.

My wife holds me aloof, my mother hates me;
The wretched finds no cover for his shame;
I am a costly horse grown old and feeble,
No longer finding comfort in my game.

Others caress the wife of one whose riches
The dice have made their irony and scoff;
Father, mother, brothers, all exclaim,
"We know him not, bind him and take him off!"

When I resolved to play with dice no more,
My old friends left me in bleak isolation.—
Still, when the dice are thrown upon the board
I am a girl seeking an assignation.

Truly, dice are armed with driving-hooks.
Deceiving men, landing them in the dirt,
They give frail gifts and then destroy the winner,
Leaving him without a cloak or shirt.

Their troop sports merrily, with mystic numbers;
Happiness of the highest heaven nears them;
They need not fear the anger of the nobles;
The King himself pays homage and reveres them.

Now they roll down and now bounce briskly upward;
Handless, they flog their servants with keen lashes;
Cast on the board, like lumps of magic charcoal,
Though cold themselves, they burn the heart to ashes.

The gambler's wife is left forlorn and wretched;
His mother mourns; he has no bed or board;
In debt and fear, friendless yet seeking riches,
He sneaks to rooms he nowise can afford.

The gambler saddens when he sees a matron,
Another's wife in her well-ordered home;
He yokes his brown dice in the early morning;
The fire sinks; then he starts once more to roam.—

"To the official or the tax collector,
The chief arch-foe, tyrant of careless youth,
I show at last my ten extended fingers;
I have no money and I tell the truth.

Do not play with dice; no, till the corn-land;
Enjoy small profits and live modestly!
These are your cattle and your wife, poor gambler;
So a wise man once instructed me.

Be my friend! Show me a grain of mercy!
Do not beat me with such fearful force!
Let the brown dice snare some other prisoner!
Take pity, officer! Have some remorse!"

x, 34

✑ NIRRITI: PRAYER FOR HEALTH [17] ✎

His life has been renewed and carried forward,
As with two in chariots, skillful at the traces,
One falls, one seeks the goal with quickened vigor;
Let Nemesis depart to distant places!

Here is a psalm for wealth and food in plenty;
Let us do deeds to bring us in good graces;
All our doing shall delight the singer;
Let Nemesis depart to distant places!

May we subdue our foes with acts of valor,
As heaven towers above earth's lowly places;
The singer has considered all our deeds;
Let Nemesis depart to distant places!

Do not leave us prey to death, kind Heaven!
But let us see the Sun and the Stars' faces;
Let our old age be passed in kindly fashion;
Let Nemesis depart to distant places!

O Lord of Death, preserve the soul within me,
Let me see the Sun at next uprising,
Lengthen the days still granted me for living;
Strengthen me with your oil, delay my dying!

Give me my sight again; give me calm breathing!
Long may I see the rising of the Sun!
Lord of Death, bless me with your kind favor,
Giving me joy, as you before have done!

May Earth restore to me my vital spirit!
May Heaven, the Goddess of mid-air, restore it!
May Pūshan show to me his path of comfort!
If soma grants me peace, I shall adore it.

"May both worlds bless you with the peace of Indra,
Kept by young mothers of our holy lore;
May Heaven and Earth uproot and sweep away
Your sin and shame, to trouble you no more!

May helpful medicines fall down from Heaven
By twos and threes upon this mortal shore!
May Heaven and Earth uproot and sweep away
Your sin and shame, to trouble you no more!

Drive forward your ox-wagon, greatest Indra,
Saving you as others saved before;
May Heaven and Earth uproot and sweep away
Your sin and shame, to trouble you no more!"

X, 59

❧ THE GODS ❧

With tuneful skill proclaim the generations
Of the great gods and their true parentage,
That one may know them when this solemn hymn
Is chanted in some far and future age!

Bramanaspati made, with blast and smelting,
Existence from pure nonexistence rise;
Gods there were before ours; but those departed;
All Regions then were born beneath the skies.

Earth sprang from the Productive Power; the Regions
Sprang from it; Infinity from Force;
After her, the gods were born unaging,
Clasping arms, as in a dancer's course.

The gods caused all existing things to grow;
They brought forth Sūrya hidden in the seas;
Eight Sons of Āditi sprang to life;
With Seven she flew to the Divinities.

So with her Seven Sons Āditi came,
Hiding the Sun God, Sūrya, far away;
But, turn by turn, brings him again to sight,
Dying and living with each Night and Day.

X, 72

ᴇᴥ§ PURUSHA [18] §ᴥᴗ

Soul of the Universe, great Purusha
Has a thousand feet, a thousand eyes;
On every side, pervading all the earth
He builds on space ten fingers-width in size.

This Purusha is all that yet has been
And all that is predestinate to be;
He waxes greater through his deathless food,
All-potent Lord of Immortality.

So mighty is the compass of his greatness
That no dimension greater could be given;
All living creatures are one-fourth of him;
Three-fourths is his eternal life in Heaven.

With three-fourths he ascended to the skies
But still the fourth of him was always here;
Thus he surpassed all living or dead things,
That eat or eat not through the changing year.

The egg was born from him, he from the egg;
No sooner was the season of his birth
Than he expanded to the East and West
Covering the surface of the Earth.

When the gods prepared the sacrifice,
The sacrificial oil was understood
As making Spring; the holy gift was Autumn;
Warm Summer was the fullness of the wood.

Out of the general sacrificial pyre
The dropping fat was gathered from the flame;
From it he formed the creatures of the air
And crawling things of earth, both wild and tame.

From it horses were born, all goats and cattle,
All living beasts with teeth in double row;
All sheep and deer, all tiny mice and rabbits,
And all that run on legs, both high or low.

When the gods divided great Purusha
What portions did they make and of what size?
What did they call his mouth and what his arms,
What did they call his feet and what his thighs?

The Brahman was his mouth; his arms were warriors;
His thighs were merchants, farmers were his feet;
The moon came from his mind, sun from his eye;
The Wind-God sprang out of his breath complete.

Indra and Agni issued from his throat;
Out of his navel the mid-air appears;
The sky itself was fashioned from his head,
Earth from his feet, the Regions from his ears.

Seven mighty Oceans then were born
Where seven fencing-sticks held up the fire
When the gods, offering their sacrifice,
Bound Purusha on their sacred pyre.

Gods, sacrificing, offered up the victim,
The earliest ordinance of which poets are telling;
The Mighty Ones attained the heights of Heaven
Where the Sadhyas, ancient gods, are dwelling.

X, 90

With myriad eyes the Goddess Night
Looks down on earth when day is done,
Putting all her glories on.

Her deathless being fills the waste;
The Goddess pierces depth and height,
Conquering darkness with her light.

The Goddess as she enters, goes,
Yields Dawn her place, as ritual says,
Then all darkness vanishes.

Dear, favor us this night with rest,
Whose transit we delight to see
As birds their nest upon a tree!

The villagers have sought their homes,
With birds and beasts at close of day—
Even the falcons, fain for prey!

Keep off the she-wolf and her mate,
Turn the roving thief aside,
In quietness let the evening glide!

Quietly she comes to my tired eyes
With richest sheen and starry frets—
Morning will cancel them like debts.

Dear Night, accept my hymn, a gift
In sacrifice to you and for
True service to my conqueror!

X, 127

◄§ CREATION §►

Once was no nonexistence nor existence;
There was no realm of air, no sky at all;
Was there some unfathomed depth of water?
What gave shelter? Where? Was there a wall?

Death was not there nor anything immortal;
No trace of day nor nighttime to divide it.
That One Thing, breathless, breathed by its own nature;
There was nothing else at all beside it.

Darkness was there, at first concealed in darkness,
A total chaos indiscriminated;
All that existed then was void and formless;
By power of Warmth the Unit was created.

Thereafter rose Desire at the high portal
Of life, Desire, germ of this persistent
Spirit of life; sages with their hearts' thought
Discovered life first through the nonexistent.

The severing lines extended forth transversely,
Higher or lower, what was fate dreaming of?
There were begetters, there were mighty forces;
Free action here and energy above.

Who truly knows or who here can declare it?
When was its birth or what was its creation?
The gods are later than this world's production.
Who can tell its first and primal station?

He, the Creator of the Universe,
Can he have formed it from a cosmic blot?
Whose eye controls this world from highest heaven,
He knows it, or, perchance, he knows it not.

X, 129

᪥ VISVEDEVAS: PRAYER IN SICKNESS [20] ᪥

Our gods, raise him once more whom you have humbled,
The man whom you have stricken and brought low,
Restore again to life the evil doer
Whom you have smitten with so heavy a blow!

Two separate winds are blowing from the Ocean
Where the beneficent in life holds sway;
May one bring strong, new energy upon you,
May one blow your malignancy away!

"I come with balms to bring you rest and safety,
I come to drive off ills, to give you ease.
Here let the gods deliver him, and the Maruts
And all things free him from his foul disease!

Waters, with your healing powers flow on him,
Waters, caress him, fair tongues bless all such!
Then, with the ten-fold branching of our hands,
Release and stroke him with our gentle touch!"

X, 137

✍ SAPATNIBADHANAM [21] ✍

I dig a plant out of the earth,
The most effectual magic known,
By which one quells the rival wife
And gains the husband as one's own.

Sent by the gods, victorious plant,
Whose vigorous leaves expand and shine,
Blow the rival wife away
Making my husband only mine!

I am the far lustier one,
Of greater strength and never blench;
She who is my rival wife
Is lower than the lowest wench.

I shall not disclose her name.
She takes no pleasure in this man.
To places evil and remote
Drive this woman, if we can!

I am the conqueror and you,
Herb, are triumphant in the strife.
Victory awaits us both;
We shall throw off that loathsome wife.

I have gained you as vanquisher,
Grasping you with my powerful spell;
As a cow hastens to her calf,
Pour out your charm! All shall be well.

x, 145

ᴥ§ FOREST GODDESS [22] ໊ᴥ

Goddess of the wilds and woods who so eludes our sight,
Why avoid our villages, why suffer so from fright?

When cricket and when grasshopper unite their treble voices,
Sounding like tinkling bells, the Lady of the Wood rejoices.

Far off, it seems, the cattle graze by houses on the plain;
At shut of day the Forest Goddess frees the farmer's wain.

Here one is calling to his cow, another fells a tree;
At twilight dwellers near the wood fear things disorderly.

The Goddess never kills unless some woodsman is oppressed
By bandits; men consume her fruits, then take their welcome rest.

Now I have praised the Forest Queen, redolent, sweet with balm,
Mother of all sylvan things, who saves us from all harm.

x, 146

Karna's
Task

BHĀSA

◈§ In 1912 Pandit Ganapati Shastri discovered manuscripts of thirteen Sanskrit plays which materially enlarged the world's understanding of the early period of Indian drama. These became known as the "Trivandrum Plays," because of their discovery in the city of Trivandrum, in South India. There was no clear evidence of their authorship and still less of their date or dates of origin, but Shastri's conjectural ascription to a poet bearing the name of Bhāsa has been accepted as at least a convenience in scholarly discourse. No one really knows who this "Bhāsa" was or whether the celebrated poet bearing this name is actually the author. Internal evidence at least suggests that all the plays are of an early date in the confused annals of the Sanskrit stage. This means that they derive not far from the beginning of the Christian era. All are strongly theatrical. A terseness in expression in contrast to the lush style later used in Sanskrit drama has even led to a conjecture that they are in some cases acting versions. Karna's Task, the play represented by the following translation, in itself, however, gives small evidence of any compromise between poetry and the theater, for it is equally impressive as a drama for acting and for reading. In this respect it resembles all the great Sanskrit drama literature, where the highest requirements of both poetry and the theater are conjointly realized.

The play's thought derives from the Bhagavad-Gita, most treasured of Indian religious texts, itself a part of the great epic, the Mahābhārata. The moral is contained in the simple statement, "Virtue is in the effort." Fortune, the poet goes on to say, may lead us where it will. If through spiritual and ethical effort we acquire the power to confront our human condition in the noblest manner, that is enough. The rest remains with fate. Such wisdom may be described as a spiritual pragmatism.

Karna, the play's hero, has a stronger conscience than most heroes in the Sanskrit epic. He is, so to speak, a Hindu Hamlet, noble in soul, fighting a civil war both within himself and in the state. He has acquired his magic armor by a ruse. Before his last fight, in which he is to fall at the hands of his arch-enemy, Arjuna, the storm-god, Indra, receives his armor as a gift, thus exposing the hero to his predestined death. Indra appears disguised as a Brahman priest, whose every request must be granted by those properly pious in the faith. Karna is troubled by the very nature of the impending conflict. He knows that circumstances lead him to combat his own kith and kin, a condition peculiarly hateful in Hindu morality. Loyalty to his chief runs counter to loyalty to his family and clan. The play is tense with all manner of irony, which in itself greatly enhances its dramatic force. The myth belongs to folklore, the thought to philosophy. A poetry which is all-powerful unites the sophisticated and the naïve.

The meter in which this heroic drama has been rendered in its English version has been suggested by that of the Elizabethan poet George Chapman, in his translation of Homer's Iliad. Although Sanskrit playwrights in their many works employing legends from the Indian epics invariably treat their material with considerable freedom, adapting it to the later periods of Indian thought, they still piously and vigorously maintain much of the spirit of their sources. All this suggests Chapman's Homer. It has, accordingly, seemed appropriate to borrow something from the Elizabethan verse-sentiment in rendering analogous material from the Orient. A more refined and sophisticated metrical system is elsewhere used in attempt to suggest the ripe and elegant verse-style achieved by the court-dramatist Kālidāsa and his followers.

MANAGER

"May Vishnu, God of Fortune, now bring you every joy,²
Whose blows the enemies of Heaven utterly destroy.
For those who see this god-like man, whether in earth or
hell,
Are terror-stricken, men and women, fiends and gods as well,
Nor any hostile multitude against his strength prevails.
He burst the demon-king's own heart with ax-edge of his
nails!"
With such a prayer as this, my lords, I must give you the
word—
What sound was that, just as I spoke? What was that noise
I heard? ³

VOICE
Ho there, tell the king of Angus ⁴—

MANAGER
                              Yes, one understands.
An urgent messenger brings Karna word with folded hands,
Duryodhana finds the fight all in a fierce uproar.⁵

SOLDIER (Entering).
Ho there, tell the king of Angus this is time for war!
Princes brave as lions advance on elephants and steeds,
And with the Pāndu battle-flag rush on to valiant deeds.⁶
Perceiving what is now at stake, the serpent-bannered herd
Led by the champion of the world, by fierce cries unde-
terred,
Comes forth; the Angus king in arms rides from king Salya's
home.
But O, why is the valorous chief in such dejection come?
Accounted first in battle-line, portentous to his foes,
He comes as one of thoughtful mind in spirit bent by woes.
Karna is the majestic sun whose once-resplendent brow
Is hidden by the summer's cloud.—But I must leave you
now.   (Exit.)

(Enter Karna and Salya.)
KARNA
No, no, have any hostile kings come in my arrow's range

And yet remained for long alive? Why should my fortune
    change?
It would please Kurus if I fought Arjuna instantly.— [7]
King of the Madras, drive my car where Arjuna may be!

SALYA

I shall.

KARNA

    My valor matches death and yet there comes an hour
When all the pomp and pride of war, before which cowards
    cower,
No longer moves my darkened breast; elephants nor horse,
Warriors charging on the foe with all their thunderous
    force,
Blade clashing blade, limb slashed from limb, ruins of em-
    pory,
Cannot relieve my blackened heart from pangs of misery.
I am not Radya's son; Kuntī was my mother;
Now I find, alas, that Yudhishthira is my brother
Along with the Pāndavas. This is now my day of days,
When in one glorious hour of war I should win highest
    praise,
But all the skill of arms I learned is at this hour deferred,
My soldier's pride blasted at last, gone at my mother's
    word.—
O Madra king, hear how I learned the bitter art of war!

SALYA

Yes, I wish to hear it.

KARNA

I went to Jamadagni's door.

SALYA

Yes.

KARNA

    I went to see that sage, pride of the Bhrigu race,[8]
The terror of the warrior class, with stern and fearful face,
With dark, rough hair, his battle ax whirling far and wide.
Humbly I saluted him, in silence by his side.

SALYA

And then?

KARNA

    I said, my lord, I come to learn of war's grim game

And how to wield each weapon best?

SALYA

And so then what said he?

KARNA

The sage was silent for a while and then reluctantly
Said he would teach only the priests but never warriors.

SALYA

Yes, he has a standing feud with leaders who make wars.
And then?

KARNA

I said I was not of the class inciting strife.
And so he taught my weapons' use for military life.

SALYA

And then?

KARNA

A few days after that we strolled in leisure hours
Through pleasant woods in search of roots, fuel, grass and
    flowers.
The aged man, being quickly tired, fell to his noonday nap,
Lying in peace beside me, his head upon my lap.

SALYA

Then—

KARNA

A voracious insect bored its teeth through both my
    thighs,
But I would not awake the sage by writhing nor by cries.
So for my master's sake I suffered long in fortitude.
Then suddenly the sage awoke in streams of blood imbrued
And in a blaze of rage cried out: "In time of greatest need
May your best weapons fail you!"

SALYA

That was a curse indeed!—
A bitter thing it was for such a mighty sage to say.

KARNA

And now let us inspect the weapons that we bear today.
These weapons all seem to lack power. And beyond this I see
Our horses stumbling wildly, as though blind by misery;
Our elephants, like wind-blown leaves trembling in afright,
Herald our disastrous end in the forthcoming fight.
The battle horns and drums are still.

SALYA

This is a dreadful thing!
These are fearful portents!

KARNA

Yet be not dismayed, good king!
The victor gains the glory, the vanquished, heaven's grace.
All's for the best, good friend. The world thinks well in
  either case.
These steeds, swift as the bird of death, of proud Kamboia
  stock,
Although they have no prospect of returning from the shock
Of dreadful war, shall yet protect me from the evil power,
Though I am past protection, in this predestined hour.
May happiness possess the hearts of priests, good wives and
  cattle! [9]
Good luck to fighting men who scorn to turn their backs in
  battle!
And good luck to my soul, though worldly luck has run its
  course!
O, I am glad! For I shall pierce the proud Pāndava force,
Capture Yudhishthira, famed for wealth and kingly craft,
And overthrow Arjuna with my resistless shaft,
Until our world will be a wood wherein all lions are slain.—
Now come, king Salya, let us mount our chariot again!

SALYA

Ah, well! Since you so wish it, I shall mount instantly.

KARNA

King of the Madras, drive my car where Arjuna may be!

VOICE

O Karna, I salute you!

KARNA

Ah, what a noble sound!
But I cannot discern the man, look as I will around.
This must be at once a priest and some great nobleman.
My slender steeds, who previously at a fierce gallop ran,
Now in delicious terror halt and at this grave, deep voice,
As figures in a picture stand, while all their hearts rejoice.
Their ears are taught; their necks are arched; those necks
  with jewels strung,

Rub their shoft chests, their warlike breasts by that sweet
      voice unstrung.
You call the sage.—No, I shall call.—O reverend sir, come
      on
Where I can see you!
          (Enter Indra, disguised as a Brahman.)
                    INDRA
      Back, dark clouds, dissolve before the sun!
O Karna, I entreat you!
                    KARNA
      I am glad, my holy friend,
I shall this day be listed among those who gain their end.
Karna salutes you; on his feet he wears the radiant gems
That one-time flashed on princely heads in royal diadems,
But prouder that his head, by your sage presence purified,
Lies in the dust beneath your feet here freshly sanctified.
                INDRA (Aside).
What can I say? If I should say, "Long life to you," he
      would
Live on interminably. But if perchance I should
Say nothing, he would certainly despise me as a fool.
On either side I must avoid extremes. No easy rule
Applies. But yes—I have it.—Karna, I salute your name!
Eternal as the sun, sea, moon or mountains be your fame!
                    KARNA
You might, with an auspicious word, have bade me to live
      long,
But you pronounced a better word; another had been wrong.
Virtue is in the effort; fortune, like a serpent's tongue,
Flickers, even in the lives of kings. That king is truly sung
Whose thoughts are on his peoples' good though bodies
      should be killed.
But, holy man, what wish of yours by me may be fulfilled?
                    INDRA
O Karna, I entreat you! I require a noble loan.
                    KARNA
I would give you a noble gift. Now hear what wealth I
      own.[10]
If it should please you, worthy priest, I'd give a thousand
      cows,

Young cattle, fit for altars, gold-tipped horns upon their
    brows,
Who, after feeding all their calves, give nectar soft as silk.

INDRA

Your thousand cows are not for me. I drink but little milk.

KARNA

Well, hear again. I'll give Kamboian horses fleet to run
A gallant race in heaven against the horses of the sun,
Bringers of luck to princes, with high valor in their breast,
Swift as the wind, without a fault, and in the battle best.

INDRA

Horses I ride but little. They would not be preferred.

KARNA

Then listen, noble sage, once more! I'll give a countless herd
Of elephants, with whited nail and glittering ivory tusk,
About whose heads the bees converge, sipping the odorous
    musk,
Elephants that resemble the Himalayan hills,
About whose brows the thunder roars and sharp-pronged
    lightning thrills.

INDRA

Elephants I ride little.[11] No, Karna, you may hold
All of these creatures.

KARNA

            What!—Then I will give you endless gold!

INDRA

Yes, I'll take that and go.—No! Karna, no, that will not do!

KARNA

Then I will conquer all the earth and offer it to you.

INDRA

What would I do with all the earth?

KARNA

                Then I'll bring every spice,
Fruit, bud and flower that on the earth fits a burnt sacrifice.

INDRA

What good were sacrificial fires and offerings to me?

KARNA

Then take my head!

INDRA

Ugh, ugh!

KARNA

Don't be alarmed, for if that fee
Falls short, forgive me, holy sage! I have another plan;
My armor like my body's strength is as a single man,
No god of fiend can pierce it with any sword or spear,
Yet I will gladly give it, with both earrings that I wear.[12]

INDRA (Joyfully).

Yes, give me that!

KARNA

So that is what he wishes! As I see it,
This may be one of Krishna's tricks.[13] But if it is, so be it!
Fie, it is unbecoming to suspect an ill.—Here, take it!

SALYA

King, your armor is your life and you should not foresake it.

KARNA

King Salya, do not check me, for life itself has shown
Great learning comes in time to nought, firm trees are
        overthrown,
The fountain from the fountain's source the droughts of
        Autumn sever,
But gifts and fair oblations last forever and forever.—
Here, take it!

INDRA (Taking the armor, aside).

Yes, I have it now, and now that by this deed
I have fulfilled what long before the gods in heaven decreed,
Namely, Arjuna's victory, I shall in peace ascend
My elephant and ride to watch this duel to its end.   (Exit.)

SALYA

You have been cheated, king.

KARNA

By whom?

SALYA

By Indra!

KARNA

Not at all!
It's I who cheated Indra, he who caused the demon's fall.
Having contented Indra, I reach my final goal,

Indra himself possesses Arjuna, flesh and soul,
Whose hands are rough with patting the celestial elephant,
To whom the twice-born painfully endless oblations grant.[14]
(Enter a Spirit disguised as a Brahman.)

SPIRIT

Indra is grateful, Karna, for the earrings and the arms
And prays you to accept a spear to shield you from all
    harms,
And with it kill one of the Pāndava chiefs.

KARNA

             O fie,
To take return for gifts free given befits not such as I!

SPIRIT

Then take it at a Brahman's wish!

KARNA

           That I cannot decline,
For any Brahman's wish expressed must instantly be mine.
I have ever thought so.—But where now can it be had?

SPIRIT

When you recall it to your mind.

KARNA

          Then thank you! I am glad!—
You may return.

SPIRIT

    So be it!   (Exit.)

KARNA

    King Salya, mount my car!
We must return immediately to where the champions are.
(They mime getting into the chariot.)

SALYA

Ah, very well.

KARNA

    I hear a sound.—Say, what can this portend?
That couch is like the ocean's roar proclaiming the world's
    end!
Can it be Krishna?—No, it's Arjuna, who with his might
To revenge Yudhishthira's fall comes on in our despite.—
King of the Madras, drive my car where Arjuna may be! [15]

SALYA

*I shall. This noble king himself complies with heaven's
decree.*

(Exeunt.)

EPILOGUE

May all good fortune reign on earth, all evil disappear,
And may our king with royal virtues rule forever here! [16]

Mālavikā
and
Agnimitra

KĀLIDĀSA

Sanskrit drama developed from plays using many of the stories and maintaining much of the spirit of the Indian heroic epics, the Māhābhārata and the Rāmāyana, to plays clearly reflecting the highly refined and sophisticated life in the courts of the Indian princes during the centuries constituting the Middle Ages in terms of the Western calendar. The plays became subtler in their sentiments, emotions, and ideas, at times overripe and also increasingly directed to learned audiences. As time advanced, the Sanskrit language itself was used by fewer and fewer persons; the very language in which the plays were written, accordingly, became more aristocratic and less popular. Naturally, the plays reflected the marked changes in the cultural climate.

The apex of Indian drama is commonly described as represented by Kālidāsa, poet and playwright, who is thought to have flourished at the beginning of the fifth century A.D. The nature of his writings shows him to have been a court poet, celebrating the pride and magnificence of the Indian princes, instilling into his works the sophistication and refinement of the aristocratic life. He was also a poet of such deep sensibility and religious inspiration that his works transcend the narrower usages of his time and place, establishing him among the world's masters. Unhappily, only three of his plays survive, Sakuntalā, the most widely known, Vikramorvaci, the most heroic in temper, and Mālavikāgnimitra, a singularly graceful play in the spirit of high comedy. It is the last that has been selected for this collection. The choice is to be explained as follows...

Although Sakuntalā is, no doubt, Kālidāsa's masterpiece and has many times been translated, it is hardly an exaggeration to say that the translations reveal, above all, the extreme difficulty which it presents to translators. It is hard to enable the modern reader to realize that the Sanskrit playwright is in fact writing a deeply religious drama dedicated to man's relations with nature and especially to the sanctity of parenthood. It is hard to escape an erroneous suspicion of romantic or even sentimental clichès. The play may, no doubt, be revealed to Western readers as a great and moving drama, but for the moment the present writer is unwilling to submit his own version to public attention. Accordingly, for more reasons than one this work, commonly accessible on the shelves of public libraries, if not found in private hands, is omitted. Vikramorvaćī is omitted, though rendered into English verse by the present writer and available in a version elsewhere, on the ground that, cast, as it is, in a distinctly epic mode and inspired by high seriousness not greatly unlike that of the preceding play in this volume, Bhāsa's Karna's Task, its presence here would necessarily introduce some duplication in tone.

Mālavikāgnimitra, or Mālavikā and Agnimitra, to repeat, is high comedy and is unquestionably the finest and most representative instance of the main road taken by Sanskrit drama in the later stages of its history. It was repeatedly imitated by Sanskrit playwrights themselves. In modern India it has probably been produced more often than any other of the Indian classics save Sakuntalā, though abroad Sūdraka's The Little Clay Cart is more commonly seen. No English rendering has, I believe, appeared outside India and none is at present in print. As a comedy, or lighthearted romance, it offers a striking contrast to the grave dramatic parable of Karna's Task. Few Sanskrit plays offer closer parallels than these two to Western conceptions in turn of the gravity and deep earnestness of tragedy, the grace and humor of social comedy.

As Sanskrit drama advanced, one convention in style, particularly valued by Kālidāsa, protruded above all others. This is a use of short poems or passages in lyric form interspersed throughout the conventional dramatic dialogue. These passages are rarely of a choral nature and are, excluding the extremely few exceptions, rarely sung. They were designed to be spoken, though presumably with a heightening in the recitational tone. Hundreds of these verse passages found their way into the popular Sanskrit verse anthologies. The spiritual value of each play is enshrined in them to such a degree that, should they be abstracted from the play, they would relate the play's story and convey the core or substance of its meaning. In the present rendering these passages are distinguished by rhyme and, as in the Sanskrit texts, numbered consecutively for each act. To this extent one of the most important formal features of the playwriting is preserved in the English rendering.

Unlike the more serious Sanskrit plays, whether by Kālidāsa, Bhāsa, Sūdraka, Bhavabhūti, or any of the acknowledged masters, this deals with flirtation rather than with deep affection. It breathes a hedonistic atmosphere at times even suggesting The Arabian Nights. Yet it is much more serious and poetic than the foregoing statement suggests and so much the more representative of Kālidāsa and his contemporaries in drama. The play, we are told in its prologue, is intended as part of the celebration of a spring festival. It is set deliberately in a cheerful, amorous key. But its leading theme, the fructifying of a tree by the ceremonial touch of a girl's foot, belongs to folklore and to devout nature worship. This play is gay but not trivial, happy but in no sense slight. Moreover, in art or refined craftsmanship it is virtually unsurpassed. It may remind us that as works of art Twelfth Night and The Tempest are in no way inferior to Coriolanus or Julius Caesar. After the gravity of Karna's Task and the hymns from the Rigveda, it appears fitting to conclude with a work which, at least in its original, contains so much grace, gaiety, and inexhaustible youthfulness of spirit.

↭ CHARACTERS ↫

KING AGNIMITRA
DHĀRINĪ *queen of the first rank*
IRĀVATĪ *queen of the second rank*
MĀLAVIKĀ *princess of Vidarbhā*
KAUSIKĪ *a priestess, formerly a princess of Vidarbhā*
KAUMUDIKĀ *maid in service of Queen Dhārinī*
BAKULĀVALIKĀ *maid in service of Queen Dhārinī*
GANADĀSA *a dancing master*
HARADATTA *a dancing master*
VĀHATAKA *a minister serving the king*
GAUTAMA *a clown, being a Brahman and friend of the king*
CHETĪ *servant to Irāvatī*
CHAMBERLAIN
TWO BARDS
MADHUKARIKĀ *keeper of the royal garden*
SAMĀDHIMATIKĀ *attendant*
NIPUNIKĀ *maid in service of Queen Irāvatī*
PRATĪHĀRĪ *maidservant in the palace*
SĀRASAKA *a woman gardener*
RAJANIKĀ *a woman from Vidarbhā*
JYOTSNIKĀ *a woman from Vidarbhā*

Act One

BENEDICTION

Lighten our darkness, Śiva, dissipate
Our ignorance, that we may find the Way!
You who wear a cloak of coarsest skin [1]
Though all the universe admits your sway;
You whose body is united with
Your love, though scorning all the senses give;
You in whom no arrogance is found
Although you are the lord of all that live!   (1)

(Enter Stage Manager. He looks behind the curtain.)

STAGE MANAGER

Actor, please come here!

ACTOR (Entering).

Sir, here I am.

STAGE MANAGER

In honor of our festival of spring
This learned audience requires today
That we present a play by Kālidāsa
Entitled Mālavikā and Agnimitra.
So summon our musicians to begin!

ACTOR

Please do not do so! Why should informed spectators
Value the product of a living poet,
Neglecting compositions of old masters,
As Bhāsa, Kaviputra or Saumila?

STAGE MANAGER

You are imperceptive, judging crudely.
No old work is better art because
Through circumstance it happens to be old;
No new work is worse for being new:
Wise men examine; fools believe what they're told.   (2)

ACTOR

This audience provides the best of judges.

STAGE MANAGER

Then hurry to prepare for our event.

I shall do as I before had promised,
Smoothing the passage for our opening scene
As this good servant of our royal mistress
Labors to serve the wishes of her queen.²   (3)

(Enter Bakulāvalikā, a maidservant.)

BAKULĀVALIKĀ

Queen Dhārinī orders me to ask
Our worthy dancing master, Ganadāsa,
What progress Mālavikā may have made,
During the short season of her lessons,
In executing the Chalita dance.
So I shall go to the recital hall.

(She walks about. Another maid, Kaumudikā, enters with an ornament in her
hand.)

BAKULĀVALIKĀ

Friend Kaumudikā, why be so abstracted
As not to notice me while you walk past?

KAUMUDIKĀ

Pardon me, dear Bakulāvalikā!
You accuse me rightly. My excuse is this:
I was gazing too intensely at
The queen's ring with the snake-design carved on it.³

BAKULĀVALIKĀ (Looking at the ring).

Your eyes are fixed upon a lovely thing
Furnishing the forepart of your hand
With rays that flash like filaments of flowers.

KAUMUDIKĀ

Where are you going, Bakulāvalikā?

BAKULĀVALIKĀ

I am going, on the order of the queen,
To ask our dancing master, Ganadāsa,
How Mālavikā fares with his instruction.

KAUMUDIKĀ

Although her lessons keep her in seclusion
The king himself has seen her, I presume?

BAKULĀVALIKĀ

Yes, in a sense, since the king observed her
Standing in a painting near the queen.⁴

KAUMUDIKĀ

How was that?

BAKULĀVALIKĀ

Listen and I shall tell you.
The queen had gone into her picture-gallery
To see the latest painting by the master,
When suddenly the king himself came in.

KAUMUDIKĀ

What happened then?

BAKULĀVALIKĀ

After their formal greetings,
The king sat on the bench beside the queen
To ask about the picture she was viewing.

KAUMUDIKĀ

What did he ask?

BAKULĀVALIKĀ

He simple asked the name
Of the unknown girl beside her in the painting.

KAUMUDIKĀ

Beauty induces wonder. Then what next?

BAKULĀVALIKĀ

When his majesty observed the queen
Paid no attention to his inquiry
He spoke again and still the queen was silent.
Finally, the little princess, Vasulakshmī,
Blurted out, "Sire, that is Mālavikā."

KAUMUDIKĀ

That is precisely what a child would do.
What followed then?

BAKULĀVALIKĀ

Why, what would you suppose?
Now the girl is more than ever hidden
Out of the eyesight of his majesty.

KAUMUDIKĀ

Friend, go about your errand. I in turn
Shall take this splendid jewel to the queen.   (Exit.)

BAKULĀVALIKĀ (Walking and looking about).

See, the dancing master, Ganadāsa,
Comes from the concert hall. I must speak to him.

GANADĀSA (Entering).

All hard-learned skills are honored but not all
Worthy of such high dignity as mine.

Sages tell us that the gods maintain
Presentational art to be our best
Eye-pleasing sacrifice, seen in two modes
Significant of energy and rest,
As Śiva and his love comprise one form,
One body and soul. Its symbols explicate
The three essential forms of human nature
With all the sentiments which these create.
Whatever differences in men we find,
Dance is the chief delight of all mankind.   (4)

BAKULĀVALIKĀ

I salute your honor!

GANADĀSA

All good fortune to you!

BAKULĀVALIKĀ

The queen inquires if Mālavikā gives you
Trouble in the course of your instruction?

GANADĀSA

Tell the queen that she is skilled and clever.
Whatever sentiments or technical
Nuances my instruction may impart,
She betters my instruction by the beauty
Of her most consummate and perfect art.   (5)

BAKULĀVALIKĀ (Aside).

Hearing this commendation, I foresee
Queen Irāvatī suffering an eclipse.—

(Aloud.)

Your pupil is most fortunate to find
Her teacher truly gratified in her.

GANADĀSA

You are the favored one. Perhaps you know
Where the queen procured this paragon?

BAKULĀVALIKĀ

She has a brother of a lower caste,
Vīrasena, whom the king appointed
Commander of a fort upon our frontier
At Mandakini river. There he captured
This girl and sent her to the queen, presuming
Her capable of mastering many arts.

GANADĀSA (Aside).
Her noble form implies a noble race.
(Aloud.)
My friend, I see I shall be famed at last.
When the professor finds a brilliant pupil
He is also certain to excel,
Just as water issuing from a cloud
Creates a pearl when falling on a shell.   (6)
BAKULĀVALIKĀ
Where is your student now?
GANADĀSA
After I taught her
The five-limb movement and its corollaries,
I ordered her to rest. Now she is sitting
On the high window-seat that overlooks
The lake and there enjoys a cooling breeze.
BAKULĀVALIKĀ
Then give me your permission to attend her
So that I may stimulate her zeal
By telling her how gratified you are.
GANADĀSA
Then go to see your friend. I, too, shall take
My interval of leisure and walk home.   (Exeunt.)

(The king is discovered with his followers. His Minister stands
beside him with a letter in his hand.)
KING (Looking at the Minister, who reads the letter).
Vāhataka, what does the Vidharbās' king
Intend?
MINISTER
His own destruction.
KING
Read his letter.
MINISTER
He answers your dispatch with this reply:
(Reads.)
"My royal brother tells me that my cousin,
Mādhāvasena, who promises to be
Brother by marriage to us, being attacked,
Was taken prisoner by my frontier guardsmen.
I am requested to set this man free

Together with his sister and his wife.
My royal brother should know well enough
The right behavior shown by kings to kings
And so should be impartial in this matter.—
The prince's sister vanished in the tumult.
I shall do my uttermost to find her.
My royal brother may at least be sure
Mādhāvasena shall be freed.
These are the final terms of our agreement:
If my royal brother will release
My brother-in-law, the Maurya envoy, now
In prison, I in turn will liberate
Mādhāvasena from imprisonment."   (7)

KING

What! does this foolish fellow bargin with me?
This intriguer, as my natural foe,
Crudely evinces his hostility.
Order my force, predestined to that end,
With Vīrasena as its general,
To root him out as one who rashly stands
Among men liable to be attacked.

MINISTER

I shall obey your majesty's commands.

KING

What do you personally think of this?

MINISTER

Your majesty speaks according to the Sastras.
Any foe recently come to power,
Taking no popular root, is rooted out
With ease, just as a tree whose roots are shallow
Is weaker than one whose roots are old and stout.   (8)

KING

Then may this saying in the treatises
Prove true, and let our general be dispatched.

MINISTER

This shall be as your majesty commands.   (Exit.)

GAUTAMA (Entering).[5]

His royal highness gave me this commission:
"Gautama," he said, "find me some ruse to meet

With Mālavikā, whose portrait I have seen
By strategy!"—Well, I have done all this
And now I shall inform him of the fact.   (*He walks about.*)

KING

Here comes a minister of another species.

GAUTAMA

Long may your highness prosper!

KING

Please be seated!
I hope your massive intellect's engaged
In finding out the pathway to our end.

GAUTAMA

Ah, ask instead of my accomplishment!

KING

How can this possibly be?

GAUTAMA (Whispers in his ear).[6]

This is the scheme.

KING

Well done, friend, to begin and I foretell
Fruition in this difficult attempt.
Even an able person needs a friend
To aid him when perplexed, although his sight
Be normal, just as one who walks in darkness
Needs assistance from a lantern's light.   (9)

VOICE (Behind the scenes).

Stop, stop your arrogant boasting! The decision
Of better or worse between us must be made
In presence of his majesty himself!

KING

The blossom on your tree of policy
Has budded, friend.

GAUTAMA

And you shall taste its fruit.

CHAMBERLAIN (Entering).

My lord, the Minister informs your majesty
That all your orders have been executed.—
Now for Haradatta and Ganadāsa:
The illustrious masters of the art of dancing,
Jealous of one another, in whom we view

The embodiment of histrionic passions,
Are both alike intent on seeing you.   (10)
                    KING
Then let them enter.
                    CHAMBERLAIN
        As the king commands.
    (*He goes out and reenters with the dancing masters.*)
    Follow me, gentlemen, this way, this way.
                    HARADATTA (*Aside*).
His majesty is hard to be approached:
It is not that I find the king unknowable
Or proud, yet I approach him fearfully,
For he seems new to me at every glance,
Mutable as the surface of the sea.   (11)
                    GANADĀSA
The luster of the illustrious king is blinding:
Although his door-guards granted me an entrance,
Although attendants showed me all compliance,
The effulgence from the throne repels my gaze;
Here am I, utterly reduced to silence!   (12)
                    CHAMBERLAIN
His majesty is there.—Approach the throne!
                    BOTH
Victory to the king!
                    KING
        Welcome!—Guards, give them chairs.
Why do you both besiege my throne together
When you should be attending to your pupils?
                    GANADĀSA
Hear me, king! I learned dramatic art
From a great teacher, have given learned lessons
To pupils, and been thanked by king and queen.
                    KING
We know it well.
                    GANADĀSA
        Now I have been insulted
By Haradatta here in the full presence
Of all your court and called not worth the dust
Beneath proud Haradatta's insolent foot.

My lord, this man was first to rouse my anger,
Saying the difference between him and me
Was that between the ocean and a pond.
So let your majesty examine us
In theory and in practice of our art.
Your majesty alone can judge our merits.

GAUTAMA

This man has made an excellent proposal.

GANADĀSA

Your majesty need only listen closely.

KING

Stop a while! The queen may think us partial.
This should be tried in presence of the queen
And that most learned lady, Kausikī.

GAUTAMA

You say quite right.

BOTH

Be it as the king desires!

KING

Chamberlain, inform them of this matter;
Call the queen here with the wise Kausikī.

CHAMBERLAIN

I shall obey.

(Goes out and re-enters with the queen and the priestess.)

QUEEN (To the priestess).

Learned lady, what is your opinion
Of the quarrel of Haradatta and Ganadāsa?

PRIESTESS

Do not fear your faction will be losers.
Ganadāsa cannot be defeated.

QUEEN

Even if that be true, the royal favor
Must surely give his rival the advantage.

PRIESTESS

But think, you have the title of our queen.
Assistance from the royal sun in heaven
Grants the fire the brilliance of its light,
While the moon also wins its queenly splendor
When favored by the grandeur of the night.   (13)

Look, here comes the queen, preceded by
Your chamberlain and the learned Kausikī.
KING
Yes, here's my queen, Dhārinī, coming toward us:
She is clad in her auspicious ornaments
While Kausikī in her aescetic dress
Shines like the incarnate soul of the three Vedas [7]
Attended by transcendent blessedness.   (14)
PRIESTESS
Victory to the king!
KING
Holy one, I salute you.
PRIESTESS
May you be husband for a hundred years
Of queen Dhārinī and the holy Earth,
Support of living creatures, strong in patience,
Alike in majesty and noble birth!   (15)
QUEEN
Victory to his majesty!
KING
Welcome, queen.
Reverend lady, take your honored seat!
(All sit down according to their dignity.)
Lady, Haradatta and Ganadāsa
Both claim superiority in knowledge.
You must serve as judge in their dispute.
PRIESTESS (Smiling).
Do not jest with me! When a town is near
Do men have jewels tested in a village?
KING
Lady, no, no, you are a learned scholar
Whereas the queen and I are clearly partial
To Haradatta or to Ganadāsa,
BOTH
His majesty speaks wisely. Reverend lady,
You should adjudicate the case between us
In all disputes of merits or defects.

KING

Well, then, let the argument begin.

PRIESTESS

King, the science of dramatic form
Lies chiefly in its practice, so what use
Can these mere verbal arguments possess?

KING

What does the queen think now?

QUEEN

To tell the truth,
I abominate all chatter on aesthetics.

GANADĀSA

The queen must not rate me with that impostor!

GAUTAMA

Lady, let us see these rams embattled!
Why should we grant them pasture-land for nothing?

QUEEN

Indeed, you take an evil joy in wrangling.

GAUTAMA

Don't say that, angry lady! How can peace
Exist between two drunken elephants
Until one of the two destroys the other?

KING

Surely, you have seen the strong emotions
Presented by these teachers in their acting.

PRIESTESS

Indeed I have.

KING

What more can they present?

PRIESTESS

I was on the point of saying this:
Some excel in action, some in precept;
Some are best in doing, some in preaching;
Some in each. Those admirable in both
Are also the most excellent in teaching.   (16)

GAUTAMA

Gentlemen, you have heard the lady's words,
Which mean your trial must be based on skill
In actual teaching.

This seems fair to us.
GANADĀSA
King, it is so agreed.
QUEEN
But if some artless
Pupil disgrace the instruction of her teacher,
Is the good teacher then to bear the blame?
KING
It is necessary that it should be so.
GANADĀSA
The improvement of a pupil without promise
Shows the sharp discernment of the teacher.
QUEEN (Looking at Ganadāsa; aside).
What's this? (Aloud.) Desist from humoring my husband.
That only serves to aggravate his passions!
Spare yourself the trouble!
GAUTAMA
You speak wisely.—
Ganadāsa, since you now are guzzling
The sweetmeats offered to our god of learning,
Sarasvati, under the pretense
Of being a teacher of acting, why do you
Enter the lists in danger of defeat?
GANADĀSA
O yes, that is the sense of the queen's words.
But listen to a saying highly apt:
We call that man no better than a huckster
Who shrinks from contests because he possesses
Merely the means of servile livelihood
But lacks just pride in all that he professes.   (17)
GAUTAMA
Your pupil has been lately given to you
And so it proves unfair to put on trial
Instruction that is not as yet concluded.
GANADĀSA
So much the more my merit will appear.
QUEEN
Well, then, both of you show your best instruction
For the venerable lady's eyes alone.

PRIESTESS

No, that is wrong. Even an omniscient man,
Taking responsibility upon him,
May make mistakes.

QUEEN (Aside to the Priestess).

You are a foolish pedant! Do you wish
To lull me asleep when I am wide awake?
(She turns aside in anger. The king calls the attention of the Priestess to the
petulent queen.)

PRIESTESS

Why should you, moonfaced lady, turn away
Your countenance from your husband without cause?
Even those haughty wives who rule their husbands
Await some ground to break sound marriage laws. (18)

GAUTAMA

No, there is good reason, for she believes
She should uphold the faction which she favors.
(He looks at Ganadāsa.)
I congratulate you on the fact
That you have been protected by the queen,
Pretending to be angry. Not all scholars,
However learned, are also skillful teachers.

GANADĀSA

Listen, queen. You hear what people say:
If in this dispute you do not let me
Show how I communicate my art,
I shall presume that in this disputation
You have assumed a frankly hostile part. (19)

QUEEN (Aside).

What strategem or refuge have you left?
(Aloud).
You have authority over your pupil.

GANADĀSA

I have long been suspicious without reason. (Looking at the king.)
Your queen at length has counseled me to let
Your majesty command me in what precinct
Of art I should exhibit my instruction.

KING

The reverend lady must determine this.

PRIESTESS

The noble queen has something on her mind.
I am afraid to speak.

QUEEN

O no, speak boldly.
I am mistress only of my own attendants.

KING

Say you will be mistress of me also!

QUEEN

Sacred and reverend lady, speak your mind.

PRIESTESS

King, the Chalita dance is in four parts.
Let the two masters give that composition.
That will contrast their differences in skill.

BOTH

Just as your reverence shall order us.

GAUTAMA

Then both of you return into our theater.
After your arrangements for the music,
Send your servant to announce your coming,
Or better, the loud drum will rouse us up.

HARADATTA

So be it.

(He rises. Ganadāsa looks at the queen.)

QUEEN

Ganadāsa, I am not
Hostile to you as you have supposed.

(Both teachers start to go away.)

PRIESTESS

Come here a moment, erudite professors.

BOTH (Turning around).

We are here.

PRIESTESS

I speak in my capacity as judge.
Let your pupils come without stage dresses
So that we may watch their limbs in action,

BOTH

It was unnecessary to tell us this.   (Exeunt.)

QUEEN (Looking at the king).

How glorious if your majesty would show

As great intelligence in affairs of state
As you have exercised today in this!
                    KING
Lady, you should not judge me so severely.
You know the cause from which this quarrel came.
My clever wife, we find it customary
That learned men are jealous of their fame.   (20)
            (A sound of drums behind the curtain.)
                    PRIESTESS
Ah, the dramatic overture begins!
The drums whose sound is like the peacock's cry
Inspire our hearts by sounding low or loud.
Hear that delightful middle tone, as peacocks
Lift their arched necks at the dark thunder-cloud!   (21)
                    KING
Lady, let us go and not be late!
                QUEEN (Aside).
            GAUTAMA (Aside to the king).
How little this rude king observes decorum! (All rise.)
Walk slowly and calmly, otherwise the queen
Will violate the compact she has made.
                    KING
Though I endeavor to be calm, this sound
Of drumming stirs me. Primal intuition
Knows it the echo of my soul's desire
Entering the path to its fruition.   (22)
                                                          (Exeunt.)

Act Two

(After the arrangements for the concert are completed, the king enters, along with Gautama, Queen Dhārinī and attendants, according to their rank.)

KING

Reverend lady, which of the two masters
Shall we see first exhibiting his skill?

PRIESTESS

Although the two seem much alike in learning,
Ganadāsa should be seen the first.
He should be preferred, being the elder.

KING

Well then, my chamberlain, instruct them so
And go about our business with dispatch.

CHAMBERLAIN

All shall be as your majesty commands.   (Exit.)

GANADĀSA (Entering).

King, there is a dance-play by Sarmishtha
Given in four parts, in medium tone.
Your majesty should hear the fourth part of it
With close attention.

KING

                    Yes, I am attentive,   (Exit Ganadāsa.)
Especially for the eminent teacher.
                    (Aside to Gautama.)
                                    Friend,
My eyes long for a girl whose sight I lack.
Oh how I yearn to push that curtain back!   (1)

GAUTAMA (Aside to the king).

Pure honey for your eye is near at hand
But the queen-bee is near, so please take care!

(Enter Mālavikā, whose costume and movements are inspected by the teacher.)

GAUTAMA

My lord, her charms confirm her picture.

KING

                    Friend,
My heart was fearful that her real form
Compared with what the painter drew would fail

To gratify me, but instead I find
The artist's own conception weak and frail. (2)
                    GANADĀSA
Do not be bashful, child! Compose yourself!
                    KING (Aside).
She holds her posture faultless in the dance:
Her face and gaze are like the autumn moon,
Her arms show gracious curves of womanhood,
Her chest is strong, her ample breasts are firm,
Her graceful sides are smooth as polished wood,
Her waist is measured by the clasp of hands,
Her hips are elegant and broad of beam,
Her feet are delicate, with rounded toes:
This figure is a dancing master's dream. (3)
        MĀLAVIKĀ (After completing the prelude, she sings and dances.)
Do not yearn, my heart, for one so hard
To win! Though my left eye in sharpest pain
Throbs auspiciously, I must not hope
One hard to see, impossible to obtain,
Can ever love me. Yet, dear friend, consider
I long for you as the Earth longs for rain. (4)
            (Her dance expresses the sentiments of her song.)

                    GAUTAMA (Aside).
Ha, ha! This woman throws her heart to you
In singing the finale of her song.

                    KING
Friend, two hearts together beat as one:
Certainly when she pointed to her body
And sang, "Dear lord, consider how I long
For you," she used a ruse. Since Queen Dhārinī
Is present, she has reached me with a song. (5)
            (At the end of her song Mālavikā begins to go out.)

                    GAUTAMA
Stop, lady! In your exit you omit
The strict decorum. I should like to question
You of it.

                    GANADĀSA
        Stop, dear child, then you may go
After your fault in going has been corrected

Or your performance has been rated faultless.
(Mālavikā *returns and stands motionless.*)
KING (*Aside*).
Her beauty gains fresh splendor with each pose:
Her body as a statue wins more charm
Than all its glory in her rapid dance.
I note the delicate placing of her wrist
On her left hip. I note her perfect stance.
Golden bracelets dangle from each arm,
Her right arm curving like a bending branch.
Her upper body itself is proud and straight
And yet she casts her modest eyes below
Upon the inlaid pavement where she pushes
A fallen blossom with an agile toe.   (6)
QUEEN
I fear the noble teacher takes to heart
The reservation of his lordship's friend.
GANADĀSA
The contrary is true. Helped by the king,
His friend will easily gain a sharper sight.
Even a stupid scholar becomes brilliant
Who knows wise men, as muddy streams are free
From base pollution and grow crystal clear
When showered by blooms from a kataka tree.   (7)
We are all waiting for your lordship's judgment.
GAUTAMA
Ask of the learned lady who has watched
The whole performance. Later I shall mention
The omission that I previously observed.
GANADĀSA
Reverend lady, give us your opinion
Whether her art was a success or no.
PRIESTESS
All was faultless and in full accord
With the immutable aims and rules of art.
Through the poetic movement of her limbs
She perfectly expressed the known emotions.
In the smooth operation of her dance
Were no unseemly fidgets or commotions.
Passion banished passion in her acting,

All held in measure to the dancer's pace.
The gentle motions of her legs were perfect
Embodiments of feeling and of grace.   (8)

GANADĀSA

What does his majesty conclude from this?

KING

Ganadāsa, we are among those
Whose confidence in their faction has been shaken.

GANADĀSA

This proves I am a master of the dance,
No common, ordinary dancing-teacher.
Good men call that instruction by a teacher
Pure when it shines unsullied in your sight,
As gold is only valid gold when tested
By flames that in a crucible burn bright.   (9)

QUEEN

I must congratulate you, honored sir,
On satisfying your examiner.

GANADĀSA

Ah, the queen's favor is my greatest prize.
        (Looking at Gautama.)
Now tell us, Gautama, what is your objection?

GAUTAMA

In the first presentation of a work
A Brahman's worship is obligatory,
But that you have unhappily forgotten.

PRIESTESS

Ah, the learned questioner has plumbed
The very essence of dramatic art.
        (Mālavikā smiles; the others laugh.)

KING

My eye now holds its object of delight.
My joy is to have seen her smiling face,
Teeth shining, half-displayed, her eyes drawn wide,
Just as a lotus with fresh filaments
Half-seen while the full flower is undescried.   (10)

GANADĀSA

Great Brahmana, this display was not
A public stage-performance; otherwise
How could we not have offered you this honor!

GAUTAMA

I am the foolish bird who lived on raindrops
And asked a draught of water when the sky
Was filled with thunderclouds and still no rain.

PRIESTESS

That is quite true.

GAUTAMA

The ignorant should place
Their confidence in the judgment of the wise.—
If the holy lady believes that this performance
Was perfect, may I offer her this present?
(He takes a bracelet off the king's arm and offers it to her.)

QUEEN

Stop! Why should you give away this jewel
Not knowing the true value of her service?

GAUTAMA

Why, just because it belongs to someone else.

QUEEN (Looking at Ganadāsa).

At least we know it is because your pupil
Shows such consummate mastery of art.

GANADĀSA

Come, Mālavikā, let us leave, my child.
(Mālavikā and Ganadāsa go out.)

GAUTAMA (To the king).

My genius now has served you to its limits.
The rest is for yourself.

KING

O, never say
That your superior power has reached its limit.
The curtain that concealed this dancer fell
Upon my own good fortune, sealed my eyes
And quenched my heart's festivity as well.   (11)

GAUTAMA

You are like some poor, sick man who should beg
A miserly physician for his cure.

HARADATTA (Entering).

King, will you kindly judge my pupil now?

KING (Aside).

The motive for my seeing is concluded.

(*Aloud.*)

Haradatta, we shall eagerly await
Our judgment of her.

HARADATTA

I am highly honored.

BARD (Behind the curtain).

Victory to the king! The sun has reached its zenith:
Now flamingos with their half-shut eyes
In the bright lotus-pond seek grateful shade;
Pigeons leave the rooftops of the palace
Which the sharp, blistering rays of noon have made
Insufferable. Peacocks shun the heat,
Drenching themselves under a cooling shower
Thrown by the water-wheel. The sun shoots forth
Its splendor vying with your royal power.[8]   (12)

GAUTAMA

Ho! the hour for bath and food has come!
Our doctors blame us if we dare desist
From honoring it.

KING

Then tell me, Haradatta,
What shall we do?

HARADATTA

It's not for me to say.

KING

Then we shall view your artistry tomorrow
And now retire to rest.

HARADATTA

As you command.   (*Exit.*)

QUEEN

Your majesty, perform the noontime rites
As these concern the bathing ceremony.

GAUTAMA

And do you make special haste, great lady,
In good arrangements for our food and drink!

PRIESTESS (Rising).

Health to the king! We beg to take our leave.
(*Exeunt the queen, the priestess and attendants.*)

GAUTAMA

Ah, Mālavikā, I perceive, is matchless
Not only in her beauty but her art.
KING

When the creator furnished her with knowledge
As well as beauty he prepared a shaft,
Steeped by the god of love in bitter poison.
I am wounded and trust solely in your craft.   (13)
GAUTAMA

But you should also think of my own comfort.
My stomach is like a hot pan in the market.
KING

That's so. But you must labor for your friend.
GAUTAMA

You have my promise but must clearly know
Her visit hangs on Queen Dhārinī's will.
She is a moon obscured by dusky clouds.—
Your majesty amuses me by asking
To have your will fulfilled when you are hovering
Like some poor bird about a slaughterhouse
Simply too timid to consume the meat.
KING

Friend, how can I not be deeply grieved
Now that one beauty is my sole resort
While I experience no grain of pleasure
From all the lesser beauties of my court?   (Exeunt.)

Act Three

SAMĀDHIMATIKĀ (Entering).[9]
The reverend lady ordered me as follows:
"Samādhimatikā, get a melon
And bring it to me so I may present it
In token of my homage to the king."—
Now I must look for old Madhukarikā,
Keeper of the royal pleasure-garden.   (Looks about.)
Ah, there stands Madhukarikā, tending
The gold asoka-tree. I shall speak to her.
                    (Madhukarikā enters.)
How do you like the shrubbery, Madhukarikā? [10]
                    MADHUKARIKĀ
Good day to you, dear Samādhimatikā!
                    SAMĀDHIMATIKĀ
Listen, friend! Our gracious lady said
That common folk like me should not approach
The Wealthy One and come with empty hands,
So I shall give his majesty a melon.
                    MADHUKARIKĀ
Indeed, I see we have the fruit at hand.
Tell me, which of the rival dancing masters,
After their instructions flowered in practice,
Did the venerable lady favor?
                    SAMĀDHIMATIKĀ
Each of them is learned, shrewd, proficient
In presentational arts, but as a teacher
Ganadāsa towers above his rival
Owing to his pupil's excellence.
                    MADHUKARIKĀ
Does the court gossip about Mālavikā?
                    SAMĀDHIMATIKĀ
Indeed we do, concluding that it's certain
His majesty is much in love with her,
But out of courtesy to Queen Dhārinī
He takes no opportunity to meet her.
Mālavikā, too, is seen to fade

Like some jasmine-garland proudly worn
Then rudely thrown aside. I know no more.
Let's be going.

MADHUKARIKĀ

Take this melon with you
Hanging upon this vine.

SAMĀDHIMATIKĀ

Friend, may you win
A high reward from this most saintly lady
Far greater than the fruit which I shall bring!

(Starting to go.)

MADHUKARIKĀ

Come, let us go together. I will also
Inform the queen of this asoka-tree
Long ago fertilized but vainly longing
To burgeon into its enchanting bloom.

SAMĀDHIMATIKĀ

You are right. It is your duty to report it,
Being the mistress of this royal garden.

(Exeunt.)

(Enter the king, depressed, with Gautama.)

KING (Observing himself).

Not having clasped the body of my love,
Well may my body be emaciated;
Not having seen the figure of my love,
My weeping eyes may well be inundated.
But since our hearts are no way separated,
O fawn-eyed girl, why should mine be prostrated? (1)

GAUTAMA

Stop these futile lamentations, hostile
To your naturally firm and steadfast mind!
Meeting Mālavikā's dearest friend,
Bakulāvalikā, I have told her
The word your majesty intrusted to me.

KING

And when you told her, what did she reply?

GAUTAMA

She said to tell you she would gladly do
You service. But that wretched girl is watched
More strictly by the queen than hitherto,

A priceless jewel guarded by a serpent,
Hard to be reached. Still, she will do her best.

KING

O sacred God of Love, why do you strike
Me down so sorely that I cannot live long,
Holding an image in my yearning breast
Focused upon the unobtainable?
What possible relation can there be
Between the shaft of love and dart of fire,
The sweet and bitter of the bow of passion,
The cruel weapon of the god Desire?   (2)

GAUTAMA

Do not say that, for I have found the means
To ensure the goal you long so to attain.
Therefore, your majesty, compose yourself!

KING

Since my customary business irks me,
How shall we pass the remainder of the day?

GAUTAMA

Irāvatī has just sent to you
Some crimson kurabaka flowers to prove
The first appearance of the gorgeous spring.
She adds a message through Nipunikā
Hoping to join you in the garden swing
And frolic in the pleasures of the year.
You have promised to do as she desired,
So let us walk into the pleasure-garden.

KING

How could I possibly do as she wishes?

GAUTAMA

Why not?

KING

My friend, women are keen by nature.
How will your friend, even as I embrace her,
Fail to perceive my heart belongs to another?
I know of many plausible excuses
Why it is better for me to ignore
Such intimacy than court a clever woman,
Even though more ardent than before.   (3)

GAUTAMA

You should not discontinue your civility
Shown to the many ladies of your palace.

KING

Then lead me to this springtime pleasure-garden.

GAUTAMA

Here is the way, your majesty, this way.

(They walk about.)

Spring pushes out her tendrils that are fingers
Beckoning your highness to this garden,
Fanned and favored by a friendly breeze.

KING

Spring is surely noble. Look, my friend:
She makes the southern wind, fragrant with blossoms,
Play on my limbs like a hand's gentle touch;
She makes the cuckoo, drunk with warm compassion,
Inquire how my weak heart endures so much.   (4)

GAUTAMA

Pass through this garden-entrance into peace.

(They enter the garden.)

Look, dear friend, look carefully around:
Surely the beauty of these pleasure grounds,
Aiming to cure you of unhappiness,
Puts on a robe of many-colored flowers
Shaming the splendor of a woman's dress?

KING

Indeed, I note it with warm admiration:
The crimson dye upon a woman's lips
Is far surpassed by this azalea bough;
The kurabaka blossom, blue, white, red,
Transcends the mark upon a woman's brow.
The eye of the tilaka flower is fairer
Than any painting at a woman's eye;
The bees cling to it like collyrium.
All this vernal beauty can defy
The decoration of a woman's face,
Showing that gardens wear the greater grace.   (5)

(They admire the garden. Enter Mālavikā.)

MĀLIVAKĀ

I am ashamed to find I love the king,

Whose sentiment for me I cannot know.
How can I tell this love to my dear friend?
I cannot say how long the god of love
Will leave me in such miserable pain.
                        (Walks a few steps.)
                        (Recollecting.)
Where was it I was going now? Oh, yes!
I have received an order from the queen.
She told me that in falling from a swing,
Owing to Gautama's carelessness,[11]
She bruised her foot and can no longer move it.
So she has asked me to perform the ritual
Causing the gold asoka-tree to blossom.
She tells me that if within five nights' time
The tree puts out its flowers she will present me
With gifts that gratify my heart's desire.
                        (She sighs.)
O, here I am at the appointed place.
In this secluded garden for a moment
I may give my secret sorrow vent,
Till Bakulāvalikā comes to dress me,
Carrying fitting ornaments for my foot.

GAUTAMA

Here the sweet juice of sugarcane is ready
For one already sourly drunk on rum.

KING

Friend, what is this?

GAUTAMA

        Why, there stands Mālavikā
At no great distance, lightly dressed and pale
As one who is afflicted, and alone!

KING

What, Mālavikā?

GAUTAMA

        Surely, it is she!

KING

Now at last my life finds some support.
My distracted heart takes hope once more,
Knowing that my loved one may be here;

So a parched traveler's withered heart revives
When bird-sounds hint a shaded river near.   (6)
GAUTAMA
Here she arrives, walking directly toward us,
Emerging from a row of flowering trees.
KING
My friend, I see her, just as you have said:
She with the almond eyes comes to me now,
This flower-like woman whom I love the best,
Broad in her rounded hips, gracefully slender
In waist, wide-swelling in her ample breast.   (7)
My friend, this girl comes in a different state
From that in which I saw her first, bedecked
With jewels for her ceremonious dance.
Her cheeks are pale, like stalks of withered grass;
Her limbs are weak, her ornaments are scarce;
She seems depressed, like early jasmine bowers
Decked with few pallid leaves and fewer flowers.   (8)
GAUTAMA
She, like your highness, must be weak through love.
KING
It is your friendship only that sees that.
MĀLAVIKĀ
This asoka, waiting pregnancy,
Still unadorned by amplitude of bloom,
Is like myself thrown in a state of yearning
Expectancy, a strange, delirious gloom.—
I'll sit on this stone slab beneath its shade.
(Sits down.)
KING
Even that does not prove your own conjecture.
This gentle breeze from the Malayan mountain
With pregnant pollen, breathing without pause,
Its light rain blessing faint, unfolding buds,
Creates a longing even without cause.   (9)
My friend, conceal ourselves behind this arbor.
GAUTAMA
I think I see far off somebody coming
Who seems from here to be Queen Irāvatī.

ANCIENT POETRY FROM INDIA/401

The elephant who spies a lotus cluster
Disregards a snapping alligator.

(Gazes at Mālavikā.)

MĀLAVIKĀ

Why should my heart be tortured with desire
When every hope of pleasure must be vain?

(Gautama looks at the king.)

KING

My good friend, note the irony of love:
It does not show the cause for which it yearns;
No conjecture proves it obviously,
Yet I have felt that this dear woman's grief
Unequivocally points to me.   (10)

GAUTAMA

At last your highness may be freed from doubt
For here comes Bakulāvalikā, she
To whom I gave the message of your love.

KING

Do you think she remembers my request?

GAUTAMA

What, can you believe the daughter of a slave
Could overlook a message from a king?
Why, even I have not forgotten it.

(Bakulāvalikā enters, carrying foot-ornaments.)

BAKULĀVALIKĀ

Do things go well with you, dear Mālavikā?

MĀLAVIKĀ

Ah, Bakulāvalikā! Welcome, friend!
Sit here beside me.

BAKULĀVALIKĀ

Dear, on this occasion

You have been commissioned by the queen
To bring to pregnancy this gold asoka.
Stretch your foot out so that I may tint it
Crimson and clasp these golden anklets on it.

MĀLAVIKĀ (Aside).

I am not proud that this uncommon honor
Falls upon me; I cannot free myself
From this persistent, gnawing melancholy.—
Your gifts will be my funeral ornaments.

Why should you hesitate? The queen is eager
That the asoka should put forth its flowers.

KING

What, is all this preparation only
For the fertility of an asoka?

GAUTAMA

Why, do you believe the queen without some cause
Would ever have this simple girl adorned
With ornaments drawn from the royal harem?

MĀLAVIKĀ (Raising her foot).

I beg your pardon!

BAKULĀVALIKĀ

Dear, you are my life!
(She begins to decorate Mālavikā's foot.)

KING

Friend, observe the streak of moistened color
Bloom at the tip of my beloved's foot.—
The emerging blossom on Love's sacred tree,
When Śiva's eye consumed it, bud and root!   (11)

GAUTAMA

The truth of your remark is absolute:
This girl might strike two objects with her foot,
Its white nails gleaming for a fresh assault:
A gold asoka not as yet in flower,
A kneeling lover humbled by his fault.   (12)

GAUTAMA

You will find occasion to offend the lady.

KING

I accept the omen: Brahmans speak the truth.
(Enter queen Irāvatī in disordered dress and mildly intoxicated, attended by
her servant, Nipunikā.)

IRĀVATĪ

Nipunikā, my friend, I sometimes hear
Intoxication fits a woman well.
Do you accept the common belief as true?

NIPUNIKĀ

Mere rumor once becomes the truth today.

IRĀVATĪ

Stop your flattery! How did you know

The king preceded me into the swing-house?
NIPUNIKĀ

I judged it from his constant love for you.
IRĀVATĪ

Come, come, enough of your servility!
Speak to me with impartiality.
NIPUNIKĀ

The illustrious Gautama wants his spring present
And told me of it. Do make haste, my mistress!
IRĀVATĪ (Walking as well as she is able under her condition).

My impulse urges me to meet my husband
But my intoxication holds me back.
NIPUNIKĀ

But see, we are already at the swing-house.[12]
IRĀVATĪ

Nipunikā, his lordship is not here!
NIPUNIKĀ

Look closely; I suspect his majesty
Conspires to play a trick upon your highness
By hiding in a hedgerow. So let's enter
This arbor, sitting down on this stone bench
Under thick shade of the asoka tree,
Intertwined with pale wisteria creepers.
(Irāvatī does so.)
NIPUNIKĀ (Walking about and observing).

Look, queen, while gathering the mango sprouts
I see we are bitten by these wretched ants.
IRĀVATĪ

Do you speak symbolically?
NIPUNIKĀ

Yes indeed!

Under the shade of these asoka boughs
Here is Bakulāvalikā painting
Mālavikā's foot with crimson lac.
IRĀVATĪ (Suspicious).

This is not Mālavikā's proper place.
What do you infer from such a thing?
NIPUNIKĀ

Now I remember. Queen Dhāriṇī, falling
Out of her swing, severely bruised her foot,

So ordered Mālavikā to perform
The ceremony needed to bring forth
The gold asoka to its pregnancy.
Otherwise how could Queen Dhārinī give
Her servant anklets she herself had worn?
                    IRĀVATĪ
That is a mighty honor, I must say!
                    NIPUNIKĀ
Why do you not try to find the king?
                    IRĀVATĪ
Because my legs refuse to move. Besides,
My mind is wavering. Ah, I am suspicious!
                    (Looking at Mālavikā.)
My heart is jealous in the proper place.
          BAKULĀVALIKĀ (Showing her the foot).
Are you pleased with the beauty of the lines
Of color I have painted on your foot?
                    MĀLAVIKĀ
Being on my foot, I blush to praise your art.
Who taught you this fine skill of decoration?
                    BAKULĀVALIKĀ
In this I am a pupil of the king.
                    GAUTAMA
Hasten to get the king's acknowledgment.
                    MĀLAVIKĀ
I praise you that you are not proud of it.
                    BAKULĀVALIKĀ
But I shall be proud now, having obtained
Feet so worthy of my highest art.
                    (Looking at the color, aside.)
I have accomplished half of my commission.
                    (Aloud.)
Friend, one foot is finished; it is only
Needed to breathe on it and that is easier
Because the garden welcomes the spring winds.
                    KING
Look, look, my opportunity has come
To serve her by my breathing on her foot
Where the coloring still is fresh and damp,
Here by the asoka's shaded root.   (13)

Do not be troubled, my most honored friend,
The intimacy you enjoy today
Will prove a joy that shall not pass away.[13]

BAKULĀVALIKĀ

Your foot is like the flower of the red lotus.
May you rest blissfully on the king's lap!

(Irāvatī looks at Nipunikā.)

KING

I also say this prayer and give this blessing.

MĀLAVIKĀ

What you say, my friend, is most improper.

BAKULĀVALIKĀ

I spoke just as the circumstance requires.

MĀLAVIKĀ

Surely, you love me.

BAKULĀVALIKĀ

I am not the only
One who loves you.

MĀLAVIKĀ

Tell me of another.

BAKULĀVALIKĀ

Why, his majesty, who loves your virtues.

MĀLAVIKĀ

That is untrue. Such merits are not mine.

BAKULĀVALIKĀ

Certainly they are yours. And this is proved
By his palor and his limbs' emaciation.

NIPUNIKĀ

The wretch, it seems, has got her answer pat.

BAKULĀVALIKĀ

Note the proverb, "Love is proved by love."

MĀLAVIKĀ

Why do you speak with so much willfulness?

BAKULĀVALIKĀ

I do not do so. All you apprehend
Is the king's thought in the mirror of my speech.

MĀLAVIKĀ

I lose my reason thinking of the queen.

Foolish girl, would you refuse to make
A blossom of the mango-tree a charm
To ornament your ear when spring has come
Merely because a bee was clinging to it?

MĀLAVIKĀ

Well, wicked girl, at least you try to help me.

BAKULĀVALIKĀ

Really, I am a garland of spring flowers
Growing more fragrant with more frequent friction.

KING

Bakulāvalikā, you do well:
You have brought her under your control
By answering whatever she avers,
Following the humors of the mind,
Sensitive to every thought of hers.
It is natural that successful lovers
Rely upon their female messengers. (14)

IRĀVATĪ

Look, my friend, where Bakulāvalikā
Puts Mālavikā on the path to love.

NIPUNIKĀ

My lady, such indoctrination stirs
Desire even in persons free from passion.

IRĀVATĪ

My heart was jealous in the proper place.
I shall determine further on the facts.

BAKULĀVALIKĀ

The decoration of your second foot
Is finished. Now to put the anklets on.
(She does so.)
Come, friend, rise up; comply with the queen's orders;
Make the asoka burgeon into bloom!
(Both rise.)

IRĀVATĪ

You heard the queen's command. Then do it now.

BAKULĀVALIKĀ

See what is standing flushed, prepared for pleasure.

MĀLAVIKĀ. (Joyfully).

What, his majesty?

BAKULĀVALIKĀ (Smiling).
No, not his majesty
But this cluster on the asoka's bough.
Make it an ornament to grace your ear.
GAUTAMA
Did your highness hear her?
KING
Yes, and this
Is quite sufficient to discourage love:
Complete destruction of those lives whose passion
Is equal but who have no prospect of
Ever attaining their desire is better
Than union with one obdurate in love.   (15)
(After Mālavikā has placed a cluster of blooms over her ear, she gracefully puts
her foot forward to strike the asoka.)
Look at what the girl has done, my friend.
She graced it with her foot and graced her ear
With blossoms such as loving hands arrange.
I am the luckless one computed by
The just equality of their exchange.   (16)
MĀLAVIKĀ
I hope our ritual will be rewarded.
BAKULĀVALIKĀ
You cannot be at fault. The asoka tree
Must indeed be barren were it slow
To bloom, being caressed by such a foot!
KING
Her foot is soft as a young lotus bloom,
Her tinkling anklets give a joyful sound,
If, when the slender-waisted girl has touched
Your sides, asoka-tree, there are not found
Immediately an infinity of blossoms
Upon you, you are not of those who find
Delight, as others confidently know it,
In the felicitous acts of womankind.   (17)
Friend, I want a favorable moment
To join the others in their conversation.
GAUTAMA
Come, I will play a comedy with her.
(They cross the stage.)

Mistress, look, his majesty is there!
IRĀVATĪ

This is what my heart anticipated.
NIPUNIKĀ

Madam, you should not have kicked the tree
Dear to the king.
BOTH (Confused).

O, look, the king is here!
GAUTAMA

Bakulāvalikā, why did you,
Who knew the facts, not keep the audacious girl
From such an act of impropriety?
(Mālavik shows her fear.)
IRĀVATĪ

How can a poor Brahmana earn a living?
BAKULĀVALIKĀ

Sir, she obeyed an order from the queen.
She is not responsible in this.
Let the king himself be satisfied.
(She bows before the king and induces Mālavikā to bow also.)
KING

If this is so, you are not the guilty one.
Rise to your feet again, my fortunate girl!
(He takes her hand and lifts her up.)
GAUTAMA

The queen should be respected in this case.
KING

Girl with such graceful thighs, I hope your foot,
Soft as lotus filaments, thin and frail,
Suffered no bruising from the tree's rough trunk,
Marring the tender skin and tinted nail.   (18)
(Mālavikā seems bashful.)
IRĀVATĪ (Spitefully).

His highness has a heart as soft as butter.
MĀLAVIKĀ

Come, Bakulāvalikā, tell the queen
That we have done precisely as she wishes.
BAKULĀVALIKĀ

Then ask his majesty your leave to go.

KING

My good girl, you may go. But learn my wish
Which now has full occasion to be heard.

BAKULĀVALIKĀ

Listen well and let the king command.

KING

For a long time I have been unable
To put forth such a flower of happiness.
The nectar of your touch alone is joy;
That hand alone can satisfy and bless.   (19)

IRĀVATĪ (Abruptly coming forward).

Ah, satisfy! This tree now shows its flowers,
But time will show not only flowers but fruit.

(All show confusion.)

KING (Aside to Gautama).

Friend, how can we escape this tumult now?

GAUTAMA

No way, except by taking to our heels.

IRĀVATĪ

Bakulāvalikā began well.
You, Mālavikā, do as the king says.

BOTH

We beg your royal pardon! Who are we
That the king should fall in love with us?

(Exeunt.)

IRĀVATĪ

O faithless men! I never knew the truth
When I followed this deceiver's word,
As antelope come at the hunter's whistle.

GAUTAMA (Aside to the king).

Defend yourself! Being a burgler caught
In the act, you ought to say that you explored
Thieves' art in order to discourage thieves.

KING

My beautiful queen, I had no real intentions
With Mālavikā. I amused myself
Somehow, because you were so long delayed.

IRĀVATĪ

You be trusted! I did not suspect

My husband had so excellent a pastime,
Otherwise I had spared you this annoyance.
GAUTAMA
Do not rebuff the courtesy of the king!
If merely talk with servants of the queen,
Seen here by chance, is held to be a crime,
This is your new law, and we must obey it.
IRĀVATĪ
Well, call it talk! I'll trouble myself no longer.
(Goes away in anger.)
KING (Following).

Forgive me
(As Irāvatī staggers forward, her feet become entangled in her girdle.)
Beautiful queen, it is not right
For you to disregard your constant lover.
IRĀVATĪ
Traitor, your love is not to be relied on.
KING
With that word "traitor" let all anger end.
Dismiss your violent temper, I entreat!
Look where even your girdle begs for peace,
Lying, prone and prostrate, at your feet!   (20)
IRĀVATĪ
Even this wretched girdle takes your side!
(She lifts the girdle and threatens the king.)
KING
The fiery woman with the streaming eyes
Beats me with a gold girdle for a thong,
Just as a bank of raging rainclouds strikes
The Vindhya Mountain with its lightning's prong.   (21)
IRĀVATĪ
Would you provoke me to a further fault?
(She lifts her hand with the girdle.)
KING
Curly-haired woman, why do you withdraw
Punishment from your slave who bears the blame?
You magnify your beauty by your rage.
(Aside.)
This should quench her anger's surging flame.   (22)
(He falls at her feet.)

These are not your Mālavikā's feet
That gratify your longing for a touch.

(*Leaves with her attendants.*)

GAUTAMA

Rise up! You are blessed.

KING (*Getting up and not seeing Irāvatī*).

What, is the dear one gone?

GAUTAMA

Happily she went away, but did not
Forgive you for your fault. So let us go
Quickly before she comes again with vengeance
Striking like the angry planet, Mars!

KING

Look at the inconstancy of love:
Since I am captivated by a new
And happier love, rejection leaves me free;
I may as well neglect the angry queen
Though she pursues me so incessantly.   (23)

(**Exeunt.**)

Act Four

(*Enter the king and a female attendant, Pratīhārī.*)

KING

May love's tree—that when I heard her voice
In my enamored heart took sturdy root,
That put forth buds when I observed her first,
That when I touched her promptly came to shoot
Shudders of joy throughout my every limb—
May this tree at the last yield savory fruit.   (1)
Hear me, Gautama!

PRATĪHĀRĪ

Victory to the king!
Sire, Gautama is not near at hand.

KING (*Aside*).

I sent him to bring news of Mālavikā.

GAUTAMA (*Entering*).

Victory to the king! I have returned.

KING

Servant, find where Queen Dhārinī is
And how she suffers from her wounded foot.

PRATĪHĀRĪ

I shall obey your majesty's commands.

KING

Ah, friend, what's the condition of the lady?

GAUTAMA

That of a cuckoo captured by a cat.

KING (*Sadly*).

What do you mean?

GAUTAMA

That the poor wretch is thrown
Into a dungeon, like the jaws of death,
As the woman with the flashing eyes commands.

KING

Is this because I merely spoke with her?

GAUTAMA

Undoubtedly it is.

KING

Friend Gautama,
Who was so evil-minded as to plant
This blazing anger in Dhāriṇī's heart?

GAUTAMA

Listen! The ascetic lady tells me
That yesterday the lady Irāvatī
Went to the queen inquiring of her health,
Since she had hurt her foot.

KING

Well.

GAUTAMA

The queen said
She had not lately seen you. Then she told her
The reason for your absence which, she said,
Is that her servant is so dear to you.

KING

This makes the queen jealous of Mālavikā,
Regardless of the truth.

GAUTAMA

Then she, being pressed,
Told the queen everything of your misconduct.

KING

She is obdurate in anger. Tell me more.

GAUTAMA

What is there more to say? Poor Mālavikā
And Bakulāvalikā lie in chains,
Incarcerated, where no daylight comes,
Like two snake-maidens prisoned underground.[14]

KING

The sweet-voiced cuckoo and the honey-bee,
Companions in the budding mango-tree,
Are driven to its hollow by a gale
Of wind, accompanied by rain and hail.   (2)
Friend, is there any plot to alter this?

GAUTAMA

How is it possible? Stern Mādhavikā,
The jailer, has an order from the queen
Never to let the wretched prisoners free
Unless she sees her royal signet-ring.

KING (Sighing).
What possible relief can we apply?
GAUTAMA (Thinking).
There is one even here.
KING
What can it be?
GAUTAMA (Looking around).
Someone might overhear our conversation;
I shall tell it to you in your ear.
(He does so.)
KING
My, what a clever plan! Carry it out!
PRATĪHĀRĪ (Entering).
Lord, the queen is resting on her bed,
In open air, her wounded foot all plastered
With thick, red sandal paste and held on high
By servants, while the venerable lady
Amuses her by reading moral stories.
KING
That makes a good excuse to visit her.
GAUTAMA
Then go, my friend, and meanwhile I shall get
Some flowers to offer to the ailing queen
So that I may not meet her empty-handed.
KING
Before, inform the servant of our plan.
GAUTAMA (Whispers in her ear.)
This it is, good lady.
KING
Now, my servant,
Show me the porch on which the queen is resting.
PRATĪHĀRĪ
Here is the way.
(The queen is seen lying on her couch with the Priestess and attendants ac-
cording to their rank.)
QUEEN
Lady, you have read a story
With an absorbing plot. What happens next?
PRIESTESS (Looking around).
I shall take it up another time.

His majesty the king has come.

QUEEN

Ah, king!

(Tries to rise.)

KING

Omit the ceremony, noble queen!
O sweet-voiced girl, you should not pain your foot
And me at the same time. It is not used
To being bare of ornaments. When not
On its gold footstool it appears abused.   (3)

PRIESTESS

Victory to the king!

QUEEN

May the king prosper!

KING (After saluting the Priestess and taking a seat.)

Lady, is the pain endurable?

QUEEN

Thank you, there is some improvement now.

(Enter Gautama, alarmed, with his thumb tied with his sacred cord.)

GAUTAMA

Help, help! I have been bitten by a snake.

(All turn pale.)

KING

Where did this fearful accident occur?

GAUTAMA

I went into the garden to pick flowers,
As usual on visiting the queen.
O help me, help me!

QUEEN

A terrible mischance!
I have placed a Brahman's life in danger! [15]

GAUTAMA

As I put out a hand to pluck a cluster
Of red asoka flowers, death in snake's guise
Came from a cavity and bit my finger.
Look here and see the twin marks of its teeth.

(Shows the bite.)

PRIESTESS

The rule is that the first thing to be done
Is to cut out the bite. Let us do this.

The cutting or the burning of the limb
Or letting blood have proved the only right
Remedies for men attacked by snakes
And elsewise due to perish of the bite.   (4)
KING
This is the business of the poison-doctor.
Servant, bring Dhruvasiddhi quickly here!
PRATĪHĀRĪ
As you command!
(Exit.)
GAUTAMA
Ah, Death has come to take me!
KING
Don't be afraid! The bite may not be poisonous.
GAUTAMA
How can I help it? All my limbs are shaking.
QUEEN
See how the poison wracks his limbs! Support him!
(The attendants support him, with fear and trembling.)
GAUTAMA (To the king).
Your highness, I have been your friend from childhood;
Remember this. Care for my helpless mother!
KING
Don't be afraid! The doctor soon will see you.
Only be quiet!
PRATĪHĀRĪ (Entering).
King, Dhruvasiddhi asks
That Gautama be taken to him promptly.
KING
Carry him to the doctor and support him
Carefully in the arms of the court eunuchs.
PRATĪHĀRĪ
It shall be as your majesty commands.
GAUTAMA (To the queen).
Lady, whether I live or die, forgive me
For any fault that I may have committed
Serving his majesty!
QUEEN
May you live long!
(Exeunt Gautama and Pratīhārī.)

PRATĪHĀRĪ (Entering).

Victory to the king! Dhruvasiddhi orders
That something with the image of a snake
Be placed upon the snake-wound and it then
Be subject to a ritual bath of water.

QUEEN

Here is my ring with a gold serpent on it.—
Take it and afterwards return it to me.

(Hands over the ring.)

KING

Servant, report the progress of the cure.

PRATĪHĀRĪ

It shall be as your majesty commands.

(Exit.)

PRIESTESS

My heart pursuades me that he has recovered.

KING

I pray it may be so.

PRATĪHĀRĪ (Entering).

Victory to the king!
Gautama is cured and healthy as before!

QUEEN

Fortunately I am cleared from blame.

PRATĪHĀRĪ

The minister Vāhataka requests
That public matters now may be considered
And therefore asks the favor of a visit.

QUEEN

Go, my lord and may you be successful!

KING

Lady, this porch is open to the sun.
Cool treatment is thought proper for your pain.
So have your couch removed.

QUEEN

Attendants, do
As the king orders.

ATTENDANTS

Queen, it shall be done.

(Exit the queen, with her attendants, and the priestess.)

                              KING
Servant, lead me to the pleasure-garden
Along a secret path.
                            PRATĪHĀRĪ
          This way, my lord.
                              KING
Has Gautama accomplished his designs?
                            PRATĪHĀRĪ
No doubt of it. That is as usual.
                              KING
Although I find the strategy well planned,
With its fulfillment shrewdly carried out,
My heart is still on tenterhooks. I feel
Uncomfortable restlessness and doubt.   (5)
                      GAUTAMA (Entering).
Victory to the king! I have completed all.
                              KING
Servant, you may go about your work.
                            PRATĪHĀRĪ
I do as you require.
                            (Exit.)
                              KING
          Friend, the old jailer
Is shrewd. Didn't she ask you any questions? [16]
                            GAUTAMA
How could she, when I showed her the queen's ring?
                              KING
I am not disrespectful to the ring,
But she ought naturally to have asked the cause
For liberation of the prisoners
And why you were commissioned for the purpose
Rather than the queen's own messengers.
                            GAUTAMA
Yes, I was asked these questions. I replied,
Using my usual aplomb of thought.
I said, astrologers have told the king
That deep misfortune threatens his estate
And urged that all the prisoners be released.
I said that when Dhārinī learned of this,
Wishing to spare Queen Irāvatī's mind,

She ordered all the prisoners be freed.—
Hearing this, the guard was well contented.
KING (Embracing Gautama).
Friend, I recognize you love me dearly.
What friends accomplish is not done alone
Through intellect; the love itself of friends
Traverses a pathway to success
And by hard work accomplishes its ends.   (6)
GAUTAMA
Hurry, my lord. I have placed Mālavikā,
With her attendant, in the summerhouse.
KING
I shall welcome her. Walk on.
GAUTAMA
Here is the house.
KING (Anxiously).
There comes the maid Chandrikā, who attends
On Irāvatī, busy gathering flowers.
Hurry! Hide ourselves behind this wall!
GAUTAMA
Thieves and lovers must avoid the moonlight.
(They hide.)
KING
Gautama, is your friend there waiting for me?
Let's observe her through this narrow window.
(They observe.)
(Mālavikā and Bakulāvalikā are seen.)
BAKULĀVALIKĀ
Friend, salute the king, who stands in profile.
KING
I judge that she is showing her my portrait.[17]
MĀLAVIKĀ (Joyfully).
King, I salute you!
(She looks toward the door and expresses disappointment.)
But where is the king?
Oh, you have cheated me!
KING
Friend, I am pleased
Both with the lady's joy and disappointment:
All at once my loved one's lotus face

Assumed two aspects that no heart forgets:
One, with the brilliance of the rising sun,
One with sadness when the sun has set.   (7)

BAKULĀVALIKĀ

Indeed his majesty is in the picture.

BOTH (After bowing to him).

Victory to the king!

MĀLAVIKĀ

I did not gratify
My thirst for viewing the splendor of the king
That time I saw him in the theater
So completely as I do today,
For now I look at him in perfect leisure
With all attention that one gives a painting.

GAUTAMA

Did you hear that? The lady says you look
Much better in the picture than in life.
Now your arrogance of youth is vain,
Like a casket proud of holding jewels.

KING

Women are curious but by nature bashful:
These wide-eyed women, though they wish to see
Their lovers freely the first hour they meet,
Keep their eyes closed through natural modesty,
As persons who are timid or discreet.   (8)

MĀLAVIKĀ

Who is that girl who turns her face aside,
At whom the king is looking lovingly?

BAKULĀVALIKĀ.

Surely, that woman must be Irāvatī.

MĀLAVIKĀ.

Friend, he seems wanting in civility
Since he has so much set his eyes on her,
Neglecting all the ladies of his palace.

BAKULĀVALIKĀ (Aside).

She is angry at his majesty
In pictured form, assuming him alive.
Since this is so, I shall amuse myself.

(Aloud.)

She is the favorite of his majesty.

MĀLAVIKĀ

Then why should I disturb myself at all?
(She turns angrily aside.)
KING

See, my friend, her gestures and expression:
In the gesticulation of her hands
She shows the lessons of her drama tutor,
With quivering lip and knitted eyebrows, bent
In angry fury at a faulty suitor!   (9)
GAUTAMA

Be ready to propitiate her now!
MĀLAVIKĀ

Here is the Brahman, waiting on the king.
(She again shows her wish to look in another direction.)
BAKULĀVALIKĀ (Preventing her).

Certainly you are not angry now.
MĀLAVIKĀ

My friend, if you consider I've been angry
Too long, I certainly shall cease to be so.[18]
KING (Coming forward).

Why are you angry with me, lotus child,
Just for a picture which you chance to view?
Here is indeed your servant in true life,
Devoted to no other girl than you.   (10)
BAKULĀVALIKĀ

Victory to the king!
MĀLAVIKĀ

Was I angry at the king
As painted in a picture? Lord, forgive me!
(Expressing bashfulness, she joins her hands in supplication. The king seems
distracted by love.)
GAUTAMA

Why do you seem distracted?
KING

Because your friend
Is so unstable.
GAUTAMA

Do not doubt her.
KING

Listen:

She appears in dream, then vanishes in a moment;
She comes within my grasp, then fades away;
How can my heart, that suffers from love's torture,
Find in this phantom any trust or stay? (11)

BAKULĀVALIKĀ

You have deceived his majesty too far.
Now is the time to fortify his trust.

MĀLAVIKĀ

I am an unfortunate, who found
Union with the king hard even in a dream.

BAKULĀVALIKĀ

King, answer her.

KING

What use in a reply?
All I had to give to love I gave.
Fires of love consume me. I am not
Her master, but in secret am her slave. (12)

BAKULĀVALIKĀ

I thank you for her.

GAUTAMA (Walking about in agitation).

Bakulāvalikā,
Here is a deer coming to eat the shoots
Of the asoka. Hurry and drive it off!

BAKULĀVALIKĀ

I see.

(She starts to go.)

KING

Be always careful for our safety.

GAUTAMA

That caution is superfluous for me.

BAKULĀVALIKĀ

Noble Gautama, I'll conceal myself,
While you will watch the door.

GAUTAMA

All this is right.

(Exit Bakulāvalikā.)

I shall sit here on this polished stone.—
I find it strangely pleasant to the touch.[19]

(He sleeps.)

Ah, lovely girl, put off your bashfulness,
Be like a vine whose arms clasp ardently
A trunk that long has been its one support.
You are the vine and I the mango tree. (13)

MĀLAVIKĀ
I dread the queen and so I fear to do
What I should dearly wish.

KING
Don't fear, don't fear!

MĀLAVIKĀ
You are a fearless man but yet you seemed
To fear like me when you faced Irāvatī.

KING
Politeness is traditional with lovers
And I, my sweet-lipped girl, depend on you,
The girl who views me with long, almond eyes,
To whom I am perpetually true. (14)
So accept me as your constant lover.
(He starts to embrace her; Mālavikā avoids him.)
(Aside.)
Young women behave charmingly with lovers:
She trembles and draws back my eager hand
Busy about the girdle at her breast;
She covers this with her own hands when all
My body leans against her, closely pressed;
She turns away her face, shutting the lashes
Of almond eyes when I would force a kiss:
She gives me joy, fulfilling my desire,
Jesting in forms of love's antithesis. (15)
(Enter Irāvatī and Nipunikā.)

IRĀVATĪ
Nipunikā, did Chandrikā really say
She saw Gautama sitting all alone
Upon the terrace of the summerhouse?

NIPUNIKĀ
If she did not, how could I dare to tell
Your majesty that such a thing was true?

IRĀVATĪ
Then let us go there to inquire the health

Of his high majesty's most faithful friend,
Just rescued from the fearful claws of death.

NIPUNIKĀ

My mistress has some further words to say.

IRĀVATĪ

I'll ask the pardon of his highness' portrait.

NIPUNIKĀ

Why not rather ask the king himself?

IRĀVATĪ

Foolish girl, his majesty's whole heart
Is given to another, so to me
He is no better than a painted figure.
My aim is to atone for incivility.

NIPUNIKĀ

If this is what you wish, be on our way.
(They walk about.)

CHETĪ (Entering).

May my mistress prosper! The queen says
That this is not the time for her to show
Her jealousy, that she put Mālavikā,
Together with her friend, in iron chains
Only to show the high respect in which
Your majesty is held. If you agree
To aid his majesty, she also will.
So let her know your wishes in this matter.

IRĀVATĪ

Chetī, tell the queen that I cannot
Obey, that she has shown me a true favor
Imprisoning her servants and that no one
Does me a greater service than herself.

CHETĪ

I shall deliver these instructions to her.
(Exit.)

NIPUNIKĀ (Moving about and observing).

Lady, look here! By the pavilion door
Gautama is sitting fast asleep,
An old ox drowsing in the market place.

IRĀVATĪ

Ah, I can hardly believe the ill effects
Come from the poisoned snake-bite can remain.

NIPUNIKĀ

Judging by his face, he looks at ease.
Besides, having been drugged by Dhruvasiddhi,
Nothing dangerous possibly can touch him.

GAUTAMA (Dreaming).

Mālavikā—

NIPUNIKĀ

Mistress, did you hear?
This rogue, this rascal, this insatiable glutton,
Avid of hearing any talk of eating,
Stuffed to the throat with sweetmeats that we gave him
Out of pure reverence, now, in drunken sleep,
Prattles only about Mālavikā.

GAUTAMA

I pray that you may checkmate Irāvatī.

NIPUNIKĀ

Ha, what's this I hear? I'll hide myself
Behind this pillar and scare this wretched Brahman.
The means will be this crooked stick of mine,
Since he is frightened half to death by snakes.

IRĀVATĪ

The rascal well deserves your punishment.

(Nipunikā drops the stick on Gautama.)

GAUTAMA (Waking up abruptly).

Help, help, help! A snake has fallen on me!

KING (Suddenly appearing).

Friend, take heart, take heart!

MĀLAVIKĀ (Following).

King, do not rush
So thoughtlessly away! He only says
He sees a snake.

IRĀVATĪ

Oh, oh, his majesty
Himself is rushing to the rascal's help.

GAUTAMA (Laughing).

Why look! the snake turns out to be a stick!
I thought the snake-bite that I imitated
By scratches with a thorn had turned a true one.

(Bakulāvalikā enters, tossing aside the curtain.)

BAKULĀVALIKĀ (Confused).
Where is the snake? Don't take a step, your highness!
Here is something crooked like a snake.
IRĀVATĪ (Coming forward and addressing the king.)
I hope your assignation has been pleasant!
(All are confused on seeing Irāvatī.)
KING
What an extraordinary form of greeting!
IRĀVATĪ
Bakulāvalikā, happily
You have fulfilled your role as go-between.
BALULĀVALIKĀ
Pardon, my lady! Does the great god, Indra,
Neglect his love, the Earth, when frogs cease croaking?
GAUTAMA
Do not say that! His majesty forgets
The scorn you showed him kneeling at your feet
Merely by seeing your rare loveliness,
While you as yet are not at peace with him.
IRĀVATĪ
What shall I do now, when I still am angry?
KING
You should not be angry without cause:
When was your face and your still fairer body
Ever the seat of anger without cause?
How should the night obscure the perfect moon
Unless the eclipse invokes celestial laws?   (16)
IRĀVATĪ
Doubtless his majesty was correct in saying
That I was angry without proper right.
Henceforth if my property is stolen
And I am angry, I am ridiculous.
KING
You are mistaken. I see no cause for rage.
Servants ought not to be held in prison
On days of popular festivity.
Moreover, when the prisoners are released
Their duty is to pay respects to me.   (17)
IRĀVATĪ
Nipunikā, inform the queen Dhārinī

That I have found her partiality
To Mālavikā.

NIPUNIKĀ

I shall do so, madam.

(Exit.)

GAUTAMA (Aside).

Ah, what bad luck! A pigeon that escaped
Its cage has fallen into the hawk's beak!

NIPUNIKĀ (Entering).

Mistress, I have just met with Mādhavikā
Who told me how the matter came about.

(She whispers in her ear.)

IRĀVATĪ (Aside).

Well, well, I see this rascally Brahmana
Conceived and executed the design
Of capturing the fortress, Mālavikā,
Through policy of the Minister of Love.

GAUTAMA

If I have read a word of policy
May I forget the words of Holy Writ!

KING (Aside).

How can I possibly escape my troubles?

(A servant enters in confusion.)

SERVANT

King, the little princess, Vasulakshmī,
Was running for her ball when a brown monkey [20]
Frightened her terribly out of her wits
And even though sitting on Queen Dhārinī's lap
Now trembles like a twig in windy weather
And has not yet regained her natural spirits.

KING

What timid creatures all we children are!

IRĀVATĪ (Confused).

Hurry, your majesty, to comfort her
And do not let her terror-tantrums grow.

KING

I shall easily bring her to her senses.

(He walks rapidly about.)

MĀLAVIKĀ

Friend, my heart trembles thinking of the queen.

I cannot tell what more I have to suffer.

VOICE (*Behind the curtain*).

Marvelous, marvelous! The gold asoka
Is flourishing with blossoms long before
Five nights after the ritual have passed.
I must tell the queen immediately.

(*Both show delight.*)

BAKULĀVALIKĀ

Dear, be at rest! The queen has kept her word.

MĀLAVIKĀ

Then let us follow the old gardener.

BAKULĀVALIKĀ

Yes!

(Exeunt.)

Act Five

(Enter a woman gardener.)

GARDENER

I have fenced in this gold asoka tree
That answers to the purifying spell.
Now I must inform the queen of this.—
Ah, fate should be more just to Mālavikā!
Perhaps the angry queen will feel compassion
On hearing that her loved asoka flowers.
Where can she be?—Ah, here is Sārasaka,
The hunchback, belonging to the queen's attendants,
Come from the palace with a box in hand,
Sealed with red lac. I shall at once ask him.

(The hunchback enters.)

Sārasaka, where are you going now?

SĀRASAKA

Madhukarikā, here is the monthly treasure
Accumulated for the learned Brahmans.
I'm carrying it to the high priest.

MADHUKARIKĀ

But why?

SĀRASAKA

Ever since the queen heard Vasumitra
Was made the officer to keep strict guard
Over the sacrificial horse, she has given
Eighteen gold pieces to the learned men
To insure the preservation of its life.

MADHUKARIKĀ

That's as it should be. Where's the noble queen?

SĀRASAKA

She is sitting in the sacred hall
Hearing her brother Vīrasena's letter
Sent to her out of the Vidarbhā's country,
Read out to her by her learned scribes.

MADHUKARIKĀ

What news comes from the king of the Vidarbhās?

SĀRASAKA

The loyal army Vīrasena leads
Has overwhelmed the lord of the Vidarbhās
Freeing his relative, Mādhāvasena.
This man has sent as present to our king
Wagons filled with jewels and attendants.
Most of the girls are well trained in the arts.—
The ambassador will see our king tomorrow.

MADHUKARIKĀ

Go on your business. I shall see the queen.

(Exeunt.)

PRATĪHĀRĪ (Entering).

I am ordered by the queen to tell the king
She wishes him to join her to inspect
The fresh-blown blossoms on the asoka tree.
I shall address him when he comes to judgment.

TWO BARDS (Behind the curtain).

We hail his majesty, who by his might
Tramples the heads of all his enemies.

FIRST BARD

You pass the spring in those delightful gardens
Flourishing on Vidīshā's fertile shore
Loud with delightful chanting of the cuckoos,
Blessed by the god of love whom all adore.
Brave giver-of-gifts, your unexampled valor,
Your matchless prowess, bows your enemies low,
As, where your victory-elephants are fastened,
Tall trees bend down in humbled overthrow.   (1)

SECOND BARD

Your victories over the Krathakaīsikās
Are celebrated in our god-like songs.
Pure in your love of courage, with your might
You pillaged them of riches; men of Sauri
Suffered also when, with war's alarms,
You carried off their champion, Rukminī,
With strength of trees in his four massive arms.   (2)

PRATĪHĀRĪ

Here comes his majesty with his procession,
Acclaimed by shouts of joy and victory.

I shall place myself a step aside
Protected by the archway of this terrace.
(She stands aside. The king and Gautama enter.)

KING

When I consider how my love is cold
And hear of the Vidarbhās overpowered,
I feel my heart a lotus now in sun
And now by summer tempests overshowered.   (3)

GAUTAMA

I believe your pleasures will be absolute.

KING

Friend, how can I anticipate that blessing?

GAUTAMA

Today your queen, Dhārinī, interviewed
The venerable priestess, Kausikī,
Deeply skilled in decorative arts
Concerning marriage dress among Vidarbhās
Fit for the gracious limbs of Mālavikā.
Now she is robed in glorious attire
And the good queen may gain her special wish.

KING

Friend, that indeed is likely, for the queen
Has long been free from petty jealousy
And shown compliance with my own desires.

PRATĪHĀRĪ (Coming forward).

Victory to the king! Your noble queen declares
That she will be rewarded for her labors
If you will keep her company in viewing
The blossoms on the gold asoka-tree.

KING

Is she already there?

PRATĪHĀRĪ

Indeed she is.

First, after distributing awards
To all the harem ladies, she dismissed them.
Now she is waiting for you in the garden,
Her retinue headed by Mālavikā.

KING

Friend, lead us there.

GAUTAMA

This way, your majesty.

(*They walk about.*)

My friend, the spring here in your splendid garden
Seems almost past its youth.

KING

Yes, that is true.
The passing of the spring provokes regrets:
The mango tree is bending with its load
Of fruit, while lesser trees are richly decked
With fallen petals the kurabak bestowed.   (4)

GAUTAMA

This gold asoka with its clustered blooms
Is like a bride with many ornaments.
Please look at this!

KING

These later blooms are best,
For now they show their ripest splendor. See:
The beauty of the flowers that shone before
On earlier blooming trees is now distilled
In these; the virginal promises of April
Are now in this last, perfect bloom fulfilled.   (5)

GAUTAMA

Be confident. Dhārinī has observed
Our coming and on that account speaks kindly
To Mālavikā, standing by her.

KING (*Joyfully*).

Look!

Dhārinī, with great modesty, is rising
And walking towards me, followed by her band
Of maidens, Mālavikā at their head,
Like Lakshmī, with no lotus in her hand.   (6)

(Enter the priestess, the queen, Mālavikā and their followers, according to their
rank.)

MĀLAVIKĀ (Aside).

Although I know the reason for this rich
And fanciful decor, my faint heart trembles
Like a drop of water on a lotus leaf;
But then, auspiciously, my left eye quivers.

GAUTAMA

Ah, unquestionably Mālavikā
Radiates splendor in her marriage dress.

KING

I see her in her gorgeous ornaments:
Robed in a silken garment not too long,
Hung with few ornaments, though gleaming bright,
She is the moon of spring among star-clusters,
Shining through a clear, unclouded night. (7)

QUEEN

Victory to the king!

GAUTAMA

Long may your highness flourish!

PRIESTESS

May victory attend your majesty!

KING

Venerable lady, I salute you!

PRIESTESS

May all your dearest wishes be fulfilled!

QUEEN (Smiling).

I offer this asoka to my lord
To serve him for a springtime rendezvous,
Attended by the women of his court.

GAUTAMA

Oh, you are indeed propitiated.

KING (Walking reverently around the asoka).

This asoka certainly deserves
Her special worship, chosing to defer
Blossoming in the early days of spring
Until its vernal impulse came from her. (8)

GAUTAMA

Be cheerful; look at her who gleams with youth!

QUEEN

Who might this be whose youth glows so upon her?

GAUTAMA

Surely, the flowering, gold asoka tree!

(All sit down.)

KING (Looking at Mālavikā, aside).

Ah, we are divided and yet near.
I am the bird who only meets its mate

By day; my dear one now is in my sight;
But Queen Dhārinī is a bird of prey
Or some divisive spirit of the night.   (9)
                    CHAMBERLAIN (Entering).
Victory to the king! The minister
Reports through me that in the caravan
Sent from the conquered country of Vidarbhā
Were two accomplished girls, not first presented
Because fatigued by hardships of the journey.
They now are in a fit state to appear,
So may his majesty permit their entrance?
                    KING
Let us see them.
                    CHAMBERLAIN
          You shall be obeyed.
      (He goes out and returns with the two women, Jyotsnikā and Rajanikā.)
Come this way, young ladies, come this way!
                    JYOTSNIKĀ
Dear Rajanikā, I am in a trance
Of joy to see the splendor of this court.
                    RAJANIKĀ
Friend Jyotsnikā, I feel just as you.
There is a proverb saying that one's heart
Truly foretells a coming joy or sorrow.
                    JYOTSNIKĀ
I trust this may apply to us today.
                    CHAMBERLAIN
Here are the king and queen. Enter, my ladies!
(They come forward. Mālavikā and the Priestess exchange glances on seeeing
                    them.)
                    BOTH (Bowing).
Victory to the king! May the queen long flourish!
                    KING
Greetings to you both. Be seated here.
                    (Both sit.)
Ladies, I hear that you are skilled in arts.
What may be your chief accomplishments?
                    BOTH
We are trained in music.

KING

Queen, take one of them.

QUEEN

Look, Mālavikā, would you like to have
A partner in your singing?

BOTH

Ah, the princess!

(They bow and break into tears. All look surprised.)

KING

Who are you and who may this girl be?

JYOTSNIKĀ

King, she is the daughter of our prince.

KING

How can that be?

BOTH

King, listen to us. This
Is Mālavikā, younger sister of
Prince Mādhāvasena, whom your arms released
From prison, when your forces overthrew
The king of the Vidarbhās.

QUEEN

Ah, a princess!
I find I have defiled pure sandalwood,
Having transmuted it to humble shoes.

KING

How did the lady fall to this condition?

MĀLAVIKĀ (Sighing, aside).

By the resistless ordinance of fate.

RAJANIKĀ

Listen, king. When Mādhāvasena
Was rescued by his friends, this noble lady
Was taken by the minister, Sumati,
Leaving behind such servitors as us.

KING

I have known this before. So then, what happened?

BOTH

We cannot say what happened afterwards.

PRIESTESS

I, an unhappy woman, can report it.

Princess, the voice we hear appears to us
Like that of our old mistress, Kausikī.

MĀLAVIKĀ

Yes, this is she.

BOTH

Still, it is hard to tell
Our mistress in this plain ascetic dress.
We, too, salute the venerable lady.

PRIESTESS

Welcome, my girls!

KING

What, are these young women
Acquainted with the venerable priestess?

PRIESTESS

Indeed they are!

GAUTAMA

So you will kindly tell us
What still remains of Mālavikā's story.

PRIESTESS (Sadly).

Then listen. You should know that lord Sumati,
The loyal minister of Mādhāvasena,
Was actually my elder brother.

KING

Well,
All this is understood. What happened next?

PRIESTESS

He carried off this girl and me together,
After her brother had been lost, and meant
To take her in the company to Vidīshā,
Offering her in marriage to your highness.

KING

Then what happened?

PRIESTESS

When the merchants finished
Their business, they encamped beside a wood
To rest, long overwearied by their travels.

KING

And then?

PRIESTESS

Then suddenly a band of robbers,
Armed with quivers, ready for the fight,
Wearing peacock feathers on their caps,
With bows in hand and armor shining bright,
Attacked with such a furious assault
They terrified us by their very sight. (10)
(Mālavikā seems afraid.)

GAUTAMA

Do not be alarmed! The reverend lady
Is only telling of an action past.

KING

And so what happened?

PRIESTESS

Soldiers to protect
The caravan fought bravely for a time
But soon were put to flight.

KING

My reverend lady,
I judge we'll hear a tale of sadness.

PRIESTESS

Then
My brother, who was faithful to his lord,
Entered valiantly into the strife
To save the girl from capture but was helpless
And for his loyal service gave his life. (11)

JYOTSNIKĀ

So our good lord and master now is dead.

RAJANIKĀ

This explains the troubles of our princess.
(The princess weeps.)

KING

This is the common fortune of mankind.
Do not grieve too deeply for your brother
Whose loyal death repaid his master's care!

PRIESTESS

I fainted; then, recovering, found the lady
Was out of sight.

KING

You have had great troubles, madam.

I burned my brother's body. In deep sorrow,
Like widowhood, I came into your country
Wearing the saffron garment of religion.

KING

That is a fitting life for pious people.
Then what occurred?

PRIESTESS

This lady was delivered
Out of the robbers' grasp by Vīrasena
And sent by him a handmaid for the queen.
So I met her here when I was granted
Admission to the palace. This is all.

MĀLAVIKĀ (Aside).

Now what can be his majesty's response?

KING

Ah, misfortunes bring us to disgrace!
One treated as a servant rightly owns
The title and the service of a queen.
A noble garment of the finest silk
Was put to kitchen uses, base and mean.   (12)

QUEEN

You should have told me, venerable lady,
That Mālavikā was of noble birth.

PRIESTESS

Do not say that. You are wrong. I had good reason
To keep the secret.

QUEEN

What could that have been?

KING

Tell us, then, if that is now permitted.

PRIESTESS

A divine sage of supernatural powers,
Who has assumed the body of a man,
Long ago, when her father was alive,
Declared that she would suffer for one year
The labors of a servant and would then
Acquire a husband fitting for her rank.
So when I recognized this prophecy

Would be fulfilled, I bided my own time,
And so by doing believe that I was right.
KING

You acted prudently to wait in patience.
CHAMBERLAIN

King, the minister dispatched this message
Which I have been commissioned to report
But could not do so for these interruptions.
He says that the Vidarbhās stand in judgment
And now desire to hear the king's decision.
KING

Chamberlain, my wish is to establish
The brothers, Vajnasena and Mādhāvasena,
In equal rule of the Vidarbhās' country.
Let them hold the northern and the southern
Shores of their river in an equal sway,
Just as the moon and sun in peace divide
Between themselves the nighttime and the day.   (13)
CHAMBERLAIN

I shall report this to the ministers.
(The king agrees by moving a finger. The chamberlain goes out.)
JYOTSNIKĀ. (Aside to Mālavikā).

Princess, I give you my felicitations.
Your brother now possesses half a kingdom.
MĀLAVIKĀ

Rather I ought to think it a prime blessing
That he is rescued from the threat of death.
CHAMBERLAIN (Entering).

Victory to the king! The ministers admit
The king's decision as magnanimous.
Further, your loyal ministry declares:
Two princes sharing in the royal splendor
Will serve as tractable and firm compeers,
As horses serving underneath your yokes
Guided by their skillful charioteers.   (14)
KING

Go, tell the council to dispatch Vīrasena
With written memoranda to this end.
CHAMBERLAIN

I shall.

(He goes out and reenters, holding a letter and a jewel.)

The order of the king has been performed.
Here is a letter from Prince Pushpamitra,
Together with a gift. King, look at it.
(The king places the jewel on his head, then passes it to an attendant and opens the letter.)

QUEEN

Ah, my heart looks eagerly to that.
After good wishes for the royal health
I shall hear messages of Vasumitra.
The general gave my son a princely rank.

KING *(Sits and reads.)*

"May you be fortunate! I, Pushpamitra,
Commander in the sacrificial court,
Commend me to the son of Agnimitra,
Embracing him with absolute affection,
There in the territory of Vidīshā.
Hear, then, that I have now initiated
The sacrificial ritual of the horse,[21]
Let loose and free from all impediments,
To be returned after a year, appointing
Vasumitra as its guardian,
Aided by a hundred janissaries.
This steed when by the right bank of the Sindhu
Yavanās threatened with a thousand horse.
Then ensued a sharp, heroic battle
Between their army and our smaller force."   (15)

(The queen shows dismay.)
KING *(Aside)*.

Could such a conflict possibly have happened?
(He continues reading.)

"Then Vasumitra, the resistless archer,
Defeating the invaders, brought to safety
My noble horse, already in their hands."

QUEEN

My heart revives.

KING *(Still reading)*.

"So now that through my grandson
My horse returns to me, as Amsumat
Brought back Sagara's steed, I shall begin

The sacrifices. You, rejecting anger,
Must join me speedily, bringing in your troop
The daughter-in-law whom I sincerely love."
I am satisfied.

PRIESTESS

Praise to the king and queen,
Happy in the victory of their noble son!

(Looking at the queen.)

Your husband elevates you as the chief
Of wives his sacred majesty has won,
But honor as the mother of a hero
Comes to you through the triumph of your son.   (16)

GAUTAMA

How happily your son follows his father!

KING

Observe, my chamberlain, the elephant's young
Imitates the leader of the herd.

CHAMBERLAIN

Not even his most valiant deeds produce
Wonder, since his body and soul arise
From you, as Aurva is the quenchless fire
Before whose violence even water dies.   (17)

KING

Chamberlain, free the noble brother-in-law
Of Vajnasena and all the other prisoners.

CHAMBERLAIN

The orders of the king shall be obeyed.

QUEEN

Jayasenā, go to Irāvatī
And all the lesser ladies of the harem
Telling them of the triumph of my son.

PRATĪHĀRĪ

The queen shall be obeyed.

(She begins to leave.)
QUEEN

But stay a moment!

PRATĪHĀRĪ (Returning).

I am here.

QUEEN (Aside to Pratīhārī).

Tell Queen Irāvatī

From me what I have promised Mālavikā
When I engaged her to perform the rite
Of fertilizing the asoka-tree.
Tell them also of her noble birth
And move her by reminding her she must not
Through any motive deviate from truth.
PRATĪHĀRĪ
The queen shall be obeyed.
(She goes out and returns.)
Lady, I bring
A casket that contains the precious jewels
That ladies of the harem handed me
In honor of the victory of your son.
QUEEN
What is there wonderful in that? This triumph
Alike is common to themselves and me.
PRATĪHĀRĪ (To the queen).
Irāvatī furthermore requests
That you shall alter nothing you have done.
QUEEN
Priestess, I beseech you for permission
To bestow Mālavikā on the king,
As good Sumati formerly designed.
PRIESTESS
Henceforth you have her in your own command.
QUEEN (Taking Mālavikā's hand).
Let his majesty have Mālavikā
As due reward for bringing happy news.
(The king modestly remains silent.)
QUEEN (Smiling).
Why does his majesty so overlook me?
GAUTAMA
New bridegrooms, it is said, are always bashful.
(The king looks at Gautama.)
Or better, the king wishes Queen Dhārinī
To give the title "Queen" to Mālavikā
Before he entertains her as his bride.
QUEEN
The title of a queen is hers by right
Of birth. What is the use of repetition?

Do not say so, my queen, do not say that!
You are fortunate, for jewels taken
Directly from the mine we never hold
As worthy until polished, but thereafter
As fit to be united with pure gold.   (18)

QUEEN

The venerable lady will forgive me,
For I was overwhelmed with happy news.—
Servant, go, and fetch silk garments for her.

PRATĪHĀRĪ

The queen is answered.
       (Goes out and returns with a silk garment in hand.)
           Lady, they are here.
      QUEEN (Robing Mālavikā with the dress).
Now let his majesty accept her freely!

KING

Lady, your goodness leaves me without words.

PRIESTESS

She is at last accepted by the king.

GAUTAMA

How obedient the king is to the queen!
        (The queen looks at her attendants.)
      ATTENDANTS (Approaching Mālavikā).
Victory to the queen!

PRIESTESS

       These actions are not strange.
Chaste women serve their husbands, bringing them
New brides to be their rivals, dutifully,
Much as rivers draw a thousand brooks
Downward in beauty to the lordly sea.   (19)

        NIPUNIKĀ (Entering).
Victory to the king! Queen Irāvatī says
She acted to her lord with disrespect
And now that she has won her dearest wish,
She should win full pardon and forgiveness.

QUEEN

Certainly the king will grant her plea.

NIPUNIKĀ

I shall report it as the queen requests.
(Exit.)

PRIESTESS

King, if you will grant me such a grace,
I wish to visit Mādhāvasena, now
So happy in his recent league with you.

QUEEN

Reverend lady, do not leave us now!

PRIESTESS

I am your dependent through your love.

QUEEN

May his majesty deign to inform me
What further service I can do for him?

KING

What more could I desire? But be this added:
Angry and beautiful, I beg of you,
But rather ask it of my other wife,
Your rival, that both may, out of your goodness,
Be favorable to me all my life.
Surely, no evils can afflict my subjects
Nor any malice nor misfortune fling
The six calamities of ill upon them
While Agnimitra serves them as their king!   (20)
(Exeunt omnes.)

Notes

POEMS BY TU FU

1) This poem was written in recognition of Assistant Secretary Chia Chih's audience in the morning ceremony at the Imperial Ta-ming Palace. His father had held the same position.

2) This poem was presumably written during September, 756, when, owing to the rebellion headed by An Lu-shan, the poet was living in the capital Ch'ang-an, and his family in Fu-chou, many miles distant.

3) This poem records the poet's reunion with his family after their separation occasioned by the civil war ravaging China in 757. Such wars provided the subject for many of Tu Fu's compositions.

4) Li Po, most celebrated of Chinese poets contemporary with Tu Fu, was his close friend. Li had a brief, brilliant career at court, after which he passed many years in exile.

5) This poem was presumably written in 750, when Tu Fu became keenly aware of the disastrous price paid for aggressive campaigns conducted on China's far-flung borders.

6) This poem has been dated differently by its commentators. William Hung assigns it to 758, when Tu Fu was elated at the prospect that the rebel An Ch'ing-hsü would be overcome and peace be soon restored to the Empire.

7) This poem is best understood as Tu Fu's humorous rebuke of himself. Frank expression of political opinion at Court damaged both his own fortunes and those of his friends.

8) Horses long supplied a favorite subject for Chinese painters and sculptors.

9) Ssu-ma Hsiang-ju was one of the most celebrated literary figures of the first century B.C., after which his house was preserved as a memorial. The poem epitomizes his romantic career.

10) This is one of Tu Fu's occasional expressions of ideas commonly found in Asian religions endorsing quietism. Taoist doctrines appear to have been uppermost in his mind here.

11) Chinese painting and poetry stand in the most intimate relation. Descriptive poems were commonly written on pictured scrolls. Picture and poem show a common imagery.

12) This poem describes the deplorable conditions in China immediately before the outbreak of the An Lu-shan rebellion in December, 755.

13) This poem appears to have been written in 757, very shortly after Tu Fu ended his laborious journey of some 215 miles from the temporary capital at Feng-hsiang to his home in the village of Ch'iang. It is to be understood as a circumstantial account, resembling notes in a diary.

14) This poem may be regarded as a poetical epistle in the typical Chinese manner. It constitutes an apology for a considerable part of Tu Fu's career.

15) Confucius.

16) Self-depreciation constitutes a humorous convention in much Chinese verse. See also the poems, "Drunk, I Fell from Horseback," page 89, "Twenty Rhymes to Dispel Gloom," page 83, and "Just a Note," page 87.

17) Written during political disturbances in 766.

18) By "Confucius' school" Tu Fu refers to imitators of the Book of Songs, selections from which are given on pages 137–199.

19) The "Brilliant Emperor" is Hsuan-tsung (685–762), who flourished during the early years of Tu Fu's life and whose downfall constituted the most important political event of the period. He was a lavish patron of all the arts.

20) This poem well illustrates Tu Fu's relation to orthodox religion. Its teachings and practice supplied him with welcome periods of release but he was first of all both poet and man of action. Even when visiting among the contemplatives in their monasteries, he found his chief satisfaction in study of his craft as poet.

21) This familiar quotation refers in figurative language to the view that a man's death should be accomplished with honor and dignity.

22) This line expresses the orthodox view of the intimate and harmonious relation assumed to exist between the cosmos and the Imperial rule.

23) This expression voices an ancient Chinese ideal that political power though firm should be exercised with an imperceptible sway.

24) This expression of the charms of informality accords with the idealism of the poet Li Po, to whom the lines are addressed, and reflects obversely on the heavy burdens of Chinese decorum and convention.

25) The "Eight Immortals" are in reality Tu Fu's drinking companions, all eminent figures in the current life of the Imperial Court. They are not the sages and mystics to whom the words usually apply.

26) This poem is written in accord with the Chinese literary convention that makes a virtue of retirement and non-action. The poet Li Po mentioned in the last lines was himself a celebrated exponent of this view.

27) The "sea-gull" stands for Tu Fu. The poet especially enjoyed such understatements regarding himself. Compelled to travel often, he thought of himself as migrating with the birds.

28) The lines describe a famous shrine dedicated to the Buddhist deity, Kuan-Yin.

29) The Milky Way.

30) This poem describes a young member of the Imperial family who hid from the victorious rebels during the rebellion of 756.

31) This poem describes the capital, Ch'ang-an, when it was dominated by the forces of the rebel leader An Lu-shan during the year 757.

32) These lines describe the ruins of a palace built for the Emperor T'ai-tsung in 646.

33) Petitions for aid are extremely common in Chinese poetry, which often frankly displays a utilitarian purpose. See also "Staying in the Boat," pages 94–95.

34) "Cowboy and Weaving Girl" refers to the popular myth which relates that once a year these lovers, both celestial deities, effect a

meeting, crossing "The River-in-the-Sky," namely, the Milky Way.

35) This poem is to be understood in the light of the inveterate animism of Chinese mythology. Even a cane shares the vitality and precarious existence of a living plant.

36) This poem concerns the famous statesman Chu-ko Liang (181–234 A.D.), who contributed heroic service to the First Ruler of Shu. He is also known by the name K'ung-ming. The minister is depicted as providing the timber for the Imperial edifice.

37) "The Bright Concubine" is Wang Chao-chün, who lived in the first century B.C. She experienced many undeserved misfortunes, the chief of which was to be sent out of China and to become a concubine of a barbarian monarch. She enjoyed playing the guitar and is often so represented in paintings. Although buried in the desert, her grave was said by a miracle to be "forever green."

38) William Hung, in *Tu Fu, China's Greatest Poet*, suggests that in this poem the poet likens himself to an eagle who declines to be lured into service of any feudal master but instead remains faithful only to the Emperor. Whatever may be the local allusion, the lines clearly have poetic eminence by virtue of the strength of their explicit imagery.

ODE TO THE LUTE

1) This familiar conception of intercourse between the spirits in nature, each material phenomenon animated by a soul, was popularized in Chinese thought by the native cult of Taoism and through influences coming from India as expressed in such Buddhistic literature as *The Lotus Sutra*.

2) The romantic scenery in this and the immediately following stanzas is consciously in accord with the mountain scenery especially beloved by the classical Chinese painters. The poetry and painting sprang from a common source.

3) Buddhist doctrine teaches the transmigration of the soul but regards the crowning blessedness as the attainment of nirvana, or ultimate unconsciousness—a point of no return.

4) These and several lines following illustrate the intimate association in classical Chinese thought between aesthetic sublimation and detachment as realized in religious meditation.

5) These lines reveal the solicitude of Chinese thought for adjustment of the arts to a pattern of living or way of life. Art, according to this view, does not exist in a vacuum; it is as much an integral part of life as the blossom of the plant which it adorns.

6) The words "inebriate crew" may be understood literally. Chinese romantic thought gave serious regard to the notion of spiritual inspiration through wine.

7) It is to be noted that musical values are in Chinese thought, as in Indian philosophy, intimately associated with those of the dance.

8) This passage well illustrates the Chinese version of the doctrine of the mean. Note also number 136 in the *Book of Songs*: "much is much too much." The idea is characteristically Confucian.

9) It is noteworthy that this ode expressing the classical Chinese ideal of "the complete gentleman" assigns to him some skill in each art. He is to concern himself with music, gardening and the writing of poetry.

10) A further testimony of the relation of art to morality. It is not held, as by Plato, that art teaches morality. Chinese doctrine holds that each derives from a common source. The thought is summarized in the last line of this panegyric on the lute: "The noble soul alone can master it and play."

11) Although the immediately preceding stanzas express a highly idealistic aesthetic, it should be observed that this stanza voices a relativistic view: each person gains from art the virtues that are his private and particular commitment.

12) It is noteworthy that this stanza enlists for the arts the services of the three major realms of the cosmos as generally understood in Chinese thought: earth, air and water.

BOOK OF SONGS

1) This song well illustrates the convention of variations played on phrases in the first and last lines of stanzas.

2) This lyric through metaphorical expression deals with the unfortunate position of concubines in the household of a nobleman whose first-rank wife enjoys the favored place.

3) Bernhard Karlgren in his edition of the *Songs* explains the imagery of this poem as referring to game wrapped and hidden carefully by a poacher.

4) It is noteworthy that in this poem the refrain, commonly found in Western lyrics at the end of each stanza, appears at the beginning.

5) This poem expresses the conflict in the mind of a girl shortly to be married between her impatience to arrive at the city of her future husband and the rigid demands of decorum in her marriage journey.

6) The fox and the raven are regarded as creatures of evil omen.

7) This is essentially a dynastic hymn. A state is founded upon its cultural ideals: trees to provide materials for musical instruments and silkworms to provide elegant garments.

8) This poem gives an especially lucid instance of the crescendo or montage typical of the *Songs*.

9) This song describes a rash, unceremonial betrothal, a pleasant courtship and its termination in an unhappy marriage. The wife's family scorns her. She sadly journeys back to her parental home over the same road by which she has left it.

10) It was customary at festivals for each man to dance carrying a flute and a plume. See also Song 136.

11) This song is to be understood as a lament for youthful indiscretions.

12) The sentiment in this song is satirical. The lover is depicted as rich, pretentious and, his eloquence notwithstanding, in reality cold.

13) It will be observed that this lyric and Song 96 are surprisingly close to the manner of the *aubade*, or dawn song, as composed in Europe during the Middle Ages.

14) Commentators differ as to whether this poem is imagined as spoken by a man or woman. The question, however, does not seriously affect the meaning.

15) Imagery in this poem is symbolic and, as often in the *Songs*, means more than is openly stated.

16) A courtier is reluctant to leave his mistress at dawn.

17) This song is imagined as advice to a lover whose sweetheart has been duly married and taken to the town of her husband. The lover is advised to accept his fate.

18) In this song, fish, as they often do, symbolize fertility. The image was much used in marriage ceremonies.

19) The refrain in this lyric signifies that life should flourish with exuberance.

20) "Buzzards" signify the sovereign's misguided ministers who force the nation into war.

21) The note of friendship between men sounded in this song is one of the conspicuous features not only of Chinese poetry but of the Chinese classical conception of human values.

22) Pepper seeds were held to have magical properties, the chief of which was to induce spirits to descend to earth.

23) "Lady Ts'i from Sung" was traditionally said to have possessed unmatched beauty.

24) The refrain here indicates that the girl in question though admirable in her own right has grown up in inauspicious circumstances.

25) A girl is reluctantly leaving her lover behind her.

26) In this poem, as often in the *Songs*, the refrain underlines the main theme by stating its precise contrary. The cuckoo is crafty, the lover faithful.

27) This song voices the lament of an abused wife.

28) The ejaculation of the deer is understood as an expression of deep satisfaction.

29) This poem celebrates quietism and restraint. Its outlook anticipates much in the later development of Chinese philosophy and religion.

30) Crane and fish are traditional symbols of wisdom and sagacity. Here whetstones and the hammering of jade connote superfluous activity.

31) In this and the succeeding lines heavenly constellations useless to men are likened to rich but unworthy political leaders; the Lady of the Milky Way is "The Spinning Maid."

32) This poem outlines the conflict between Confucian morality and Taoist passivity.

33) This stanza is to be understood as ironical.

34) Many professional musicians were blind. Compare the "blind bards" of Western tradition.

35) Note that this song implies farming on a communal plan.

36) The song accompanies court dances in which the dancers are masked as stallions.

37) This song, intended for court rituals, gives a valuable picture of the elaborate orchestra employed in such ceremonies.

THE MANYŌSHŪ

1) The earliest Japanese commentaries describe this poem as presented by a messenger to the Emperor Jomei on the occasion of a hunting party on the Plain of Uchi. Its author, the Empress Kogyoku (593–641), was Empress-consort of the Emperor Jomei and mother of the Emperors Tenji and Temmu. Twice she was herself Empress-regnant.

2) The Empress Yamato-himé was Empress-consort of Emperor Tenji and granddaughter of Emperor Jomei.

3) Princess Nukada flourished in the second half of the seventh century. She was a favorite of the Emperor Temmu and regarded as foremost among the women poets of her times. Thirteen of her poems are in the Manyōshū.

4) This anonymous poem is said to have been written by the wife of a courtier present during the Imperial visit to the region of Lake Biwa.

5) Kakinomoto Hitomaro, author of this and the four poems following, is the most celebrated poet represented in the Manyōshū. Although the dates of his birth and death are unknown, he flourished from approximately 670 to 720. He held an official post of the lower rank. His works include long poems and short, several hundred of which have survived.

6) This poem was written on the occasion of a hunt held by Prince Naga, son of Emperor Temmu, in the neighborhood of Lake Kariji.

7) This poem was written for a religious festival and ceremony on the breaking of ground for a new house.

8) The word "Shami" signifies a lower rank in a Buddhist monastic order, somewhat similar to the word "brother" in Christian terminology. The author of this poem is thought to be Yamada Mikata, who in the latter part of his life joined a monastic order. He was active approximately

from 700 to 720. After studying in Korea, he was appointed tutor in the Japanese Imperial household. He composed Chinese as well as Japanese verse.

9) This anonymous poem is said to have been composed by one of the workmen engaged in the building of the Palace of Fujiwara, which became the seat of the Imperial court. It belongs to the early eighth century.

10) Prince Yuhara, author of this and the following poem, was grandson of the Emperor Tenji. Many well-known poems are ascribed to him. He was active in the early years of the eighth century.

11) This poem is said to have been written on the occasion of men climbing Ikuji Hill to drink beneath a pine tree. Prince Ichihara, its author, flourished in the second part of the eighth century, when he enjoyed a high reputation as poet and man of letters. Among his important posts was that of superintendent in the construction of the celebrated Tōdai-ji Temple.

12) Kasa Kanamura was a notable court poet in the first half of the eighth century. He is represented in the Manyōshū by nearly fifty poems.

13) These lines celebrate a visit of the Emperor Shōmu to his palace at Naniwa during the year 725.

14) These verses were presumably composed on the visit of the Emperor Shōmu to his palace at Yoshinu in 724. The author, Ōtomo Tabito (665–731) was appointed Grand Councillor of State in 728. The Manyōshū contains a large number of his poems, thirteen being in praise of saké. Most of his pieces, however, are of a grave and somber character, qualities inconspicuous in the selections given here.

15) This stanza alludes to an episode in Chinese history. The Emperor Taitsung forbade the drinking of saké, whereupon those who drank it called diluted saké "the wise man," and pure saké, "the sage."

16) Lady Ōtomo of Sakanoé was a prolific poet of the mid-eighth century. Her work shows great sensitivity and depth of feeling.

17) Ōtomo Yakamochi (718–785) was eldest son of the celebrated poet Tabito. The Manyōshū contains as many as five hundred of his works, all written in the early part of his career. He is considered one of the most moving and skillful poets of his times.

18) This praise of Mount Futagami is said to have been written with much spontaneity on the occasion of a visit, on March third, 747.

19) This poem is held to have been written at the Emperor's order during the poet's journey, in 751, to Nara, the capital, for delivery at an Imperial banquet.

20) Yamambé Akahito, a leading poet of the so-called Nara Period, is thought to have died approximately 736. He excels in the briefest forms of verse, wherein he shows himself master of an extraordinary grace.

21) Yamanoé Okura (659–733) visited China in 702 and returned in 704, having taken part in a cultural embassy. In 721 he became tutor to the Crown Prince. He wrote both Japanese and Chinese, using prose and verse. Chinese thought and especially Chinese humanism strongly attracted him. He was distinguished as a humanitarian, scholar and thinker. He compiled an anthology unhappily lost.

22) This poem was composed as a prayer for the safety and welfare of the Japanese ambassador to China, Tajihi Hironari, on the event of his departure from Japan in 733. The poet had himself been on a mission to China thirty years before.

23) This poem describes a provincial folk-festival on the day of *kagai*, when men and women danced together, sang love-songs, and enjoyed considerable license.

24) The author of this poem is said to have been the wife of a provincial guardsman, Mononobé Mané.

25) On the night appointed for the annual rice-offering, the men of a village were by long-established tradition denied admission to their houses.

26) This is one of several poems in dialect ascribed to frontier guards, recorded but not composed by the scholar-poets, to whose catholic taste we owe their survival.

27) This and the following poem relate to an astronomical myth well known in both China and Japan. Once a year the Oxherd rows his boat across the Milky Way to be united with his love, the Spinning Maid. The event takes place on the seventh night of the seventh moon, the harvest moon of Autumn. It is celebrated with an elaborate popular festival.

ATSUMORI

1) The samurai were the military and aristocratic caste in the feudal society of Japan.

2) A stupa is an icon symbolic of the Buddha, frequently consisting of a single piece of carved wood.

3) The Pure Land is the paradise reserved for the faithful according to a popular cult known as Pure Land Buddhism.

4) With this passage begins a long episode describing the journey of the hero to his ultimate destination. Such passages constituted a singularly persistent feature of the Japanese stage. The actor mimes the journey by circumventing the stage, at the same time that he recites lines having, as a rule, symbolic significance.

5) By this line it is understood that Renshobo enjoyed the hospitality of famous monasteries as stations on his long journey.

6) "The child" in this line is Atsumori.

7) "The Womb-Store" signifies a Buddhist doctrine of cosmology.

8) Amitābha is one of the peculiarly merciful and auspicious manifestations of the Buddha. A leading sect in Japanese Buddhism bears his name.

9) A "bodhisattava" is a soul already risen above mortality but not as yet entered into the ultimate Buddhahood. Bodhisattvas were objects of veneration and devotion somewhat as saints in Christian medieval practice.

10) In this line may be seen at the same time the Japanese recognition of the more ancient Chinese culture and their own pride and confidence in the younger civilization.

THE RIGVEDA

1) Ushas, goddess of dawn, is one of the few female deities addressed in the Rigveda. She is daughter of Dyaus, god of the sky. The personification insofar as mythical lore is concerned is rudimentary. Dawn dances and is of great beauty. This Indian deity is closely related to analogous figures in religions of Western Asia.

2) This hymn has been variously interpreted. Some scholars take it to be a satire on Brahman priests. The prevailing opinion, however, is that frogs are worshiped as bringers of rain, their cries likened to priestly invocations. According to this view priests are in no way demeaned, while the frogs are reverently praised. The Indians think highly of animals; nev-

ertheless, a humorous element should not be disregarded. Gaiety and piety are reconciled.

3) This famous hymn bears witness to the powerful fascination of cosmology for the Indian mind. On the one hand, it curiously foreshadows a purely physical explanation of the universe; on the other hand, it is both metaphysical and monotheistic. The conception of Prajapati approximates the god of the Old Testament. In short, the hymn holds an important place in the development of theological thought. It anticipates the subsequent religious works of the Hindus, such as the Upanishads and the sacred books of Buddhism.

4) Maruts are a group of storm gods, offspring of Rudra, god of thunder and lightning, who later became Śiva, and of the cloud-cow, Prisni. Of a fierce and militant nature, they are attendants on the supreme Storm God, Indra. They possess the dual function of bringing the welcome rains and of befriending warriors. Clad in gorgeous military accouterments, they drive war-chariots with great speed across the sky.

5) Sūrya, called "the all-creator," one of the chief sun deities in the religion of the Rigveda, is described as husband of the Dawn. He is also an aspect of Agni, god of fire. Among his beneficent functions is the driving away of evil dreams and diseases.

6) Indra, dominant deity in the realm of air, is more frequently invoked in the Rigveda hymns than any other god. Immoral, capricious, and violent, he kills his father and destroys the chariot of Dawn. He is saturnine, impetuous and unpredictable, fond of strong drink, and ferocious in battle. His chief enemy is Vritra, a demon of darkness, whom he slays in constantly repeated combats.

7) Agni, one of the principal deities in the Rigveda, is god of fire. He is born from lightning issuing from the raincloud and in volcanic flames imagined as burning beneath the ocean. He rejoices in conflagrations, especially forest fires. All gods honor him, since it is he who brings them the burnt sacrifices by which their lives are maintained. At times he is depicted as creator of the universe; at other times, as guardian of house and family. He is worshiped by the sacred flame and protects the domestic hearth. He reigns in heaven, on earth, and in the sea.

8) Rauhina is a demon of drought.

9) Pūshan, a pastoral deity, associated with the sun, rides on a car drawn by goats. Among his functions are the protection of roads, the safety of cattle, and the escort of souls to the abode of bliss.

10) Indian mythology gives special attention to the divine property of

water, both as rain and as running streams. There is a general deity of Waters bearing this name, along with innumerable river gods and goddesses, all conceived as beneficent. The personification of the most sacred of the Indian rivers, the Ganges, occurs, however, only in books of later origin than the *Rigveda*, which was largely compiled before the Aryans had reached Eastern India.

11) This hymn evinces the synthetic character of Indian mythology. A hymn to any major deity tends to present him as all-powerful and endowed virtually with the functions of the entire pantheon. Occasionally, as here, many gods are addressed simultaneously. The worshiper is generally more distinguished by his zeal than by a disposition to distinguish one god from another.

12) The name of this sky-deity is thought to signify "all-encompassing." He is supporter of both physical and moral order throughout the universe, governing the motions of sun, moon, and stars and the laws concerning human conduct. He metes out punishments and awards, showing mercy to persons who implore pardon for their offenses.

13) Parjanya is one of the many gods of rain celebrated in the *Rigveda*. The word signifies "raincloud." He is often imagined in the form of a bull.

14) The Ādityas constitute a group of beneficent gods and goddesses, offspring of the goddess Āditi, Varuna being their chief. The word "āditi" signifies "liberation." These deities delivered man from various afflictions.

15) The word "soma" is used to signify a plant, an intoxicating beverage, and a deity. The ritual in which soma was drunk constituted one of the major ceremonies during the period in which the *Rigveda* was compiled. A large proportion of the hymns deal with this theme. The drink was thought to enhance the zeal of the devotees and delight the gods. Although the conception is of great force in Indian religion, the personification itself remains far less vivid than that, say, of Bacchus, inasmuch as the drink was of the essence. The plant flourishes chiefly in northwest India. As the Aryans swept across the subcontinent, it became increasingly difficult to procure. The cult flourished chiefly in earlier years of Indian religion. "Pavamāna" is the name adopted by a family or clan in which the cult was especially cultivated. The word signifies "free flowing." Many hymns ascribed to this family are found in the ninth book of the *Rigveda*.

16) This is one of the few relatively secular poems in the *Rigveda*. From earliest times Indian literature bears witness to a national passion for gambling. Deceit in a gambling-match provides the main episode in the

earliest of the great Indian epics, the Mahābhārata.

17) The goddess Nirriti is the chief deity of the underworld appearing in the *Rigveda*.

18) Purusha is a primeval giant, a man rather than a god, but indubitably supernatural, having a thousand heads and feet. He is sacrificed to create the universe. This poem is commonly known as a "hymn to man," since it suggests a homocentric universe. Stanza ten signifies that from Purusha are derived the four castes of the Indian social system. Stanza eleven derives all the gods from him.

19) The theology of the *Rigveda*, founded on a frank naturalism, conceives Night and Day as primary deities. They are regarded as realities rather than as myths. In other words, the personifications are secondary; the essential meaning lies in the direct references to nature.

20) Like many hymns in the *Rigveda*, this is a prayer addressed to a number of healing deities. See also the hymn addressed to "Various Deities," page 338.

21) This hymn is one of a vast number of early Indian poems which are actually magic charms to be recited for eminently practical purposes, in other words, cures in verse.

22) This is a hymn to Aranyani, the nymph who animates the forest. In the warm Indian imagination of the *Rigveda* hymns, all natural phenomena are conceived as human.

KARNA'S TASK

1) This prayer by the stage manager complies with a convention that the producer of a play introduce it with a petition for the welfare of players and audience.

2) Vishnu is one of the chief gods of the Hindu pantheon. A sun deity, he is celebrated for three strides which he took through the elements establishing them for the welfare of humanity. He is vanquisher of demons. He has many incarnations among good men, the great hero of the Rāmāyaṇa being the most conspicuous. He is invoked as the supreme protector of mankind.

3) The stage manager's prayer is by a well-established tradition interrupted by a voice or sound from behind the scenes.

4) Words from offstage frequently precede the entrance of a character who by a convention of the theater immediately repeats on stage the phrase that has already been heard from behind the curtain.

5) Duryodhana is leader of the Kurus.

6) The Pāndus, or Pāndavas, led by Yudhishthira, are arch-enemies of the Kurus.

7) Arjuna is one of the most redoubtable of the Pāndava faction. He is reputed a son of the rain-god Indra. This in part accounts for Indra's favor to him in the present play.

8) The Bhrigu were, according to Indian legend, a venerable race of priests especially devoted to the fire-sacrifice.

9) This line refers to the sacred place traditionally held in Indian religious thought by the cow.

10) In Indian tradition a just and pious man must to the limit of his ability fulfill whatever request is made by a Brahman.

11) This is a deliberate falsification. Indra is in the custom of riding a massive elephant that he holds in special regard. Later in the play he declares that he will ascend this elephant and ride to heaven.

12) Earrings constituted an important part of Indian costume or adornment. They often had symbolic significance or magic potency.

13) Krishna is one of the chief heroes aligned with the Pāndavas. His shrewd advice gains them their final victory over the Kurus. Regarded as an incarnation of Vishnu, he is held by a large Hindu cult as a major deity to the present day. He is witty, amorous, and irrational.

14) The twice-born are the favored ones who are presumed to be on the road to blessedness. Arjuna is depicted as offering sacrifices to the elephant that is his father Indra's favorite vehicle.

15) This line, occuring three times in the play, amounts to a refrain. It epitomizes the action, Karna's final exercise of free will.

16) Each Sanskrit play not only begins but ends with a prayer. The final prayer usually includes a petition for the prosperity of the reigning monarch.

1) Literally, elephant hide.

2) Transitions of this nature between the prologue and main body of the play are a convention of the Sanskrit stage.

3) This line shows a typical device in Sanskrit play construction. In Act Four the ring with the snake-design becomes an important feature of the plot.

4) Paintings often become significant in the conduct of the action of Sanskrit plays.

5) Gautama is a stock character, the vidūshaka, or clown, friend of the hero but as unlike his friend, the prince, as possible. He is completely lacking in ideals, save for his loyalty to the king. A glutton, coward, hypocritical Brahman, and prodigy of ugliness, but endowed with a low form of cunning, it is he who steers the intrigue that in the end gains the prince the goal he desires. He is alternately shrewd and ridiculous. When, as sometimes, his errors are injurious to the king, the king invariably defends him. Opposites meet in complete harmony.

6) Characters in Sanskrit drama often whisper words unheard by the audience, who are expected to surmise the imagined communication.

7) The Vedas are books held in orthodox Indian tradition as possessing the utmost religious sanction and authority.

8) The acts of Sanskrit plays frequently end or begin at stated periods of the day. Special music is also provided to designate special hours.

9) Acts in Sanskrit drama frequently begin with forescenes in which only minor characters appear. These help to advance and explain the action.

10) By stage convention, gardens are scenes for many episodes in Sanskrit plays.

11) It is understood by the audience that Gautama deliberately brought about the queen's injury to advance his intrigue in behalf of the king.

12) The ladies in Sanskrit drama are much addicted to entertainment provided by swings.

13) The clown in Sanskrit drama frequently makes prophecies which by an invariable convention of the stage prove true.

14) Snake spirits, or nāgas, are associated with the underworld. The females are represented with special frequency as benign and beautiful.

15) To cause a Brahman's death was held the greatest possible misfortune.

16) The jailer is a woman inasmuch as she officiates in the royal harem.

17) The elaborate and highly artificial stage business of this episode is typical of much action in Indian dance-drama. All the plays provide for considerable miming. Note also the much used convention whereby actions take place simultaneously on two parts of the stage.

18) Note that Mālavikā confesses that much of her conduct is simply affectation. She teases the king.

19) By stage convention the clown takes every possible occasion to sit, lie down, or even sleep. He is as lazy and slothful as his friend the hero is restless and energetic.

20) The audience knows that Gautama played the role of the brown monkey frightening the child. This is another of his tricks to aid the king. The clown's likeness to a monkey was a commonplace in Sanskrit drama.

21) The horse sacrifice, as here described, is one of the chief religious rites depicted in Sanskrit epics. It is mentioned often in the plays.